BEHOLD · THIS · IS · THE · LAW · OF · THE · HOUSE. · · · ·

PUT · UP · THY · SWORD · FOR · ALL · THEY · THAT · TAKE · THE · SWORD · SHALL · PERISH · WITH · THE · SWORD · & · HE · TOUCHED · HIS · EAR · & · HEALED · HIM

Books by *William Keisling*

We All Fall Down
Helping Hands
When the Levee Breaks
Maybe Four Steps
The Meltdown
The Sins of Our Fathers
Solar Water Heating Systems
Three Mile Island: Turning Point

We All Fall Down

A Chronicle of an Impeachment Foretold

By William Keisling

Yardbird

FIRST EDITION, First Printing

This book was printed on acid-free paper and was Smyth
sewn. Set in Galliard with Shelley Andante Script display faces.
The artwork on the cover dust jacket is found on the front wall
of the state senate chamber of Pennsylvania and was painted in
1917 by Violet Oakley. The black and white friezes found
inside the book are sketches drawn by Oakley detailing the
senate chamber series.

Yardbird Books can be found in any good book store.
We encourage our readers to order books directly from
us at a savings. Copies of this book can be purchased for
$19.95, including shipping, by calling Yardbird Books at
1-800-622-6044. Or write us at:

Yardbird Books, 601 Kennedy Road, Airville, PA 17302.
Pennsylvania residents please add six percent sales tax.

Digital versions of our books are available. E-mail and orders
can also be sent to: info@yardbird.com. Visit our web page at
http://www.yardbird.com

Library of Congress Cataloging-in-Publication Data

Keisling, William.
    We all fall down : a chronicle of an impeachment foretold /
by William Keisling. -- 1st ed.
        p.   cm.
    ISBN 1-882611-08-X (alk. paper)
    1. Larsen, Rolf, 1934- --Impeachment. 2. Zappala, Stephen A.
3. Trials (Impeachment)--Pennsylvania--Philadelphia. 4. Judges-
Pennsylvania--Discipline. 5. Judicial corruption--Pennsylvania.
I. Title
KFP525.5.I4K45 1996
347.748'014--dc20
[347.480714]   96-16274

Table of Contents

For
Maximilien Robespierre, Georges Danton,
Jean Paul Marat
and all the boys of the Committee of Public Safety
who planned the menu

Dr. Joseph Guillotine
who sliced the vegetables

Charlotte Corday
who drew the bath

and Napoleon Bonaparte
who served the main course

THE·LAND·HE·SAW·THE·TRADE·OF·
SLAVERY·WAS·A·GREAT·EVIL··•

Part One

I felt weightless. I felt nothing would happen to me. I felt that anything might happen to me. I was looking straight ahead, running, trying to keep up, and things were occurring along the dark peripheries of my vision: there would be a bright light and then darkness again and the sound, constantly, of something else breaking, and of movement, of objects being thrown and of people falling.

Bill Buford
Among the Thugs

If you want peace, work for justice.

Bumper sticker seen on highway

CHAPTER 1

Judicial La-La Land

A judge of the court who has lost touch with reality and flipped his proverbial wig is a frightening thing, but how common of an occurrence can it be? On the afternoon of October 13, 1992, in the city of Pittsburgh, Pennsylvania, not one, but two judges with a loose grip on reality sat down for a chat.

It would seem, other than the loose grip of reality that they shared, and that the two sat on the same court, the Supreme Court of Pennsylvania, the two judges had little in common.

The one judge, state Supreme Court Justice Stephen A. Zappala, was physically a large man who enjoyed a rich family life. His father had been a well-regarded attorney and a state representative. His brothers were successful businessmen, and his children were on the way to successes of their own. The other justice, Rolf Larsen, was of slight build, with a much more difficult family history, plagued by depression and illness.

On that day in October, about three in the afternoon, Justice Zappala had walked a short distance down the hall to the offices of his fellow jurist Justice Larsen. Zappala's intention had been to deliver some bad news. Perhaps Zappala hadn't completely flipped his wig, as he seems to have foreseen trouble coming. He seems to have taken care not to unduly ruffle feathers. He'd later characterize his visit to Justice Larsen as a courtesy. He'd had his secretary call ahead to ask if Justice Larsen was available for the tête-à-tête. Justice Larsen replied he had some time and volunteered to come to Justice Zappala's office. Zappala, perhaps to underscore his mission of courtesy, replied no, he would come to see Justice Larsen.

So Justice Zappala walked the few feet down the hall to

Larsen's suite of offices. Larsen met his fellow jurist at the front of his office, near the secretarial pool. The two judges walked into a small kitchenette near the secretaries and sat down at a table.

Zappala would remember the meeting as lasting no more than five minutes. Others, in Larsen's office, would later tell investigators that the meeting lasted closer to forty minutes. No one overheard what was said. The two justices would in large part later disagree about what was said. They could only agree on the following: Zappala announced that three justices, including himself, had voted to reprimand Larsen for a small breach of judicial ethics that had occurred some years before. After years of investigation the state's judicial disciplinary board had found Larsen guilty of improperly talking to another judge about a pending case. Larsen's brethren on the high court, including Zappala, had just voted to sustain the reprimand. The reprimand was really not that much of a big deal, a minor discipline, a slap on the wrist, carrying with it no great stigma or consequence. The voters of Pennsylvania probably wouldn't even care about or remember the reprimand when Justice Larsen was set to stand for his retention election some five years in the future, in 1997.

Even so, Zappala would confess to some degree of apprehension, a "concern," as he would call it, that some ill would come to him now that he was the bearer of the bad news. You didn't cross Rolf Larsen without something bad happening. Over the years Larsen had filed many lawsuits against those he perceived as having slighted him. There had been an ongoing defamation suit against the state's two largest newspapers and their reporters. Larsen had even filed a lawsuit against a developer who had had the misfortune to plan a condominium in the same neighborhood as Larsen's own condo. The issue at hand, this matter of the reprimand that the two now met in the kitchenette to discuss, had been no less litigious.

"He and I had sat down," Zappala would later remember, and "I told him the court had reached a verdict. I said that you may not like it, but we are going to sustain the reprimand. I think we are absolutely correct. I think it will do justice to you and the court."

Larsen told him he did not like it, Zappala would recall. Common criminals got fairer treatment than he did, Zappala remembered him saying. "Then he said, 'I'm going to do what I have to do.'" There seems to be something missing from both mens' accounts of the conversation, for emotions suddenly over boiled.

"You do what you damn well please," Zappala says he told him. He'd say he couldn't stand the political heat in the kitchenette and got out. "At that point I got out of the place. That was the extent of any conversation."

Larsen remembered things differently. Later the investigators and members of the state legislature would say Larsen had flipped his wig. They'd hint his mind had been warped by illegally attained prescription drugs. The investigators and the members of the legislature were as much in denial of reality as the other two men in this chapter.

Larsen would report that Zappala, rather than get up and go, had stayed for some time in the kitchenette to console, and to bear his soul. He remembered it this way: that Zappala expressed empathy with his predicament, that Zappala said he himself was in hot water. Zappala, Larsen said, blithely told him he too had handled cases improperly, that he'd arranged financial windfalls for his brother, and subsequently had fixed several court cases to prevent the financial ruin of his brother's clients. And now the feds were closing in, he'd say Zappala confessed.

If Larsen was crazy, as Pennsylvanians were about to be told time and again, Zappala was living in his own judicial la-la land. Zappala seems to think he was free to dance into that kitchenette and play the role of disinterested lawgiver. The reality was that Zappala was hampered by his own serious liabilities. Zappala had a sixteen ton weight hanging over his own head. It was a miracle it hadn't fallen on him yet. Not seeing his own vulnerability, Stephen Zappala was as much out of touch with reality as his fellow justice, Rolf Larsen.

That afternoon, when he got back to his chambers,

Zappala telephoned two other justices. He told them he had broken the news to Larsen. "He's going to do what he's going to do," he told them.

That these judges were mad is beyond dispute. The nature of their madness depends on your definition of the word. Were they crazy, were they angry, or were they merely power mad? Maybe a little of each.

CHAPTER 2

Seven Little Indians

What Justice Larsen did was to sit down and write what were to become his most famous petitions of recusal. Some people write sonnets, others excel at writing bonds. Rolf Larsen had become somewhat a master at the legal document known as the petition of recusal.

In Pennsylvania complaints of misconduct involving members of the judiciary, like the complaints now lodged against Larsen, were first investigated by the Judicial Inquiry and Review Board. The review board then may, or may not, recommend discipline to the state's high court, which makes the ultimate decision of guilt, innocence and punishment.

The current investigation of Larsen's conduct had dragged on for more than six years, since 1986, in no small part because Larsen had filed an avalanche of petitions of recusal. If a litigant can raise questions about a judge's behavior or fairness, the judge often will recuse him or herself from the case. Larsen had filed nearly a score of recusal motions and related documents claiming conflicts of interests and other irregularities involving those on the review board and later on the court who would render judgment on him. At one stage Larsen had filed a motion asking for the disqualification of every member of the review board. He'd also filed an outside court challenge that served to slow proceedings. Somehow the matter finally got out of the review board, with the recommendation that the high court reprimand its justice. As I said, the reprimand really was just a slap on the wrist.

Larsen refused to take the slap.

The results of the inquiry now out of the review board, the

proceedings wound their slow way to fruition at the state Supreme Court. Larsen filed petitions of disqualification against two of his fellow justices. His litigiousness threatened not to stop with recusal petitions. Larsen lately had been intimating to his brethren, including Zappala, that he was preparing a lawsuit charging that his civil rights had been violated in all this.

It had become a game of ten little Indians. Rather, seven little Indians, the number of justices on the court.

Of seven state Supreme Court justices, Zappala found himself the bearer of the bad news of the reprimand because, in the lengthy game of recusal skittles Larsen had been playing, Zappala was one of the few pins left standing. Following motions filed by Larsen, Chief Justice Robert N. C. Nix had recused himself from the proceedings, as had Justice John P. Flaherty. The proceedings had taken so long that a third justice, James T. McDermott, had died in June 1992. His replacement on the court, Justice Frank Montemuro, recused himself since he'd served on the review board while the Larsen matter was first investigated. And Larsen, of course, must recuse himself in a vote concerning his own discipline. That meant of the seven justices, four had been knocked out of deliberations, leaving only three.

This had left only Zappala, Justices Ralph Cappy and Nicholas Papadakos to vote on whether to accept or reject the review board's recommendation for a reprimand. In the end, Zappala and Cappy voted for the reprimand, while Papadakos dissented, saying he had reservations about the procedures used in the matter. Zappala, the most senior of these three, found himself the bearer of the bad news. The three justices thought it would be best not to, in lawyer parlance, "blindside" Larsen. It wouldn't do to have their litigious fellow justice find out about the decision through some newspaper reporter after the order had been filed.

"There was a concern on my part as to the reaction of Justice Larsen," Zappala later would remember. "I was pretty sure that if he didn't like what we did, something was going to happen. There had already been threats about his civil rights suit. (Threats) including (to) yours truly that he was already preparing, quote, his civil rights suit. The only question was who was going to be in the shotgun? Nobody seemed to know at that point. I sure knew that somebody, including yours truly, was in the sights after that order was put down."

It wouldn't take long to find out what Larsen had in mind. Shortly after the meeting in the kitchenette Larsen sat down to write what would become his most famous petitions of recusal. His aim certainly, at the very least, was to have Zappala and Cappy recuse themselves so that, Indians #5 and #6 out of the way, only a favorable Justice Papadakos would remain, and Larsen presumably wouldn't be reprimanded.

In my mind's eye I don't know whether to picture Larsen merrily or studiously or angrily writing away. How much of what was about to happen was accidental is also hard to say. He may have been aware he was about to ignite a firestorm. When you keep in mind Larsen's long history of litigiousness it's even hard to say whether this batch of recusal petitions was more or less fair than the others. What is safe to say is that Larsen, for all his thin-skinned charges of unfairness, seemed not totally aware of the lion's den he was now about to enter.

In his petition Larsen wrote that Zappala and Cappy should recuse themselves from the reprimand vote because they harbored ill-will against Larsen. Both justices, he wrote, were attempting to make him look bad with a reprimand to sabotage Larsen's chances of one day becoming chief justice of the court. If he had stopped there chances are everyone would have shrugged it off and the events that were to follow almost certainly wouldn't have happened. But Larsen's paper was itchy for his pen.

He went on to write, among other things, that Zappala had been fixing court cases to the benefit of Zappala's bond underwriter brother, that Justice Zappala had helped get bond work for this brother, and that Zappala himself received what Larsen called "indirect kickbacks" from this misbehavior. Larsen hadn't voted the way Zappala had wanted on several of these decisions, he wrote, and so he'd earned Zappala's wrath. For good measure he wrote that Zappala was illegally recording conversations in his chambers. As for Justice Cappy, Larsen charged he was no more than Zappala's pawn, that he similarly had it in for Larsen, and had fixed a case with the design of hurting Larsen. A week or so after he filed these inflammatory petitions, Larsen filed another saying Justice Zappala, presumably enraged by the initial salvo of recusal petitions, had tried to run Larsen down with a car in front of an upscale Philadelphia hotel.

In my mind's eye I try to imagine Larsen sitting back in his quiet chambers awaiting a favorable outcome from these petitions of recusal.

CHAPTER 3

Political Justices

The uninformed might come to see this story simply as a vintage 1992 bureaucratic passion play between two justices, Zappala and Larsen. In reality the passion play includes a cast of countless seething and frustrated court observers, including the state's largest newspaper, and stretches back in time almost fifteen years, nearly a generation.

This would be no pauper's crucifixion. The stations of the cross (by careless reckoning) begin in the Pittsburgh high-rise office suite kitchenette, trail through several cartons of legal papers filed in some of our state's most august court houses, and end in impeachment within the gold-leafed state legislature in Harrisburg. Yet this impeachment would have no immaculate conception. It didn't spontaneously ignite. Premonitions of what was to happen passed some lips ten years or more before the final event.

I knew little of either man, Larsen or Zappala, before this began. Of the two I was more familiar with Larsen. I first heard Larsen's name in the late 1970s, when I was a young newspaper reporter trudging the streets of Harrisburg. Back then Justice Larsen's name popped up with increasing regularity stuck alongside a string of controversy. In the early '80s he was accused of misbehavior. This first round of charges would ultimately be dismissed. Even so this first round would set the stage for the charges that would cause the blowup in the '90s. In the first round there were conduct board hearings, and fights with, and lawsuits against, the state's two biggest newspapers. Particularly in his home region, the western part of the state, the name Rolf Larsen seemed to generate increasing heat.

Later, with the endless hearings, the motions and the counter-motions, there would be bushels of smoke. Contentiousness and controversy were becoming no strangers to Rolf Larsen. They were his modus operandi, his partners. Larsen was learning to thrive, to advance his career with the use of controversy.

It is not easy to fairly tell Rolf Larsen's story because so much of it is under contention. As I say, there were charges and counter-charges. Contested hearings and contested votes, leading to seemingly endless more hearings and more votes. The paper trail can't make up its mind about Larsen. The documents are spread from one end of our state to the other, some of them confidential and beyond the reach of the public. Not that anyone would want to lay one's hands on all the documents at once — your back would break from hauling the records. If you were to somehow put them all in one room the documents pertaining to Larsen would weigh in the hundreds of pounds. In the end what stands out is the very contentiousness of the records. About the only thing that really isn't contended is the contentiousness.

In the cauldron of Rolf Larsen's story bubbles our state's mix of politics and justice. In 1974, having practiced law in Pittsburgh for more than a dozen years, Larsen ran for a seat on the Allegheny County Court of Common Pleas, and won. Once on the bench he gained publicity by cracking down on fathers who'd fallen behind on child support. "He threw lots of fathers in jail," one state lawyer and long-time Larsen watcher told me. "Some of them were pretty good men, too, just unfortunately out of money." Off to jail they went, and for his crackdown Larsen soon found himself receiving favorable national media attention. He'd hit upon the first part of a formula for elective judicial success: take a popular, law and order stand and you'll get attention.

The second part of his success formula involved politics. In 1977 Larsen sought a seat on the state Supreme Court. The Democrats had already endorsed another candidate, a controversial Philadelphia woman. State legend has Larsen traveling to see Philadelphia Mayor Frank Rizzo, making a deal with hizzonna, who agrees to pull the plug on the woman in favor of Larsen. Another political observer recalled that Larsen's campaign that year included television commercials with images of slamming jail cell doors. Perhaps those images were prescient.

In any event, Larsen won the election, and found himself a Supreme Court justice. From then on he just can't seem to keep his hands off politics.

His legend has him returning to Pittsburgh to teach other lower court judges how it's done. The mugwumps they must talk to, what they must do to get elected to the high court. First he helps Common Pleas Judge John Flaherty (elected to the Supreme Court in 1979), then Common Pleas Judge Stephen Zappala (elected justice in 1982), and then Common Pleas Judge Nicholas Papadakos (who ascended to the high court in 1983).

"These protégés followed Larsen's formula of taking populist or law-and-order stances to get attention," one lawyer told me. "Papadakos, for example, focused on mortgage foreclosures." Zappala, the Inquirer wrote at the time of his 1982 election, "sounded tough on law-and-order issues." The extent to which, once elected, his protégés would, like Larsen, resort to politics would be of increasing controversy.

The whole time Larsen is seen by his growing list of enemies as politicking to build a power base in hopes of becoming chief justice. In our state's high court the chief justice post is awarded by seniority. At the time, in the early 1980s, the next in line for the chief justice's job was Robert N.C. Nix Jr., having served on the Supreme Court since 1972. In Pennsylvania the Nix family breaks ground. Nix's father, Robert Sr., in 1958 became the first black to win a seat in the state's congressional delegation. Junior Nix now was all that stood between Rolf Larsen and the chief justice's chair.

It was around this time, the early '80s, that the charges against Larsen began flying fast and heavy. This is where the paper trail begins to seriously kill trees. Larsen found himself accused before the Judicial Inquiry and Review Board of employing politics and racial slurs to see that Nix would lose his

1982 retention election. Larsen was accused of traveling around the state making unholy political alliances to advance his claim on the chief justice's seat. Nix nonetheless won retention and in 1984 became chief justice. The residual charges against Larsen would drag on for years, and would ultimately be dismissed, though Larsen's enemies would say the disciplinary board had been controlled by Larsen and his machinations.

One attorney who served on the disciplinary board at this time was Robert Surrick, who practices outside Philadelphia, and who himself has run unsuccessfully for state Supreme Court.

I met Surrick early on while researching this book. I was making the rounds of various groups interested in judicial reform in Pennsylvania. Surrick also was making the rounds, promoting his idea of splitting the state into multiple judicial districts. Pennsylvania's Supreme Court justices are elected on a statewide basis, giving the metropolitan areas of Pittsburgh and Philadelphia an inordinate representation on the court. Surrick was a quick-smiling, twinkled-eyed reformer. When I met him he was carting around a map that depicted Pennsylvania carved up into seven or so districts. He argued that these judicial districts would give all areas of the state an equal voice on the court.

Surrick's interest in reform, and his involvement in Larsen's disciplinary problems in the early '80s, give him a unique perspective to comment on the ongoing problems of the high court.

Surrick told me he believes Larsen was "guilty of a whole bunch of stuff. The main problem was he couldn't keep his hands off politics. He was doing things like going around making alliances with the likes of the Pennsylvania Trial Lawyers Association, which has a stake in high settlements." The numerous complaints filed against Larsen were investigated for the disciplinary board by Philadelphia attorney Richard Sprague, who'd been named special prosecutor. Sprague was a former prosecutor in the Philadelphia district attorney's office. "Sprague did the investigation of Larsen and nailed him,"

Surrick contends, "but the good old boy network of judges voted to exonerate Larsen."

Surrick in this period himself became what some call a "pariah in legal circles" for unsuccessfully pushing for the early disciplining of Larsen. He seems to have been a voice in the wilderness back then.

"Larsen all along was building a power base to become chief justice," Surrick told me. "He was doing it by building his own network and by trying to undercut Nix." The Judicial Inquiry and Review Board, in the first round of complaints, would hear testimony that Larsen had threatened to undermine Nix's 1981 retention election by publicizing the fact that Nix was black. Cyril Wecht, then Allegheny County's democratic chairman and a medical examiner who gained fame by questioning the JFK single-bullet theory, testified that, "Justice Larsen again talked about his plans to first expose the fact that Justice Nix is a 'nigger,' as he put it, and that was essential because he, Justice Larsen, felt that the great majority of people, especially outside of Philadelphia, did not know that Justice Nix was black." There were other allegations involving race. A law clerk for former Chief Justice Michael Eagen testified that Larsen, during the Philadelphia MOVE trail, had said of the disruptive defendants, "They ought to hang those niggers in cages from the ceiling and try them that way." Eagen was chief justice from 1977 to 1980. The MOVE trial involved militant blacks who were bombed out of their home by Philadelphia Mayor Wilson Goode.

Larsen would vigorously dispute all these charges, and most of the people who made them. He sued Surrick for libel in 1983, the same year he filed a complaint against Surrick with the Disciplinary Board of Pennsylvania, charged with policing lawyers. That board is under the control of the state Supreme Court. Larsen would particularly dispute the charges of racism, pointing out at one of his later hearings that he once refused a complementary membership to a social club that had been extended to all the justices but Nix. As I say, Surrick was in the minority and the disciplinary board in the end voted to exonerate Larsen of this first round of charges. The political alliances behind this vote are still a matter of dispute. What is not disputed is that Larsen was making enemies.

That list of enemies was growing. During these conduct board hearings the Philadelphia Inquirer ran articles critical of Larsen. These articles were picked up by the monkey-see-monkey-do Pittsburgh Post-Gazette. In November 1983 Larsen sued both newspapers and sundry editors and writers for defamation, violating Mark Twain's dictum not to pick fights with men who buy ink by the barrel. These libel suits are pending to this day.

Larsen was making enemies, yet alliances continued shifting, making him peculiar friends. Richard Sprague, the special prosecutor who had investigated Larsen, switched sides and began *defending* Larsen before some of the endless proceedings. In 1973 Sprague himself had sued the Philadelphia Inquirer for libel over the paper's coverage of a 1963 murder investigation which Sprague had handled. Sprague's libel case dragged on in state courts for more than twenty years. In 1983 a jury had awarded Sprague $4.5 million in damages. The Inquirer won a retrial. A second jury in 1990 awarded Sprague $34 million in punitive and compensatory damages. This too was appealed. The state Superior Court in 1994 reduced the damages to $24 million. The Inquirer again appealed.

These separate libel suits brought by Larsen and Sprague, and others (including a $6 million award for libel to the estate of late Justice Frank McDermott, which was at first overturned on appeal in 1993, then reappealed) would constitute a considerable piece of the assets of the Inquirer's parent company, Knight-Ridder. These libel actions would also serve to make the Inquirer hardly a disinterested observer of what was to come.

Back on the court, meanwhile, Larsen and the three justices he'd helped to get elected formed a voting block and stripped Chief Justice Nix of much of his power. Many of the chief justice's traditional powers were taken from Nix by this "Gang of Four." Zappala, for example, took control of the court budget.

A single father, Larsen would spend his days (when not

traveling the judicial circuit or politicking) at his Pittsburgh condo, where he lived with his daughter. He'd come to work late and work well into the night. He'd hang out at his club, exercise on his rowing machine, and complete exactly 222 sit-ups every morning.

Over the years some would come to describe Rolf Larsen as almost an autocratic zealot, bent on abusing our democratic system. This doesn't ring quite true to me. Hell, as far as I can see, Rolf Larsen was the most able practitioner of democracy to come down our pike in a long while. He saw our politicized justice system for what it was, used it, and took it to the max.

By all accounts Justice Stephen Zappala, once a Larsen protégé, was a much smoother, certainly quieter, operator. Certainly he was more of a team player, less of a loner than was Larsen. "Zappala," the Inquirer wrote following his 1982 election, "who has been a judge for less than three years, comes from a family of successful Pittsburgh lawyer-politicians who provided financial backing for his campaign."

While I was researching my 1993 book on the Pennsylvania Turnpike, *When the Levee Breaks,* the name Justice Stephen Zappala first came to my ears.

I first heard the name Zappala in 1992 while a turnpike director was giving me a rundown of the many potential conflicts of interest at the turnpike. One of the two Democratic turnpike commissioners, attorney James Dodaro of Pittsburgh, was an old family friend, protégé and former law partner to state Supreme Court Justice Stephen Zappala, the attorney told me. Justice Zappala's brother, Charles, was a principal in a firm that underwrote the turnpike's bonds, he went on.

I think it sailed right over me. The turnpike administrator who told me this lifted his eyebrows and snickered, as if to say get a load of this ethical mess.

I still have my notes from that evening. The hastily scrawled arrows that pointed to the relationships: Justice Stephen Zappala, bond underwriter Charles Zappala, and turnpike Commissioner James Dodaro. All were joined with arrows.

Other arrows sailed out from these three names.

Dodaro thorughout his career had often followed in Stephen Zappala's footsteps, serving, for example, as Allegheny County solicitor after Zappala had held the post. Some in government and the state press said that Stephen Zappala helped Dodaro become turnpike commissioner in 1984. Once on the turnpike, Dodaro was responsible for sending billions of dollars of turnpike underwriting business to Charles Zappala's firm.

The turnpike administrator explained it to me like this: "Jim Dodaro championed Charles Zappala's bond underwriting to get the turnpike work. Dodaro grew up with the Zappalas. Their dad helped Dodaro get into school. Even before he got onto the commission Dodaro was lobbying to get Charles Zappala's company the turnpike's non-competitive, no-bid bond work. It's no secret. Read the newspapers back then. He spoke quite openly about it at the time. He still speaks openly about it. Then check out the campaign contributions made by Charles Zappala and his bond underwriting firm to state Senators Robert Jubelirer and Vincent Fumo." These two arrows run from Charles Zappala to our esteemed Republican and Democratic state senators. Looking back, now I see these hash marks almost as seismic stress lines of the earthquake to come.

In the turnpike game of no-bid contracts and reciprocal campaign contributions the names of state senators Robert Jubelirer (the Republican) and Vincent Fumo (the Democrat) kept popping up. Both would receive thousands of dollars in contributions from turnpike lawyers and bond underwriters. The bucks don't stop there, I'd learn. Both Jubelirer and Fumo are lawyers, and their law firms receive no-bid work from the turnpike. The Philadelphia law firm of Astor, Weiss and Newman, to which Fumo belonged until April 1993, received more than $45,690 in turnpike work from 1989 through 1993. The firm received another $112,000 in 1994 for bond co-counsel work. Senator Jubelirer's law firm, Jubelirer, Carothers and Krier, of Altoona, received $7,000 in 1989 to represent the turnpike in a personal injury case. The point is, the men who control our state senate can hardly be considered disinterested public servants or overseers. Legislative leaders Jubelirer and Fumo (and most of the leadership) are players and beneficiaries with a vested interest in this "pinstripe patronage" system.

I would come to learn that Charles Zappala's firm, Russell, Rea, Zappala & Gomulka, known as RRZ&G, had since the mid-1980s become a major contributor to Pennsylvania's political campaigns. RRZ&G is a holding company that controls RRZ Public Markets, a bondseller. They'd formed an in-house political action committee called The Committee for the Advancement of State and Local Government. They not only gave thousands of dollars to Jubelirer and Fumo. They gave hundreds of thousands of dollars to members of our legislature and other elected officials. They'd given generously to both political parties. The higher up the ladder you got in our state, the more you got from Zappala's PAC. Republican Attorney General Ernest Preate Jr., then our top law enforcement officer, had received some $19,000 from RRZ's PAC or its principals.

These political contributions had skyrocketed after 1986, when Charles Zappala's bonding firm became the main bond underwriter for a no-bid, $807 million turnpike bond issue. It was the largest bond issue ever floated by Pennsylvania, dwarfing a $370 million bond issue for veterans assistance in 1950. In the turnpike deal the profits to the bonding companies, including Zappala's firm, had been in the millions of dollars.

How had Charles Zappala's company competed to earn such profits? The answer is, they didn't. RRZ's role as chief underwriter for the turnpike deal was awarded on a no-bid, non-competitive basis. At the time the Pittsburgh Post-Gazette published a long article about it. RRZ was sponsored for the work, the Post-Gazette reported, by longtime family friend James Dodaro, the turnpike commissioner, and former law partner to Justice Stephen Zappala. In the article Dodaro defended his advocacy of RRZ by saying the firm was well qualified.

These non-competitive bond deals are by far the largest

contracts let by state government. Often both political parties will also have two bond counselors involved in an issue — each law firm, of course, kicking back sizable sums to its political sponsors.

The canard advanced by state leaders to justify this system of insider bond selling, counseling and the resultant kickbacks is that the government leaders must personally be well acquainted with the bond underwriters and counselors to ensure the quality of the services rendered. As late as April 1996, fending off growing legislative efforts to award bond counsel work to the lowest bidder, a spokesman for Governor Tom Ridge told reporters, "Purchasing legal advise on a $100 million bond issue is not like calling around for quotes from the lumber store. The quality of legal advice is an intangible that cannot be summarized in a bid but is of tremendous importance to tax-payers." Or so the high priests at the bond houses and the state's law firms would have us believe. No strangers allowed. Only the anointed, the insider, the friendly political donor need apply.

The point I'd like to make for our story here is that to justify this outrageous system of bond corruption Pennsylvania leaders time and again advance the argument that the state's highest officials must be personally well acquainted with the bond players and their track records. When matters related to these insider-funded agencies wind up in state courts, where a semblance of impartiality is required, the story changes. If one of the politically elected judges happens to be a brother or close associate of one of the politically well-connected bonding representatives, suddenly it's a different story. Suddenly there is a collective, official amnesia. Suddenly nobody knows any of these "highly trusted" buddy-buddy characters or what they're up to.

At the time when I was first learning about this lucrative subject, in 1992, I thought little of the growing rat's nest of arrows scrawled across my notes. I was uncovering so many outrageous conflicts at the Pennsylvania Turnpike that these were just a couple more. It would turn out that other people —

particularly lawyers — were already thinking hard about Justice Zappala's relationship to his bond underwriter brother.

I had another premonition of things to come several weeks later. Again the name Zappala blipped on my radar screen. I was at the home of a turnpike attorney. Justice Zappala was the turnpike's house judge, this lawyer explained, matter-of-factly. "Zappala fixed a case for us," I was told. "He's our house judge." The independence of the state courts couldn't be trusted, the lawyer warned me quietly.

I filed this away with whatever else I'd been told. I'd been around long enough to know what a house judge was. Let's say I wasn't overly alarmed. The problem of house judges strikes to the imperfect heart of our republic. Both political parties have them. It's why the parties support, nominate and run their favorites for the judiciary. When party matters get to the courts, a house judge will see things their way.

During my research three other judges besides Zappala had been mentioned as acting at one time or another as turnpike house judges. Among these three was Chief Justice Nix. Nix, I was told, had once weighed in judicially for his political patron, former turnpike commissioner Peter Camiel, an old-time Democratic boss from Philadelphia. Camiel in the 1980s was about to be tossed from the turnpike when he'd instructed a turnpike lawyer to call Nix for help with a legal maneuver. Camiel had been Nix's political sponsor and was responsible for getting him on the court. In the clutch, Justice Nix came through for his patron, offering invaluable procedural advice.

So I didn't give any particular import to talk of Zappala being a turnpike house judge. I really had no idea of the blow up that was about to come. Then again, I had no idea the extent to which Justice Stephen Zappala had carelessly, and perhaps arrogantly, injected himself in court decisions involving those entities financed by his brother. Looking back, it's easy to see that the Zappala brothers, consciously or not, had concocted their own formula for a political explosion. By voting to reprimand Larsen in the second round of disciplinary hearings, Justice Zappala himself provided the spark.

CHAPTER 4

The Club that Beats Him

Fathoming the workings of Justice Rolf Larsen's mind is impossible. Even the bare-bone facts surrounding his actions are nearly all surrounded by controversy and can leap out and bite you. It seems safe to recount the broadest brushstrokes: Justice Larsen, seeing red because Justices Zappala and Cappy voted to reprimand him, in late November 1992 filed his poison-pen recusal petitions.

The most serious allegation contained in the recusal petitions was that Justice Zappala had fixed two court cases involving the city of Philadelphia, in the eastern part of the state, and Allegheny County, in the western part of the state. This, Larsen alleged, served to protect the financial integrity of his brother Charles' business, which underwrote bonds for those municipalities. Justice Zappala stood to benefit from "indirect kickbacks" from the outcome of these court cases, Larsen wrote.

It's hard to imagine how such allegations could have been amicably investigated and disposed of by the court. Apparently Larsen never considered that these charges would take on a life of their own outside the court. Larsen and the state's high court had been operating in such a sealed vacuum for so many years that the possibility may never have entered his head that this time the seal might be broken.

The bait set out by Larsen proved irresistible to Pennsylvania Attorney General Ernest "Ernie" Preate Jr. Preate over the years was frequently accused of making political hay out of sensitive cases. Worse, he'd lately been enveloped in a growing scandal of his own. Since mid-1991 the Pennsylvania Crime Commission had been investigating Preate. The commission would come to allege that Preate, in his former post as district attorney of Lackawanna Country, had solicited campaign contributions from video poker machine operators in return for lax or no prosecution. These charges in our state weren't all that unusual. Preate's predecessor, state Attorney General LeRoy Zimmerman, was investigated for his role in a multi-million dollar bribery scheme that ended in the public suicide of our state treasurer in 1987.

Preate, himself charged with taking money and going easy on targets of other investigations, was not the Mr. Clean needed by the people to investigate Pennsylvania's high court. Attorney General Preate, as I mentioned, over the years had taken nearly $20,000 from bond underwriter Charles Zappala's PAC.

Preate now was running for governor, and seemed in a particular hurry to inject himself in the growing controversy involving the Supreme Court. On December 8 Preate wrote the high court asking for information that would aide an investigation of the charges made by Larsen in his recusal petitions. On December 10 the high court refused to cooperate with the AG. "As you are no doubt aware," Zygmont A. Pines, a court administrator, wrote back to Preate, "the justices of the Supreme Court are duty bound to make no comment regarding matters that are pending before the court. Therefore, they are precluded from responding to your inquiry at this time. Upon disposition of this matter, the court will respond in an appropriate manner."

Here was the high court telling our state's chief law enforcement officer to flip off. In theory this could be regarded merely as a posed technicality. One could argue that the justices didn't want to open themselves to charges that they were displaying bias against their brethren in this deliberation by calling in the cops. Yet potential roadblocks could spring from these technicalities. State law precluded Preate from impaneling a grand jury with subpoena power unless he had the Supreme Court's consent.

Preate planned to plow ahead anyway. Already there had

been talk of special prosecutors. Preate's press secretary told reporters for the Philadelphia Inquirer, "We are proceeding with the selection of the special deputies." The Inquirer even leaked the names of the special prosecutors the day before they were announced. The relationship the Inquirer had with the investigators and the investigated would continue to be an important part of the story.

On Friday, December 11, 1992, at a news conference at the Philadelphia Bar Association, Preate displayed his two special prosecutors. The appointed prosecutors were Philadelphia attorney and former U.S. justice department official Edward S.G. Dennis, and James E. Tierney, a former Maine attorney general. Preate and Dennis stood side by side like strange doppelgangers, their receding hairlines, shiny foreheads displayed above slick lawyer suits and evasive smiles.

Preate said outside help was necessary because he personally knew the justices in question. "I wanted independent judgment," Preate told reporters. "I know every single one of the justices on the Supreme Court, some better than others." He hinted that he himself had a conflict, though one he characterized in personal terms. He would not mention that his campaigns over the years had received $19,800 from Charles Zappala's bond brokerage interests and political action committee.

At the time Preate seemed to have given his special prosecutors carte blanche to investigate any and all charges of malfeasance on the high court. There didn't seem, at the time, to be any caveats as to what they wouldn't look into. Just the opposite: talk was they would investigate anything and everything.

"Their charge from me is to go wherever the evidence leads," Preate told reporters. "Let the chips fall where they may. Nothing is off limits. Nothing is preordained. There will be no whitewash." He added, "We anticipate it's going to be a long, drawn-out and difficult investigation and it's going to raise questions of the greatest magnitude." All this would turn out to be balderdash. The investigation would turn out to be an ugly joke, a cake-walk for overpaid lawyers drinking at the pinstripe patronage trough. One official was quoted by the Inky as saying the investigators would have a budget that would start at about $200,000. It would turn out that Dennis alone would make that much. The entire investigation, before it had run its course, would cost nearly five times that — almost a million dollars, mostly to the overpaid lawyers.

From the outset a cursory reading of the Philadelphia Inquirer's coverage revealed several telling facts. It quickly became apparent that the state's largest monopoly newspaper had it in for Larsen. Larsen, after all, had been involved in a decade-long grudge match with the newspaper and was currently suing the Inky for defamation. There would be no favorable coverage, or even a pretext of fairness, where Larsen was concerned. It followed that in this controversy, the sides being drawn, the Inquirer must side with Zappala. It would become a case study in non-objectivity. Over the months to come the Inquirer would publish a ceaseless stream of articles defending Zappala, casting him as a victim worthy of sympathy. Whenever the Inquirer did cast a critical eye it would invariably be to denigrate Larsen's claim that all was not right with our high court.

In Edward S.G. Dennis, Preate's choice of "special prosecutor," the Inquirer and its corporate overseers had its inquisitor. In the next year-and-a-half nary a mention of Dennis's name would appear in the Inquirer without reassuring its readers that he was "a well-respected lawyer." You can almost conduct a CD-ROM search of the Inquirer's coverage of this affair by entering the phrase "a well-regarded lawyer." Fawning citations of Ed Dennis invariably pop up. Later I would learn that the Inquirer would go so far as to kill unflattering stories of Dennis.

For more than a decade Edward S.G. Dennis has been knocking around the highest levels, such as they are, of Pennsylvania politics. Dennis's mentor was former governor and U.S. Attorney General Richard Thornburgh. In this conscience-deficient, morally vacuous and dim school of

Pennsylvania politics Ed Dennis's career took root and flourished.

The sketchy facts of Dennis's life are out there. He grew up in middle-class, 1950s Delaware, his father a doctor, his mother once a college teacher. Following the desegregation of Delaware's public schools Dennis was one of the first blacks to enroll in otherwise all-white Dover Central High School. He still tells stories about the burden he felt climbing the steps of the high school, the only black in his class. Pop psychologists might wonder how this experience created in him a longing to fit in, to get on, to get along with the devil.

In 1967 he graduated from the Merchant Marine Academy with a degree in marine engineering. From there he entered law school at the University of Pennsylvania, where he met the early guiding light of his career, U.S. District Court Judge A. Leon Higginbotham Jr., for whom Dennis would later serve as law clerk. Higginbotham would go on to serve as a bottomless font of pubic praise for Dennis, mentioning his protégé as U.S. Supreme Court justice material.

Dennis's big break in the spotlight came with his appointment as U.S. attorney for the eastern district of Pennsylvania in the Thornburgh era. He rose to prominence prosecuting 'Lil Nicky Scarfo, a prosecution handed to him on a platter. Smiling Mad Nicky was stuffing the bodies of mob soldiers all over Philadelphia. Dennis wrestled control of the investigation from the county D.A. and ended up putting smiling Nicky away. Scarfo's behavior was so outrageous and deserving of the Big House that books on Scarfo mention Dennis only in passing.

Dennis in this period earned an undeserved reputation as politically independent when he refused to hire the son of a local party boss into the U.S. attorney's office. The party boss's son, William Meehan Jr., enjoyed the backing of U.S. Senator Arlen Specter. The rejection of Meehan owed less to Dennis's independence as it did to Dennis's allegiance to Thornburgh. Governor Thornburgh for years had been battling fellow Republican Specter. At one point Thornburgh threatened to run for Specter's senate seat.

Specter, the story goes, eked revenge on Dennis for the Meehan business by spiking Dennis's application for a federal judgeship in 1987. Turned down for the bench, Dennis went to work as assistant attorney general in Thornburgh's notoriously politicized U.S. Justice Department. In the Justice Department Dennis had replaced future Massachusetts Governor William Weld, who'd resigned in protest of Ed Meese's ethical lapses. The pattern emerges of someone who rushes into ethical voids, carries murky water, oversees and overlooks for The Boss. He seems too busy, too thick skinned to himself notice, much less protest, a lack of ethics. Perhaps he's the ultimate political terminator: a black Republican who does what he's told, with a nose that doesn't detect internal decay.

Dennis remained third in command in the Justice Department until 1990, when he resigned to join the Philadelphia office of Morgan, Lewis & Bockius. At that time the second-in-command in the Justice Department, Donald B. Ayer, had just resigned. Ayer had resigned, he said, to protest a controversy involving black Philadelphia congressman William Gray. Thornburgh was suspected of drumming Gray out of his congressional leadership position by leaking confidential Justice Department information to the media. Ayer, in resigning, charged that Thornburgh attempted to conceal an internal Justice Department investigation of the leaks, and pointed out that two of Thornburgh's aides had failed polygraph tests. Dennis, when he left the Justice Department to go into private practice, remained loyal to Dick, saying his resignation actually had been delayed so it would not be construed as being connected with Ayer's protest.

"I was hoping nobody else would resign," Dennis told the Inquirer. "I really, really want to go home."

Dennis, in the private life that followed, kept his door open to politics. Dennis was hardly the independent, politically disinterested prosecutor state AG Preate made him out to be when Dennis was named to investigate the Supreme Court in December 1992. Ed Dennis already was involved in political fundraising for Preate. Dennis was listed a co-chairman of the

"Annual Ernie Preate Golf Tournament and Tennis Round Robin and Cocktail Reception," held on June 17, 1992, at Harrisburg's Blue Ridge Country Club. Preate collected $1,000 from each foursome at that event, and "Hole Sponsorships" at $1,000 a hole.

What's missing, when you read about Ed Dennis, is a heart, a conscience. He seems ever loyal to his sponsors. In the list of cases he has handled for the powers-that-be there never seems to be bragging rights that he made the tough calls or, on his own, did the right thing.

I still have the newspaper clipping the Inquirer's parent company, Knight-Ridder, published in its State College paper announcing the triumphal appointment of Ed Dennis. There's a grinning photo of Dennis, short-cropped hair, round Dick Thornburgh eyeglasses, mustache, schmoozing it up at some hearing or press conference, about as flattering as it gets. All that's missing is the halo. "Appointing Ed Dennis, more than anything else, tells me Ernie Preate is deadly serious about this thing," Knight-Ridder quotes an unnamed "attorney and Democratic activist." "He said Dennis is 'a solid, sound-judgment professional who has not hesitated to step forward and put his personal reputation on the line when his job required it, and I'm thinking of the convictions he obtained against Nicky Scarfo....'"

The paper went on to say that, "Dennis is likely to find his latest assignment unlike anything he has ever encountered in a career that included overseeing the probes of Michael Milken, Gen. Manuel Noriega and Ferdinand Marcos.

"The Pennsylvania Supreme Court, controversial for decades, has never before come under such scrutiny, and has never been required to respond to the questions of a determined investigator."

The Inquirer generally lolled readers into the reassuring belief that in Ed Dennis we had an experienced heavy hitter who'd get to the bottom of things. Only when one stops to thoughtfully consider the kind of cases Dennis is asked to oversee, and the inevitable results of his "inquiries," do we begin to get a better portrait of him, and the role he has carved out for himself within the system. In the Noriega episode, for example, Dennis oversaw a case involving the kidnapping of a leader of a sovereign nation and his export to trial on American soil (forgetting, or maybe even covering up, the charges that the CIA and White House aide Oliver North may have had complicity in Noriega's hijinks).

Now Pennsylvanians were expected to believe that Ed Dennis was capable of standing up to party leaders who were charged with playing games with state courts, granting no-bid bond deals and receiving the resulting flood of political contributions.

The seeds of what was to come had taken root by mid-December 1992. On December 13 the Inquirer ran an editorial stating, "It's certainly more likely that the truth will be known now that the attorney general's investigation is under way, and with two such well-regarded former officials acting, in effect, as special prosecutors." The editorial concluded, "There is no real choice other than to cut right to the heart of the matter: Are there corrupt justices sitting on the Supreme Court who should be removed?" The question would ultimately come to turn on your definition of the word "corrupt." In my mind, the soundness of a judge, his integrity or his corruptibility, should be evaluated in terms of his fairness and impartiality. Ed Dennis and the Inquirer would prove to have different priorities.

On December 20 the Inquirer ran a telling puff-piece on Justice Zappala and family. Reporters Emilie Lounsberry and L. Stuart Ditzen described Justice Zappala as "a tall, distinguished-looking man with tinges of gray at the temples." Larsen's allegations "have been disturbing to members of the Zappala family — a clan that has produced eleven lawyers." Ditzen, incidentally, reported some of the early '80s Larsen disciplinary controversies for the Inquirer. Lounsberry and Ditzen would become the Inquirer's reporters (or unreporters) for this story. If the names Woodward and Bernstein can be contracted to

Woodstein, would this crack team be Lounzen or Ditzberry?

In this story Lounzen/Ditzberry went so far as to quote a member of the Zappala family (one Richard Zappala) as saying "I have never heard anybody say anything bad about (Justice Stephen Zappala). Except, of course, what I've been reading in the papers." Inquirer readers were frothily told that good 'ol swell Justice Zappala "is extremely intelligent.... He also is quite charming. His people skills are very good."

Charles Zappala, the bond underwriter at ground zero of the controversy, was graciously allowed his two-cents worth. "This is absolutely frustrating," the Inquirer quoted Charles as saying, "that any credence could be given to this absolutely absurd stuff." No one could ever accuse this quarter of not getting their say. Throughout the ordeal to come the Inquirer's coverage of the Zappala's would he consistently flattering — embarrassingly so. The only way the Inquirer's coverage of the Zappalas could be better would be if the whole matter was just dropped — something the Inquirer and (certainly) the Zappalas would seem to have preferred from the outset.

The article added that Justice Stephen Zappala's "powers on the court increased dramatically after the justices split the court's administrative plums in 1989. Previously, Nix had handled many of those functions, including preparation of the court's budget. That key assignment eventually became Zappala's. Zappala also is in charge of the court's computerization program. He also is the court's liaison with the state legislature.

"'We refer to Justice Zappala... as the chief justice of the west,' said one appellate-court judge. 'He more or less has preempted the powers of the chief justice.' Said another official close to the court: 'Steve Zappala is running that court. Everyone in the court system knows who runs the court. Whenever we need something, we call Steve Zappala.'"

The practice of "calling Steve Zappala" would be at the heart of the controversy. But who *is* Justice Zappala? The Inquirer's reportage didn't offer a clue. Instead readers were treated to endless vitriol that insinuated Larsen was mentally unstable.

Larsen's accusations were here described by the reporters as "increasingly bizarre." They made chuckles of Larsen's charge that Justice Zappala commandeered state Senator Fumo's car and drove too close, too fast in front of the Philadelphia hotel. "He's being accused of, what, attempted murder now?" they quoted Philadelphia Democratic chairman Robert Brady as saying. "He commandeered a car? You've got to laugh. What else could you do?" Brady, himself a patronage laughfest, is also a Pennsylvania Turnpike commissioner. Brady as much as the others had a stake in making light of Larsen's attack on partisan patronage, something the Inquirer never bothered telling its readers.

"It is very touchy right now," the Inquirer quoted someone it described as a "senior court official who agreed to speak about the mood at the court only on condition of anonymity." "Where it goes from here, you can't guess anymore. I just have no idea." To my ear, this "senior court official" speaks with the clipped phrases of Justice Zappala.

If the players weren't already in the Inky's pocket, certainly by the last day of the year the final draft of the script would be in hand. On December 31, 1992, the Inquirer published another Lounzen/Ditzberry masterpiece that laid the groundwork for everything to come. The headline read, "Sources say Justice Larsen Could Face More Severe Discipline — Even Removal." The article began by reporting that Larsen "could be removed from the bench as a result of his own request for review of a disciplinary case against him, according to sources close to the court." The prospect of Larsen's removal seems not to trouble the Inquirer at all, which seems odd, since newspapers usually are seen as having an interest in defending whistleblowers. Here the Inquirer acts almost as a cheerleader for punishing the loudmouth.

"One source said that Larsen's removal was a possibility," the Inquirer seemed to revel, almost quoting the betting odds. "...Two other sources said they believed removal was likely. 'That's definitely the way they're going,' said one; they may 'bounce him like a basketball.' The second source said that Larsen, in requesting reconsideration of the reprimand, had 'fashioned the club that beats him to death.'" The Inquirer seemed delighted with the turn the mob was taking. That's probably stating the matter too lightly. Our state's largest monopoly newspaper seemed to be cheering on the lynch mob, and their club.

"Larsen," Lounzen/Ditzberry informed us, "reached by telephone, declined to be interviewed." Wonder, wonder why? At least no one can say Larsen wasn't offered his chance to comment, same as the Zappala clan. I have to wonder what Lounzen/Ditzberry's question to Larsen sounded like: "Judge, do you have any response to anonymous comments we've dredged up that you might be thrown off the court for opening your mouth?"

If some of the Inquirer quotes from anonymous sources sounded, to my ear, to have the clipped sentences favored by Justice Zappala, I apparently wasn't the only one who thought so. The first week of the new year Larsen filed a court petition accusing Zappala and Cappy as being the only possible sources of the Inquirer's article(s), demonstrating, Larsen wrote, that his two antagonists had adopted a "judicially vindictive and retaliatory posture" against him. The Inquirer, not necessarily denying the charge, pointed out that Larsen had as yet failed to provide evidence supporting any of his earlier charges. The newspaper further took Larsen to task for repeating rumors that Justice Zappala wore a body wire to surreptitiously record con-versations. From here out the Inky would make it part of its regular menu to attack Larsen's repeating of "rumors," which precisely is what the Inquirer had been doing. I don't know, but it's hard for me to recall another instance of an American newspaper attacking rumor-mongering. Lumps of rumor, liber-ally spiced with innuendo and, some have successfully com-plained to juries, red-hot libel — these historically have been the Philadelphia Inquirer's stock-in-trade. The Inquirer seems upset that a justice should sink to its level.

More importantly, at this early, crucial juncture, before a serious investigation had even begun, a healthy taste of Larsen's blood was already in the water. Larsen's removal was already being widely foretold. The implication was that his basic charge of favoritism on the court wasn't even worthy of serious public consideration.

This then would provide an interesting contradiction to the fact that the Inquirer was cheering on chief prosecutor Ed Dennis and his sidekick, James Tierney of Maine. On January 11, 1993, the Inquirer's see-no-official-evil team of Lounzen/Ditzberry filed another in their steady stream of puff pieces, this time spreading it on thick on behalf of that dynamic duo, Dennis and Tierney. They presented the two prosecutors as engaged in a no-holds-barred search for the Godawful truth. Dennis was described here as "an independent, no-nonsense" former U.S. attorney. Tierney as "a Democrat who was majority leader in the state house in Maine from 1976 to 1980, who was attorney general from 1981 to 1991."

"Our charge is to follow the evidence wherever it goes, and that's what we're going to do," Tierney told the Inquirer.

"Dennis will focus primarily on criminal allegations, and Tierney on whether there have been ethical violations," the Inquirer informed readers. Batman and Robin, look out. "Both said they were determined to show their investigation is impartial and thorough, without political considerations.

"'We're here to stay,' said Tierney. 'We're going to work hard. We're going to find out everything we can and we're going to call it straight."

Here the Inquirer specifically mentioned, among other things, Larsen's allegations that Justice Zappala had displayed favoritism on the bench by having "guided" cases involving his brother's bonding business in a "special" manner.

"We're moving on a lot of fronts at the same time," Dennis told the Inquirer. "We're touching every base. There are some things coming over the transom and we're not ignoring it."

The Inquirer informed readers that "Dennis and Tierney urged anyone who had information relevant to their inquiry to contact them. The information, they said, would be treated confidentially.

"'We want to hear from people in the state,' said Tierney."

The boundaries of the inquiry wouldn't necessarily stop with Larsen's allegations, Inquirer readers were told. "Dennis said that, depending on what they learn, the investigation could broaden."

To read all this one would suppose Pennsylvanians were about to get a thorough look-see at their high court. One thing was sure: our state's largest newspaper already had a cozy working relationship with the special prosecutors. In the months that followed it would be hard to tell who was whose lap dog. Having a pipeline and a receptive ear at the prosecutor's office certainly was handy for the daily newspaper. Having a facile large-city daily lapping at their feet would make the going easy for the prosecutors. The point is, the dynamics, the relationships, the *sides,* were already decided and in place. The Inquirer was already talking about Larsen's removal, and was all but openly questioning his mental stability.

Throughout the ordeal to follow, curiously, the Inquirer would point out that our state's high court had been plagued for decades by controversy, the object of allegations of inferiority and favoritism. Yet the newspaper obviously didn't think Larsen's charges should be taken seriously. Here Pennsylvanians had a golden, once-in-a-lifetime opportunity to look into, and reform, their high court. The Inquirer, crippled by conflicts involving its own pique and finances, cooperated with state leaders to ensure that that investigation, and that reform, would never happen. It would become the Philadelphia Unquirer.

To understand the Inquirer's one-sided rush to judgment in the early '90s you must go back and read the newspaper's coverage of Larsen's first disciplinary run-in of the early '80s. In those 1983 articles the bitterness drips from the pages. The twenty-eight months of investigation and secret hearings that came to naught. The five judges on the disciplinary board who voted to exonerate Larsen. "Five judges, marching in lockstep," the Inquirer wrote. "Mark (their) names well, in scarlet," the Inquirer wrote of the five. The three non-judge members of the disciplinary board who dissented, calling for the disciplining of Larsen — mark those three names (including Surrick's) "in a nobler color," the Inquirer wrote. After Larsen's exoneration Surrick requested the disciplinary board's records of the investigation be made public. The full Supreme Court, including Larsen himself, voted to seal the record. "And then those five judges said the facts and reasons — the truth — are nobody's business but theirs.... Those five judges then were joined by five justices of the Supreme Court — including Justice Larsen — in a ruling that had the effect of suppressing the record," the Inquirer wrote. The Inquirer then got hold of the secret transcripts and published them.

"In sum, the transcripts tell a story of sordidness — of cynicism, lying, favor-trading, squalid politicking, racist demagoguery — at the highest and lowest levels of what should be the proud temple of the law," the Inquirer told its readers.

"The details will unfold as the information is read, digested and debated. Meanwhile, one thing is clear: Pennsylvania's judicial system, and thus its entire community of the law, is beset with a terrible sickness.

"Facing that squarely will be no simple task. The diagnosis, prognosis and cures are not for the weak. Cures must be found, however, lest the sickness spread further."

And spread, that sickness did, ultimately consuming the Inquirer. These were words of rage. These are the enraged words and the embittered tone of people who are not being listened to. In an Inquirer editorial, dated May 8, 1983, we see the first expression of the black idea. "Should Justice Larsen be expelled from the court? Common sense and the testimony in the transcripts cry out yes," the Inquirer wrote.

The disciplinary board, the Inquirer wrote, "now stands impotent. Worse, useless. Worse yet, openly indulgent of the offenses it was designed to combat — a grim caricature, whitewash brush dangling in hand." From then on the Inquirer wrote over and over of the Larsen "whitewash."

Over the next several months of 1983 the word impeachment also would ricochet, this time harmlessly, around the pages of the Inquirer. On May 8, 1983, Inquirer reporter Walter F. Roche Jr., filed an article titled, "Impeachment: Often tried, seldom successful in PA." Roche reported that house Speaker K. Leroy Irvis was investigating the possibility of impeaching Larsen. The idea hung around till winter and sputtered. By mid-November 1983, Larsen filed his libel suit against the Inquirer, the Pittsburgh Post-Gazette and Surrick.

William Broom, vice president for public affairs for the Inquirer's publisher, referred to Justice McDermott's suit when he told readers in 1983, "This is the second suit by a Supreme Court justice to grow out of accurate and sound stories we have done on problems in the state's court system. We view these suits as attempts by the justices to use libel actions as a weapon to intimidate us in their court system and prevent us from writing about the way the Supreme Court administers justice in Pennsylvania. We will not be intimidated."

In late November 1983 the Philadelphia Bar Association anonymously refused to adopt a petition calling for Larsen's impeachment, the Inquirer told readers, with more than a touch of disappointment.

Wait, the Inquirer would have to wait, until that winter ten years later when Larsen would over-step himself, and lay in open, lonesome vulnerability. Their white-hot moment would come when they'd have their man. They'd have him at all costs — even the costs of fairness and basic civility. Even at the cost of a clean state Supreme Court which, after all, the Inquirer had said in the beginning was the objective. They would suffer their souls to gain their scalp. After all, they'd said this wouldn't be work for the weak.

After it would be over Robert Surrick told me with one of his toothiest grins, "Chief Justice Michael Eagen once told Inquirer reporter Dan Biddle that Larsen would be the first justice to be impeached in one hundred years."

It was, I'd learn, to be an impeachment variously foretold.

CHAPTER 5

Finding the Invisible Case

Pennsylvania political leaders started breaking open check-books, and law books, early in 1993, saying they meant to get to the bottom of Larsen's charges of favoritism and case-fixing on the state's high court. Attorneys working for the turnpike had mentioned to me in passing that Justice Stephen Zappala had given one of their cases special attention. The turnpike was widely regarded as bond underwriter Charles Zappala's most important client. I figured the least I could do was attempt to look into the matter. Those calling for an investigation of Larsen's charges might mean business, so perhaps I could per-form a small public service by looking into the turnpike case.

Several obstacles stood in the way of my public service. I returned to the turnpike attorneys who'd expressed concern about the Zappala case. The turnpike attorneys, I discovered, suddenly seemed self-conscious. There's nothing like a major state-wide scandal and the naming of a special prosecutor to make a lawyer tight-lipped. They suddenly mentioned the attor-ney/client privilege. They reminded me that they worked for the turnpike and so were ethically bound to protect their client. They just couldn't turn the suckers in. All I could get about the case was that it involved the turnpike and one of its contractors.

Only a month or two before they casually alluded to a turn-pike court case that they'd said had been improperly brought to Justice Zappala. Before the heat was on, had I been interested, they probably would have easily told me everything. Now I couldn't even get them to name the particular case that bugged and obviously frightened them. I'd have to find out on my own. Yet without the name of a case, you can't get the docket number. And without the docket number you can't waltz into the public records and read about a case.

I first tried the obvious. One balmy afternoon I arrived at the state capitol and rode the elevators near the rotunda up to the courtroom of the state Supreme Court. The capitol courtroom that day was empty. The court, if it was in session, was riding the circuit, meeting in its other chambers in either Philadelphia or Pittsburgh. The Harrisburg courtroom is an old, airy chamber with high, ornately painted walls, gold-leafed appointments, and long tables where the lawyers sit with their books. The court these days only meets in its capitol chambers a week or two a year. Now it was empty and I stood in the doorway taking in the mysteries of the empty long tables. In the hallways outside the chamber oil paintings of long-gone justices stared icily and dog-faced down from high stations on the walls. Off to the side there was a quiet office where a worker or two attended to court business. It was a quiet, out of the way place, an odd, antiquated appendix to the main public action.

I finally caught the attention of a clerk. I asked for the name of all cases involving the turnpike that had come before Justice Zappala. The clerk seemed somewhat startled, and said he couldn't help me without a docket number. So much for the easy approach.

From there I visited a law library and tried to find the case in the law books. That proved just as fruitless, and even more frustrating. I couldn't find a comprehensive listing. The arcane language of the books and the confusing cross-referencing of cases — a Babel seemingly meant to drive the uninitiated to the brotherhood of lawyers — made my research all the more daunting and frustrating. The shelves of law books rose up like a wall, separating the curious from the truth.

I finally called one of the turnpike attorneys and said it was all but hopeless. Still the attorney was tight-lipped, wanting, if any of this should ever end up in court, to be able to truthfully say that no confidences had been betrayed. At last we arrived at a compromise. The attorney instructed me to ask a second turnpike attorney about a case involving a turnpike project called the Mid-County Interchange.

So I asked a second lawyer. Without missing a beat the second attorney told me, "Oh, you mean the Wagman case."

Now I had the name. I returned to the Supreme Court office in the capitol, asked the clerk to see any records of a case involving the Pennsylvania Turnpike and a contractor named Wagman. The clerk made an inquiry over the phone, jotted down some docket numbers, then told me I'd have to walk over to the prothonotary's office of Commonwealth Court, as the Supreme Court had had only a limited involvement with the case.

Commonwealth Court has its offices in the same capitol complex, in a building adjoining the capitol known as the South Office Building. I had only to take the steps down to the capitol rotunda, passing the capitol press office. Inside reporters slowly passed the day, shuffling now and then between their desks. From the newsroom you only had to walk the great flight of steps down to the main rotunda, over to the new annex, through a short tunnel to the South Office Building, up an elevator to Commonwealth Court. A three or four minute walk from the newsroom, no more than five for a particularly paralytic reporter.

I gave the clerk the docket numbers, was ushered into the records room, perched before a microfiche, and I began reading the strange case of G.A. & F.C. Wagman v. The Pennsylvania Turnpike.

Ah, the Wagman case. For the next two years the Wagman case would occupy that growing portion of my mind reserved for the outrageous and the hopeless. G.A. & F.C. Wagman is a family owned construction company in York, Pennsylvania. In April 1989 Wagman submitted the low bid to contract a $50 million turnpike interchange outside Philadelphia. Designed to connect the turnpike to a major state by-pass called The Blue Route, the interchange hopefully would bring fresh sources of toll money to the turnpike and its investors. The project was part of the multi-billion dollar 1986 turnpike expansion plan financed by no-bid bonds underwritten by Russell, Rea & Zappala.

In June 1989, as the turnpike prepared to award the contract to Wagman and work was to begin on the interchange, the turnpike was sued by a second, disappointed bidder. The second bidder charged that Wagman failed to comply with federal minority hiring guidelines. The project, involving an interchange proclaimed by the turnpike to be the most expensive in its history, funded by the largest bond issue ever floated by Pennsylvania government, suddenly found itself held up in court. Commonwealth Court Judge Paul Lehman ordered a review of the disputed hiring regulations, threatening months of delay. Turnpike Executive Director Louis Martin responded by announcing the turnpike would rebid the job. Wagman had lost the contract, unfairly so, its managers thought. In late August 1989 Wagman sued the turnpike, demanding a halt to the rebidding. There was another round of delays, this time before Commonwealth Court Judge Doris Smith. Judge Smith prohibited the turnpike from rebidding the job until the squabble was thrashed out in her court room.

The project, funded by all those Russell, Rea & Zappala bonds, already was a year behind schedule, and now Judge Smith threatened longer delays. The turnpike responded by seeking emergency relief from none other than Justice Stephen Zappala. In a two-hour emergency telephone hearing on September 18, 1990, Zappala allowed the turnpike to rebid the job. He restarted a project that had been held up in court for months.

On the surface it looked bad enough. The project was underwritten by the justice's brother Charles. The decision benefited an entity — the Pennsylvania Turnpike Commission — governed by Commissioner James Dodaro. Jim Dodaro, after all, was a childhood friend of the Zappalas, and a former law partner to Stephen Zappala. And Jim Dodaro unabashedly tells anyone who asks that he was responsible for awarding billions of dollars in no-bid turnpike bond work to Charlie Zappala's company.

The obvious question running through my mind was this: how had Justice Zappala become involved in this case? The answer given to me by turnpike attorneys would prove to be problematic for Justice Zappala, our state courts, and the multi-million dollar no-bid bond and political contribution scheme cobbled together by our state's politicians.

Once I'd read up on the Wagman case I went back and forth to several turnpike attorneys, ultimately, with the help of public records, piecing together an amazing story. I was told by the lawyers that turnpike Assistant Chief Counsel Jacqueline Verney, who supervised the Wagman case for the turnpike, received instructions from turnpike Executive Director Louis Martin to appeal the case directly to Justice Zappala. Turnpike administrators informed Verney that Justice Zappala would be waiting for her call. Martin, in turn, had taken these instructions from Commissioner Jim Dodaro.

It was the understanding of the attorneys I spoke with that Dodaro had apprised Justice Zappala — Dodaro's mentor and former law partner — of the troublesome case. According to plan, Justice Zappala weighed in using the high court's emergency powers, disabled Wagman's court challenge, and restarted the turnpike project — *financed by his own brother.*

It didn't take King Solomon to see this case wasn't handled with fairness or impartiality. This case strikes to the heart of Justice Larsen's allegations. The Wagman construction company had a basic right to a fair and impartial handling of its complaint. Instead it got buffaloed by the old-boy network of big finance and insider justice.

I spoke with several members of Wagman's management team, as well as the firm's attorney, who left no doubt that they thought the firm had been a victim of bad justice. They still feared retribution, and only spoke off-the-record.

"Why'd they have to take this case to Zappala, to Pittsburgh?" one Wagman employee asked me.

The turnpike attorneys, for their part, told me Justice Zappala had been called in not only for reasons of the Wagman case. By bringing in their big gun they'd hoped to teach Judge

Doris Smith, and other lower court judges, a lesson. "'Don't play games with us,'" a turnpike attorney explained The Message. "'This is what we can do.'" With a chuckle one turnpike attorney said Smith probably had learned the lesson. The next time a turnpike case came before Judge Smith, I was told, she ruled favorably for the turnpike.

All this certainly seemed like a job for Ed Dennis, the special prosecutor appointed to look into Larsen's charges of case-fixing. That is, if he and his investigation were for real. The least Dennis could do, it seemed to me, was to question the attorneys who handled the case for the turnpike.

CHAPTER 6

Lynch Mob Forms

In the first few months of 1993, while I was busy talking with turnpike attorneys to learn about the Wagman case, the Big Money look-see into our high court lurched on in stops and starts. A review of the political and editorial machinations of our party leaders and the Philadelphia Inquirer during this period reveals the formative bars of the concerto to follow.

Larsen, through January, February and into March, refused to cooperate with Attorney General Ernie Preate and Ed Dennis's investigation. On January 5 Dennis and co-counsel James Tierney wrote Larsen, apparently asking the justice for a sit down.

Larsen responded by writing a January 11 letter to the court's chief counsel, Zygmont A. Pines, and by circulating the letter to the other justices, and the presumptive investigators. Larsen reminded Pines that the latter had written Preate on December 10 opining that all the justices were "duty bound to make no comment regarding matters that are pending" before the court (i.e., Larsen's pending request for a reconsideration of his reprimand). Dennis and Tierney, Larsen wrote, asked in their letter "that I ignore the ethical constraints of the Code of Judicial Conduct, defy this court's directive and talk 'privately' and 'confidentially' with them."

Larsen accused Pines and one of Dennis's assistants, attorney Eric Kraeutler, of deal making to get Larsen to talk in "strict confidence," and so induce him to violate judicial cannon. Larsen obviously seems wary of the swarming mob. Dennis and Tierney's letter revealed "serious concerns about objectivity," wrote Larsen, insofar as the two had written that

Larsen's accusations against Zappala and Cappy "created a cloud over the court."

Reporting all this, the Inquirer allows Dennis to make the point that "it's clear that he (Larsen) does not sit as a justice in his own case," painting Larsen as perhaps viewing himself as above the law. The Inquirer, spinning its perpetual cynicism of Larsen and his charges of impropriety on the court, allows Tierney to add, "We think it's important to talk to him to see if there's merit to his allegations. As a matter of law, we don't feel there's any prohibition from Justice Larsen speaking to us."

This obstacle to Larsen's cooperation was knocked out of the way on January 22 when Zappala and Cappy reaffirmed Larsen's reprimand and refused his recusal request against them. "Each of the charges...is fabricated, frivolous and scurrilous," Zappala wrote in a 12-page opinion. Cappy wrote, "A litigant cannot await the outcome of his or her case then, upon receiving a result with which he or she is displeased, move to disqualify the judge who rendered the verdict," noting Larsen had supplied "nothing in support" of his charges.

On January 29, the court sent by electronic mail an unsigned two-page letter of public reprimand to Larsen's chambers. "A jurist must avoid even the appearance of impropriety to champion public confidence in the integrity and impartiality of the judiciary," stated the letter. "No improper motive has been imputed to your conduct, but because the conduct itself created an appearance of impropriety, we must impose the sanction of this public reprimand."

(Of course, whether Zappala himself had avoided "even the appearance of impropriety" by deciding cases involving entities funded by his brother was not the subject of the day.)

Already this juicy little court spat had spilled into the attorney general's office, and now the legislature was beginning to get involved. On January 25 state Representative Christopher McNally, a Democrat from Allegheny County, home of the Zappalas, Dodaro et al, introduced the first legislation seeking Larsen's impeachment. McNally's petition cited seven charges against Larsen, including the charge that Larsen had failed to report to police his allegation that Zappala had tried to run him down with a car.

That day fireworks also went off down the capitol hallway in the upper chamber of the legislature. State Senator Vincent Fumo, chairman of the senate appropriations committee, refused to allocate a requested $1.5 million to Preate for Dennis's investigation. Fumo, friend of Justice Zappala, patron of the Zappala bonding firm (and recipient of its contributions), said the attorney general had "overstepped his bounds" in convening the investigation. Preate, said Fumo, was poking around "for political gain."

Now came the first hints that Fumo might have deeper conflicts than friendship and political contributions. Fumo's aide Paul S. Dlugolecki told the Inquirer, "Vince's position on this is that the attorney general is not the appropriate party to conduct the investigation. The role rightly belongs to the Judicial Inquiry Review Board or the House of Representatives." But the JIRB was widely viewed as having been controlled by Justice Zappala, while many of the Democrats in the state house were owned by Fumo. Fumo's blatant flub to quash the probe proved too much for even the Inquirer to stomach, which is saying a lot, since the newspaper had already displayed a cast iron stomach and swallowed just about everything else.

In the same article in which it reported that Fumo had axed funding to the AG's probe, the Inquirer's Lounzen/Ditzberry team dropped the bombshell that "it has been rumored for weeks that Fumo was at the wheel of the car that Larsen alleged had tried to hit him." If the Inky had known about this for weeks, it hadn't bothered until now to share the information with its readers. Earlier in this article Larsen is castigated for not alerting police about the incident with Zappala and the car. Now the Inquirer is shown to have sat on information about Fumo.

"Fumo has consistently refused to comment," the Inky now tells its readers. "He continued to do so yesterday — except in the abstract.

"Fumo told reporters in Harrisburg that he would not comment 'on the Supreme Court or any member thereof.'

"Asked if he ever tried to run anyone down, Fumo replied: 'I have never in my life ever tried to run anyone down in a car, in a boat or in an airplane.' Fumo smiled and added, 'You all know me well enough by reputation that I usually hit the mark whenever I try to do anything.'"

Vince Fumo, Vince Fumo. He's so outrageously self-serving that he's become his own worst enemy and the reformer's friend. He's up front about bringing in those nice gorillas behind the casinos, and quick to help his troubled pals on the bench. The rest of the self-serving pieces of work in the legislature and in the newsroom could learn much from his honesty. Vince Fumo, like all bullies, understands and deals in fear. He was a hair's breath away from jail in the early 1980s, almost sent up to federal charm school for patronage activities, but let off on a technicality. He understands fear in other people, and how to make people fearful of him. Thus he denies trying to run over a judge with his car, yet understands the allegation can only enhance his bully's reputation. Ah, Vince Fumo, Vince Fumo. Where would Pennsylvania be without him? Who else could we so self-righteously kick around? Watch Vince Fumo get involved in some outrageous conflict, watch him get scared, see him worry about the charm school boys with the keys, watch him back down.

How these juvenile minds were occupied by this distracting incident with the car! That little putt-putt would become a hobgoblin of petty minds. Good thing Jesus didn't drive into Jerusalem, or the Lounzen/Ditzberrys of this world would have loused up that story too. There were several issues in play that seem more important than the beep beep and the honk honk so ably suited to the Inquirer's reporters. By blatantly attempting to obstruct funds for an investigation of the Zappalas, Fumo set the stage for equally outrageous conflicts by prosecutors, legislators and newspapers down the road. By slapping Vince's little wrist the Inquirer set the stage for the spectacle to come: Fumo henceforth would play the role of the

naughty whipping boy. For the next eighteen months the prosecutors and newspapers would good-naturedly kick Vince
Fumo, and he would good-naturedly take it. Why not? It was a
hell of a lot cheaper, and more fun, for everyone concerned
than losing all that Zappala bond money, and influence on the
courts.

Not to worry about appropriations chairman Fumo, the
Inky's readers were reassured. The AG's office had some money
in hand to pay the overpriced lawyers in the short run, and perhaps the Republicans would force a floor vote to end-around
Fumo. The next day the Inky nailed another plank to the scaf-
fold it'd been building. For months, between the lines, the Inky
had been indirectly casting doubts about Larsen's mental
soundness. Now the Inquirer lifts a page from the script of
Joseph Stalin. The newspaper begins to directly question
Larsen's mental stability. It allows Vince Fumo, of all noble
characters, to read the lines.

"State Sen. Vincent J. Fumo yesterday...said Larsen's 'mental stability' should be examined in a house impeachment proceeding," the Inky's lead paragraph told readers on January 27,
1993. "'If impeachment proceeds, it will probably be a hearing
on the mental competence of Justice Larsen,' said Fumo, a
Philadelphia Democrat. 'I've known Justice Larsen for a long
time. This is just bizarre and unaccountable behavior. The
whole thing is.'" Later in this article Fumo fesses up to being
behind the wheel of the All-Important Automobile, but Vince
"disputed Larsen's version, saying the car had not come within
20 feet of Larsen."

Fumo here performed good services by carrying everybody's diseased water. They let Vince mumble out loud the
hitherto unspoken Stalinist cant that Larsen was insane or
worse. Yet the Inky slaps Vince's wrists again. The paper quoted
the president-elect of the state Bar Association, H. Robert
Fiebach, as saying AG Preate had "gone out of his way" to
appoint that upstanding untouchable team of Dennis and
Tierney as "nonpartisan investigators.... It would be disappoint-

ing if political issues got in the way." (This could very well be *the* ironic understatement of the year 1993.)

The newspaper then quotes one Frederick L. Voight, of the Committee of Seventy ("a public policy organization"), who compared Fumo's blocking of investigative funds with past escapades in Pennsylvania's illustrious legislative history. "Voight said that 'much the same thing' happened in the mid-1970s when former State Sens. (sic) Henry "Buddy" Cianfranni, then chairman of the Appropriations Committee, and Herbert Fineman, then speaker of the house, cut funding for a special prosecutor looking into government funding."

Cianfrani and Fineman subsequently had a run-in with the boys who kept the keys to the charm school. That is, they were prosecuted by the feds for corruption and sent to prison.

The Inquirer ran the comparison past Fumo. "Fumo countered yesterday that the situation was different because Cianfrani and Fineman had been targets of that investigation," reported the Inquirer.

Fumo, we'd soon discover, had a greater conflict in all this than being behind the wheel of The Car. It would turn out that Vince was at the epicenter of corruption charges in our state courts. We'd soon learn that Philadelphia Mayor Ed Rendell had secured an airplane for Fumo to fly up to Lake Erie to see Justice Zappala days before the justice took up an important court case involving the city.

Anyway, Fumo got the telegraph. He obviously didn't like the comparison to those jailbirds Cianfrani and Fineman. They were rattling the keys to the charm school in Vince's face. See Vince get scared.

The next day Fumo relented and gave Preate $770,000 for the investigation. "'You guys beat the hell out of me,' Fumo told reporters when asked why he had approved the appropriation," the Inquirer reported, "'and I'm not going to stand in (Preate's) way. If he wants to spend it, let him spend it.' ...Fumo said he voted against a $1.5 million appropriation at a committee meeting on Monday because the request had come suddenly and he felt 'blindsided.' He said he had never intended to try to block Preate."

From adversity comes truth. And this was about as much adversity, and truth, as we would get. Here Fumo out and out calls our state courts a Democratic tool and the investigation of same a crooked Republican plot. "Fumo still expressed doubts about the cost of the investigation, its objectivity and whether it was even necessary," the Inquirer reported. "For one, he questioned Preate's hiring of 'Ed Dennis, a Thornburgh ally, to conduct an investigation of a Democratic court."

Ah, if Vince Fumo wasn't around to say it, who would?

So the Dynamic Duo got their loot. And some loot. Dennis expected $6,000 a week for up to 40 weeks, $240,000 through Sept. 30, at $200 an hour. Nice work if you can get it. Tierney and two other lawyers (hired from Dennis's firm of Morgan, Lewis & Bockius), not milking the cow for as many hours, got the same hourly rate but only $4,000 a week or up to $160,000 each. A private investigator pulled $50,000 plus bennies, bringing the total budget to $770,000. Before it would be over this budget would swell to more than a million.

Still, through February and into March, there was no indication that our complainant, Justice Larsen, had any intention of cooperating. In this period, early February 1993, newly installed house Speaker William DeWeese began making public rumblings about once again axing the funds to Dennis's investigation and making things simple by impeaching Larsen. DeWeese opined that $770,000 was absurd. "This is not the Manhattan Project," the speaker told reporters. "We're not inventing the atomic bomb."

DeWeese, of Green County, had replaced Bob O'Donnell as speaker after the latter was deposed in December 1992. While I was working on my book about the turnpike, insiders guffawed no end about the legal work O'Donnell's firm regularly received from the turnpike. Things got more humorous shortly after O'Donnell lost the speaker's job. Turnpike employees laughed that O'Donnell's law firm no longer received the commission's legal work, though a Green County bank (in DeWeese's district) suddenly was selected to hold a $35 million turnpike liquid fuel tax deposit. State records also showed that DeWeese had received $1,500 from Zappala interests, while Fumo had taken $10,200 from his friends at the Zappala brokerage. DeWeese was another creation and servant of the big-money that had bought and sold Pennsylvania's legislature.

Nowhere, to my reading, were Fumo and DeWeese's conflicts ever mentioned in the Philadelphia Inquirer. The Inquirer at this time starts to shift into an ugly little gazette of mob justice. The positioning of the newspaper (and Democratic leaders) at this time seemed to serve three purposes: to get Larsen at all costs; to preserve the big-money interests of the non-competitive bonding scheme (read, the interests of the party leaders), as well as the corporate assets of the Inquirer's publisher, Knight-Ridder; and not to leave one's fingerprints on the body.

So it was on February 11, 1993, when the Inquirer ran a truly bizarre article relating that house Democrats had decided against naming a "select committee to investigate the court and determine whether impeachment should be the course of action." The Inquirer never bothers to explain why impeachment should be foremost on the menu. Rep. William Lloyd, a Democrat from Somerset, was quoted as urging his comrades to leave the matter of an investigation to "people who make their living investigating and prosecuting crime." We're told by Pravda on the Delaware that party leaders held "a consensus we should lay low," in the words of someone described as "one Democrat," until Dennis's investigation had been concluded. There seems to be the unspoken, yet (for now) checked, desire to simply forget any stinking investigation and straightaway lynch the bastard. Rather than form a select committee the Democrats opted to refer the matter to the judiciary committee and its chairman, Thomas Caltagirone, comrade from Berks County. "We are not a lynch mob," Caltagirone intoned.

The Inquirer abandoned all pretense of objectivity on March 2, 1993, when it published an article that was not just a

puff-piece, but PR for RRZ. Here Stuart Ditzen waxes syco-
phantic for almost two thousand words about the poor bond
underwriting firm of Russell, Rae, Zappala & Gomulka and its
current "unpleasant problem" concerning Larsen's allegations.
"For a firm that has had a meteoric rise in the realm of public
finance, the last three months have been a nasty time." Here
Ditzen serves as apologist for a corrupting insiders' game.
Politicians, ever on-the-prowl for contributions, in the 1980s
and early '90s awarded brokers like RRZ&G billions of dollars
in no-bid bond underwriting; the brokers then tendered hundreds of thousands of dollars in campaign contributions to their
political patrons.

"Thirty-one stories up, four crisply turned-out business
executives pace the floor of their airy offices and seethe," the
article begins. As we see, Inquirer reporters usually are compe-
tent enough to handle the simple counting of office floors and
bodies. The Inky's editorial mind boggles when it toadies up to
The Big Boys and the numbers get bigger.

The men of RRZ&G, Ditzen tells us, "have been frustrated
for three months by a tricky and unpleasant problem: They
believe that Pennsylvania Supreme Court Justice Rolf Larsen
has indirectly accused their firm of paying kickbacks for bond
underwriting work."

This certainly isn't what Larsen wrote in his petitions, but
never mind. Ditzen goes on to lavish paragraphs telling us of
the bold, brave men of RRZ&G. "They were baby boom whiz
kids with MBA and accounting and law degrees who got
together in the late 1970s and barged into the staid world of
investment banking, armed with computers and innovative
ideas." Ditzen, we see here, has quite a future in investment
firm public relations. So let's get to know our neighbors, the
no-bid bond traders. Ditzen continues, as if writing a script
treatment for a situation comedy:

"Two of them had prominent names in Pittsburgh: Andy
Russell, now 51 and vice chairman of RRZ&G, was a popular
former star of the Pittsburgh Steelers football team. While playing ball, Russell earned a master's degree in business adminis-

tration and launched a career in business.

"Charles Zappala, now 44, was a lawyer from a prominent Pittsburgh political family. His father, the late Frank Zappala, had been a state representative and a magistrate and was a leader in the Italian community. His elder brother, Stephen, a former Allegheny County solicitor, was then an Allegheny County judge headed for a seat on the Supreme Court.

"Soon after joining forces in 1978, Russell and Zappala, and associates Gomulka, 45, a certified public accountant, and Rea, 44, another MBA, achieved tremendous success.

"Their bond underwriting business, RR&Z Public Markets, soared to become one of the top firms in its field in Pennsylvania. And it remained there.

"Since 1980, the firm has underwritten more than 400 bond issues in Pennsylvania worth $16.5 billion, according to the Securities Data Co. of Newark, N.J., which keeps records on stock and bond markets.

"The firm's clients range from small municipalities and school districts to the state's biggest urban governments — Allegheny County and the city of Philadelphia.

"Its biggest client of all is the Pennsylvania Turnpike Commission. Between 1986 and last year, the firm underwrote 11 turnpike bond issues worth a total of $2.6 billion.

"How did it do it?

"RRZ&G and people who have done business with the firm give these answers:

"The firm cultivated politicians and local officials around the state — the people who give out bond underwriting contracts in the cities, counties, townships and school districts. Through a political action committee, it gave generously — a total of $204,000 in 1991 and 1992 — to the campaigns of governors, mayors, and county and local leaders."

It's worth noting, I think, that the Inquirer lowballs the contributions by counting only those tendered in 1991 and '92. I counted $545,805.07 in contributions from 1987 (the year after the first big no-bid turnpike deal) to 1993.

"'You must know the decision makers,'" Ditzen goes on to

quote Charles Zappala.

Ditzen then explains how the firm refinanced debt for municipalities, including Allegheny County, Philadelphia, and the turnpike, to reduce costs. He doesn't mention that any bonding firm could, and would, do the same thing, and that the bonding firms make large profits for refinancing debt.

"...The firm was recommended for turnpike underwriting work in 1986 by James J. Dodaro, a member of the Turnpike Commission, a longtime friend of the Zappala family and a former law partner of Justice Zappala's.

"'Clearly I was an advocate of theirs,' said Dodaro. 'Based on their performance, they have been involved in every issue we've done since then.'

"RRZ&G refinanced the turnpike's debt last year, selling a $570 million bond issue that saved the commission $14 million.

"In Philadelphia, RRZ&G sold $110 million in high-interest, short-term notes in 1991 at the height of the city's fiscal crisis, enabling the city to remain solvent.

"Since then, RRZ&G, with the backing of state Sen. Vincent J. Fumo and city Controller Jonathan Saidel, has been named by the Rendell administration to participate in the underwriting of city general obligation and Redevelopment Authority bonds."

The Inquirer never bothers to tell its readers that there's nothing terribly inventive about any of this. Nationwide, over the last few decades, there's been an almost universal concern about the symbiotic awarding of no-bid bonds and the resulting obligatory and reciprocal political contributions. RRZ&G certainly didn't invent this. The U.S. bonding industry came to feel so victimized by the politicians that it pushed reforms that were adopted by the Securities and Exchange Commission in 1994. These new regulations now limit political contributions.

The point is, in this article we get a totally shameless one-sided puff piece that justifies, sanitizes and elevates everything the Zappalas are up to while denigrating Larsen's complaints.

In his recusal motion Larsen accuses Justice Zappala of guiding cases in a special manner so that RRZ&G-issued bonds are rescued from risk, to the financial benefit of Justice Zappala, who, Larsen alleges, receives "indirect" kickbacks through layered corporations. Larsen, in the end, would be judged by the most literal, strictest definition of those words. Had he'd alleged Columbus sailed the ocean blue in fourteen hundred ninety-two, God help him if that mossy-green Atlantic wasn't blue.

Charles Zappala and his colleagues "emphatically deny any tie, other than by family relationship, between their firm and Justice Zappala," the March 2 Inquirer article goes on reassure us.

"In recent interviews, the RRZ&G executives said the justice had no role in any of their far-flung businesses or partnerships — all privately held — which include hydroelectric plants, landfills, cable television and real estate holdings.

"'Absolutely, unequivocally, definitively none,' said Charles Zappala." Such trust has been developed between bond underwriter and big city daily that the Inky is allowed to go through RRZ&G business records. "The firm last week made available to The Inquirer for review a list of its enterprises — 21 corporations and 12 partnerships — and the principals and shareholders in them. Stephen Zappala's name did not appear."

The Inquirer reports that Justice Zappala's financial statement filed with the state lists him as holding bonds issued by Allegheny County, Lackawanna County and the Pennsylvania Turnpike. Here's where we start to see it's A Family Affair. The bonds, we'd later find out, were sold, at market value, to Justice Zappala and his wife by their son. The Inquirer notes, "One of Justice Zappala's sons, Gregory, is director of public finance at RRZ&G with responsibilities for developing business for the firm. Another son, Stephen Jr., a Pittsburgh lawyer, formerly worked as a consultant for the firm."

The Inquirer mentions that Justice Zappala allowed the newspaper to examine records of his purchase of the bonds. The newspaper makes it a point to say the justice made the records available "through a lawyer," obviously to blunt further criticism that Zappala and the state's largest monopoly daily are in bed together. The records of the bond purchases show that Justice Zappala "and his wife had been billed and paid list prices for them — a total of $60,347 between 1985 and 1988," the newspaper reports.

In this March 2, 1993, article, and all subsequent Inquirer articles, the newspaper would take Justice Larsen to task for the *exact wording* of his complaints against Zappala. The newspaper would totally ignore the spirit of the complaint, and would time and again refuse to look into other curious cases, such as the Wagman case, where plaintiffs were denied impartial justice at Zappala's hands.

The newspaper, and finally the special prosecutors Dennis and Tierney, would only look into two specific labor cases mentioned by Larsen — a case involving the city of Philadelphia and the Pennsylvania Labor Relations Board, and a case involving the Allegheny County Port Authority.

In the March 2 article, the Inquirer presents the straw argument that RRZ&G bonds were never "rescued from risk," in Larsen's words, in either court case. It never asks the crucial question: Does it present an appearance of unfairness for Justice Zappala to rule on cases involving entities funded by his brother's underwriting? Is it fair for other Pennsylvanians to have Zappala rule on cases involving his family's interests?

The Inquirer would have us believe that it's not at all concerned about Zappala's appearance of partiality. More than a year after the publication of this tone-setting March 2 article, when Larsen was about to be impeached, it would come out, buried in the impeachment proceedings, that an Inquirer reporter had once telephoned Zappala raising ethical questions when the justice was about to rule on a third case involving interests financed by his brother. Zappala then had taken the hint, and removed himself from that case.

This interesting incident was only one of many not mentioned in the Inquirer's articles leading up to Larsen's impeachment. In this formative period our state's largest newspaper keeps hitting the same chords.

With the Philadelphia Inquirer thus running interference, our state's political nabobs obviously felt they'd been given the green light to act and do their worst. Two days after the publication of Inquirer reporter Stuart Ditzen's amazing apology for Team Zappala, house Speaker William DeWeese again raised the specter of cutting funds for Preate and Dennis's investigation, and impeaching Larsen. "DeWeese, a Democrat, strongly indicated that the best course of action ultimately may be impeachment proceedings against the man who has leveled accusations of wrongdoing about members of the state's highest court: Justice Rolf Larsen," the Inquirer reported.

"'I am loath to use the word impeachment at this juncture specifically, but in general terms that is obviously a target,' said DeWeese, who said he has become increasingly skeptical of Larsen's accusations in recent weeks."

The Inky went on to quote Speaker DeWeese: "'We do not need a $700,000 Rolls Royce investigation,' said DeWeese. If there were a need for a criminal inquiry, he said, Preate's own staff should handle it or federal authorities should become involved. But for now, he said, he sees no need for a 'retrospective' into the last 10 years at the Supreme Court. 'I have heard nothing concrete...against Justice Zappala and I think it best the Supreme Court get on with its jurisprudential challenges,' he said."

The next day, on March 6, 1993, the Inquirer published another story suggesting funds for an investigation may be cut, puffing Ed Dennis yet again, as usual, as follows: "Dennis was a career prosecutor, known for being a stickler for maintaining a U.S. Attorney's Office that acted without regard for politics."

All this — the Inquirer's incessantly rabid one-sidedness, Speaker DeWeese's subsequent itchiness to deep-six the investigation and impeach Larsen — finally hit home. Within days Larsen's attorney notified Dennis that Larsen would cooperate in "an investigation." By the ides of March 1993, Larsen would be subpoenaed to appear before a grand jury.

Already others were talking to Dennis and cohorts. James C. Schwartzman, a Philadelphia lawyer and mutual friend to Larsen, Justice Zappala and state Senator Fumo, told the state investigators he had been out to dinner with Larsen and had dropped the justice off at the Four Seasons Hotel the night Larsen alleged he'd almost been run over. Schwartzman told the investigators he hadn't seen the incident described by Larsen. That night, he said, a dark Mercedes had rolled without incident between Schwartzman's 1988 BMW and the hotel entrance. "The car went by," Schwartzman told the investigators. "We finished saying goodbye. He (Larsen) went in the hotel, and I left." After he'd dropped Larsen and was driving home, Schwartzman said, he got a call on his car phone from state Senator Fumo. Fumo explained that he and Justice Zappala had also been out to dinner, and that Fumo was dropping the justice off at the hotel, when they spotted Schwartzman dropping Larsen. Schwartzman said Fumo told him Zappala had asked the senator to drive around the block as he didn't want to encounter Larsen. Both justices were staying in the expensive hotel while the court heard cases in Philadelphia.

Schwartzman would say that Larsen hadn't known about the offending car, let alone who had been inside it, until he, Schwartzman, had told Larsen about three or four days later. "I related to him the telephone call that I had gotten from Senator Fumo," Schwartzman said. "I thought it was, I wouldn't say funny, but it was something that was worth repeating." Larsen later sent Schwartzman a copy of the recusal petition alleging Zappala had commandeered the car and had almost run him over. "I didn't understand it," Schwartzman told the investigators of Larsen's allegations. "...I just didn't understand the whole concept of 'commandeer a car.' ...I didn't understand or follow the logic."

We know about Schwartzman's taped interview with Dennis's team because on March 17, 1993, the Inquirer published liberal transcripts, described by the Inky as "a tape-recorded interview, to which the Inquirer obtained access."

Now where oh where did the Inquirer get "access" to this interview? Obviously from Dennis and Tierney, who for months had been ceaselessly puffed by the Inquirer, and who now give the reasonable impression they were returning the favor by leaking official interviews. The important thing for us to glean from this is not the banal story of the cars, but that our state's largest monopoly newspaper and the special prosecutor were not only in bed together, by this time they were well on their way to a happy and mutually beneficial honeymoon.

The Inquirer on March 25, 1993, finally got around to publishing an article that half-heartedly described the two 1992 cases to which Larsen had referred in his recusal petition. The newspaper noted that both cases were unusual in that they leapt over lower courts and received expedited treatment by the Supreme Court. Justice Zappala played "an active role" in both cases, the Inquirer pointed out, yet didn't go into too much depth on this delicate issue. This article doesn't even mention that Zappala's brother at various times underwrote bonds for the litigants of these two cases — Allegheny County and the city of Philadelphia. In fact Charles Zappala would point out to investigators that Allegheny County "stopped doing business with RRZ after Justice Zappala's intervention in the Port Authority case." Still, no use making anybody think too hard.

Instead, Larsen is castigated by the Inky for not objecting at the time to the procedural route taken by these cases. This is a tune Dennis also plays on his fiddle. "I would assume that a justice could file a dissenting opinion of presumed conflict of interest," the Inquirer quotes Dennis. "I would think there would be some documentation if such a protest was lodged."

Later I would find out for myself just how impossible, futile, and perhaps dangerous it is to bring a questionable case to the attention of the political old-boy network, including the Philadelphia Inquirer and Ed Dennis. When it came to Team Zappala, these guys for some reason didn't want to see, hear or speak any evil.

CHAPTER 7

Spooks

The spring of 1993 turned into summer. I continued writing my book about the turnpike. I planned to send a copy to Ed Dennis and the prosecutors when the book came out later that summer. That would still leave several months for the investigators to look into the Wagman case.

One day while I was writing I got a phone call from a man who wasted little time informing me that he was an acquaintance of Justice Zappala's. I'd already written two books about my state's justice system, and I'd grown accustomed to receiving letters and phone calls from people with an interest in, and distrust of, the politicians who administer Pennsylvania law enforcement. Though I usually get a name, I often don't know the background of these callers, or the interests they represent. I think of these shadowy people as "spooks."

Spooks I encounter usually have a few things in common. They're usually law enforcement buffs, and they usually brag of having friends on the inside, and special knowledge of this or that. Spooks I run across usually are of World War II vintage, they usually think the country is going to hell, and they're usually brimming with conspiracy theories.

Often, if I'm not careful, the spooks will start bending my ear and begin laying on the conspiracy theories. In the early 1990s the spooks I'd encounter were all lathered up about the death of a freelance writer who had been found dead in a Virginia motel, the victim, the police said, of an apparent suicide. The dead writer had been working on a book called The Octopus, in which he was supposedly going to tie President George Bush and his attorney general, Richard Thornburgh, to all sorts of misbehavior involving the CIA, the mafia, and scandals of the day running from Jeb Bush, the savings and loan fiasco, the Inslaw affair to BCCI. All the world's evils and ills were tied together in the dead writer's lost and unpublished book, the spooks believed, with Bush and Thornburgh at the center of countless tendril conspiracies. Hence the term, Octopus. A true red-blooded spook will tell you that The Mob had bumped off the freelance writer at the behest of the Republicans. The often repeated canon of the spooks is that the writer had been on his way to his publisher on the day he died, that his manuscript and notes had been stolen. As time went by the Octopus scandal became more far-reaching. To hear the spooks tell it, the pope, Henry Kissinger, Queen Elizabeth, Henry Aaron, Betty Crocker and Mother Teresa were all going to be exposed by the dead writer. In this grand conspiracy Bush and Thornburgh controlled all, down to the whales who spoke French at the bottom of the sea, leviathans who, once given marching orders from George and Dick, were going to pull the plug at the bottom of the briny deep so that the oceans of the world would drain out and extinguish the pope's fire at the center of the earth.

This spook, who was the acquaintance of Justice Zappala, spewed all that and more. He was a loud braggadocio. It turned out (predictably) that he hated Bill and Hillary Clinton. This spook claimed close friendships with U.S. Senators Orrin Hatch and Dennis DeConcini, as well as contacts with unnamed (of course) Secret Service agents. He spewed the usual garbage about Hillary Clinton, whom he seemed to particularly dislike. He also disliked homosexuals. It was the damn faggots who were ruining the country, the acquaintance of Justice Zappala confided to me. Just look at the annual Gay Pride Parade in Washington. "A bunch of damn faggots giving each other blow jobs in front of the Lincoln Memorial. What in God's name this country comin' to!"

This acquaintance of Justice Zappala ended up buying several hundred dollars worth of my previous books. He said he wanted copies of my books to spread around, so that people could see what a bunch of damn crooks these Pennsylvania Republican prosecutors were. He wanted to know what I knew about Attorney General Ernie Preate and Ed Dennis. I told him not much. He led me to understand that he was on friendly terms with an investigator in the Pennsylvania Crime Commission, which Preate had fought to abolish, and which was then conducting an on-going investigation of its own into Preate's associations with the state's video poker industry. Zappala's acquaintance would spend nights at this Crime Commission investigator's house, gleaning what he could about the developing scandal involving the state attorney general.

He said he was also in touch with reporters at the Harrisburg Patriot-News, who also were currently "investigating" Preate's contacts with the state's video poker business. They were going to take care of Preate, all right, he reassured me. "They're all a bunch of damn crooks!"

These calls kept coming and, one evening, while I sat listening, this man got on another phone (he seemed to have several phones in his office) and had a conversation with someone he said was Justice Zappala, calling him "Steve." In the ensuing weeks, the acquaintance of Justice Zappala kept calling me to buy more books. He even drove up from Pittsburgh for a load of books. He led me to believe he was helping Justice Zappala by attempting to smear the Republicans, in the event Ed Dennis's investigation got serious. He offered to introduce me to Justice Zappala, saying Steve would grant me an interview for my new book. He gave me special instructions to call the justice's office, and I ended up having a brief but pleasant chat with Justice Zappala. Zappala promised to get back with me to set up an appointment for a meeting. I'd planned to discuss the Wagman case with Zappala.

Before the meeting with the justice could be arranged the acquaintance learned that I was in contact with fugitive Cambria County Judge Joseph O'Kicki. O'Kicki and been convicted of several crimes, had lost his spot on the bench, and had fled this country for Slovenia before his sentencing. Now on the lam, O'Kicki was seeking to have the state Supreme Court overturn his conviction. The acquaintance of Justice Zappala advised me to bring up O'Kicki's case with Justice Zappala during our meeting, that Justice Zappala was just the sort of decent guy who could help O'Kicki. "I'll tell Steve all about it before you meet him," the acquaintance reassured me.

This caused me to drop all attempts at meeting Justice Zappala, as I feared I was now being roped into just the sort of improper contact the turnpike attorneys had complained to me about the Wagman case. Ex parte communications, improper back channel contacts with Justice Zappala. Exactly what had landed Zappala in hot water.

So I never pressed for the meeting with Justice Zappala, but I did have one more meeting with the acquaintance. He bought me lunch one day at the Harrisburg Hilton. I brought along a bagful of my books, which he planned to distribute to God knows who. "They're all a bunch of damn crooks," the acquaintance of Justice Zappala reiterated over lunch, filling me in on the Harrisburg Patriot-News' ongoing skullduggery concerning Preate. In this man's book only Larsen earned more venom than Preate. "Larsen's a nut," he kept telling me. "There's nothing to what that nut says." I said I disagreed, that there might be something to what Larsen said.

"Do you think Steve's a crook?" he suddenly asked me.

I said only that judges had to be held to a different, and a higher standard than most politicians.

"You better let me know if you think Steve's a crook," the acquaintance of Justice Zappala told me. "Steve promised he'd help me out with a case, and I want to know if he's a crook before I get him involved."

My eyebrow may have risen, but I said nothing. I sat in the restaurant of the hotel, watching people stroll by on the sidewalk outside.

CHAPTER 8

Preparing the Noose

My book on the Pennsylvania turnpike, *When the Levee Breaks*, was published in late July 1993. The book included an entire chapter on the Wagman case. On August 6 I sent a copy to Ed Dennis. "Various individuals," I wrote Dennis, "have shared with me their concern that Justice Zappala improperly interfered in a legal case involving a Pennsylvania turnpike project. I believe you can easily and independently verify the account published in my book."

Ed Dennis said he wanted members of the public to send in whatever information they had. It seemed I had a piece of the puzzle that should interest him. Dennis merely had to pull the case, where he would find the complete court records, including the names of the involved attorneys, whom he could interview.

For good measure I called Justice Larsen's office, and the office of his attorney, and left messages that they could find copies of the book at bookstores around the state.

A few days later I got a call from Ed Dennis's secretary, who asked me to overnight a copy of my book to co-investigator James Tierney at his address in Maine.

Almost two months went by. My book sold well, and I kept busy. I heard nothing about the grand jury investigation. There were no trembles on my web. One day news came over the radio that the investigation into the state Supreme Court had been completed, and the grand jury would hand in its report in a day or two. The report said the investigators found no evidence of case-fixing on the high court, that Larsen would be prosecuted for taking drugs without a prescription, and his impeachment would be recommended. Though the report on Larsen's drug usage was shocking, it certainly wasn't a surprise. Over the summer, on August 3, 1993, the Inquirer ran a story titled "Jury looks into Rxs for Larsen." "Investigators conducting the criminal inquiry of the Pennsylvania Supreme Court are examining whether Justice Rolf Larsen obtained prescription drugs through his employees, according to court system sources," began the article. Wonder wonder who leaked this to the Inky?

I began checking around and learned that the investigators hadn't spoken with the turnpike's attorneys about the Wagman case. They hadn't even *asked*.

What this contagion called for, of course, was sunlight. If the state's newspapers would run a story about the Wagman case perhaps it would force the "investigators" to look at the case.

These days perhaps only three outlets had the muscle and visibility to force Preate and Dennis to do an honest job: the Pittsburgh Post-Gazette, the Inquirer, and the Associated Press.

That meant trouble. The Inquirer more and more is seen as a mouthpiece for party leaders. The Post-Gazette had problems of its own. At the time the Pittsburgh paper was recuperating from a debilitating labor strike. For some time the Pittsburgh Press and the Post-Gazette had been sharing resources such as presses under a government approved joint operating agreement. On May 17, 1992, the Teamster's Local 211 struck the Press and other unions walked out. The Post-Gazette's staff, including reporters, were laid off, and neither paper was published for the remainder of 1992. In the end the Press was destroyed, bought out by the Post-Gazette under a renewed government stamp of approval. The first paper published by the new Post-Gazette hit the streets January 18, 1993, in the middle of a historic Supreme Court flap that, after all, was centered in Pittsburgh. Even after the strike the newspaper seemed slow to recover. "It was a little rough at first," a Post-Gazette staffer confided to me recently. "There were lots of problems."

The reconstituted Pittsburgh paper really didn't seem to be all there. Neither of the state's remaining big city dailies was what it once was. Then there was the never-spoken matter of the defamation suit Larsen had filed against both the Inquirer and the Post-Gazette. Could these guardians of truth, justice and objectivity be expected to ride to the rescue?

I called the Associated Press. The bureau chief was Rich Kirkpatrick. I explained to Kirkpatrick that turnpike attorneys had expressed concern that Justice Zappala had fixed a case for them, and the duly appointed investigators refused to even ask them about the case. Could Kirkpatrick send a reporter to Commonwealth Court to see the file on the Wagman case? I asked.

"I don't have the resources to do that," he told me. I pointed out it was only a three-minute walk from the AP's capitol office to the court prothonotary in the state's South Office Building, next door.

He said they were busy, and didn't have a reporter to spare to send on a three-minute walk. I should try to get the Inquirer or the Post-Gazette to pick up the story, Kirkpatrick told me. *They* had the resources, he said. If one of the AP's subscribing newspapers ran the story, the AP would pick it up, he told me.

Didn't Kirkpatrick realize they were about to prosecute Larsen for drug use? I asked him. Didn't he realize this would be the first impeachment of a judge in our state in more than one hundred and eighty years? Couldn't he spare a three-minute walk to weigh for himself whether the prosecutors were ignoring evidence that Larsen was right about case-fixing? I asked.

Kirkpatrick repeated he didn't have the resources.

I called the Inquirer, and was ultimately routed (God help me) to Emilie Lounsberry. She sounded bored. You could almost hear her filing her nails. She didn't need to see no stinking court documents. She said she wasn't interested in any story

about case-fixing on the state Supreme Court. She said she
wasn't interested in talking to turnpike attorneys about any case
Justice Zappala had fixed for them. She said she didn't want a
copy of my book. I thanked her for her undivided attention,
and hoped I wouldn't get a bill for her time. No doubt she was
too busy filing a story about whether Larsen should be impaled,
pickled or merely drawn and quartered, his flesh separated,
singed, peppered and stretched over lamp shades, and there was
no use lousing up a whole year's worth of stories she'd already
filed, no use letting reality get in the way of a good smear.
She'd already invested quite a bit of blindness and lack of effort
to get things bubbling this far.

Besides, the comrades at the Politburo hadn't given Pravda
the okay. The struggle after all was against Comrade Larsen,
not Comrade Zappala.

I called Bill Moushey of the Pittsburgh Post-Gazette. He
said he was interested in talking to those involved in *Wagman*. I
thanked him, I think, profusely. Then I ran into the next problem. None of the people I spoke with wanted to talk to the
Pittsburgh paper.

This was the second time I'd run into this problem in the
same year. In the spring of 1993, when fugitive Judge Joseph
O'Kicki of Cambria County had skipped bail to seek asylum in
Slovenia, the Post-Gazette had sent a reporter across the ocean
to track down the judge. At the time the judge-on-the-run was
communicating to me regularly over the Internet. O'Kicki
didn't trust the reporter sent by the Post-Gazette. The judge
said the reporter continually displayed a bias for the other side
of the story, and refused to see the guy. An editor at the
Pittsburgh paper called me to ask if I could intercede on behalf
of their man to get an interview. It looked a trifle embarrassing
for them to be footing the bill to have some guy cooling his
heels in a hotel six thousand miles away. I honest to God tried
to help, but O'Kicki refused to talk to them. O'Kicki said the
Pittsburgh reporter had threatened to turn him over to
Slovenian authorities, or have him kidnapped. The authorities

never got their man, and the Post-Gazette never got their story. That was just another unlikely story involving the Press and the Bench in Pennsylvania.

Now those who expressed concern to me about the Wagman case refused to talk to the Pittsburgh Post-Gazette. Couldn't say I was surprised.

The best I could do was sit back and see which way the chips fell. If they decided to impeach Larsen, it seemed to me, there might be a second chance.

Already forming, I saw, was an ugly mob of disgruntled legislatures, judges, bond underwriters, high rolling political donators, reporters, publishers, and lawyers-for-hire. They would come together in court briefs, in news wires, at the club, and at the hearth. They would say that Justice Larsen had lied about case-fixing in Pennsylvania courts.

I'd learned there was plenty of reason for concern about Zappala's handling of cases. Soon a smoke screen of a thousand irrelevancies would conceal that simple truth. A mob can't concern itself with the niceties of fact. Caught up in a red rushing moment of blindness there can be no time to pause for truth. The gates and fences, the safeguards of civility, were being knocked down in preparation for the sweaty intoxicating moment when the dirty mob would get their man.

CHAPTER 9

Hangman Has a Blind Eye

The attorney general's office on October 29, 1993, filed a twenty-seven-count criminal complaint against Justice Rolf Larsen, alleging multiple violations of the Controlled Substances Act and criminal conspiracy. News began leaking of Larsen's impending prosecution before formal charges were filed. The day before the filing of charges Republicans held a social gathering in Harrisburg where party higher-ups talked openly of Larsen's impending prosecution.

The grand jury report, overseen by Ed Dennis, costing the people of Pennsylvania more or less one million dollars, was released on November 5, 1993. Preate, Dennis and cohorts threw a press conference and gave out as many free copies of their 249 page report as could be carried off by reporters. The public, however, who paid for the report, would be asked by Preate's office to pay fifty cents a page, or $125 for a copy. Not many copies circulated among the public.

Dennis's report sheds hardly any useful light on Pennsylvania courts; it instead illuminates the baseness of unchecked human nature. An attorney who was given a free copy of the report loaned his to me. Throughout the report we get vignettes of Ed Dennis traveling around the state, asking people for their cover stories, his mustached visage stone faced as they work to get their stories straight. He looks high, and he looks low, but he finds no stinkin' evidence of no case-fixin' in Pennsylvania. Even he doesn't seem to believe his own report.

He travels to Pittsburgh, and asks all the lawyers involved in the Allegheny County Port Authority case about Zappala's emergency intervention. On page 75 Dennis tells us "every attorney in the Pittsburgh city solicitor's office who was involved in the Port Authority case was interviewed." (Though, in the Wagman matter, not a single attorney with the turnpike was interviewed.) The attorneys, he says, all agree it was their idea to employ the "King's Bench" mechanism to bypass lower courts and take the Port Authority labor dispute directly to Justice Zappala.

The King's Bench maneuver, little known and seldom used, dates from British common law. It allows the state's high court to "reach down" and take a case or an issue from a lower court to dispose of it. Ed Dennis explains that "the extraordinary nature of the 'King's Bench' mechanism extends to the way in which such matters may be initiated, and the way in which they are processed by the Court. These procedures have developed according to custom rather than according to any formal, written directives.*" (Footnote reads: *"In fact, the practices may vary between the western, middle and eastern districts of the state. Given the absence of formal, written procedures, Justice Zappala was unsure as to the practices in the districts outside the western district, where his chambers are located.") "Litigants might file 'King's Bench' petitions to the prothonotary, or might approach an individual justice to hear the matter before actually filing it with the prothonotary. Thus, a litigant can essentially select the justice he or she wants to initially review the matter."

So here we have a system without guidelines, without checks and balances, rife for abuse. Equally problematic for Pennsylvanians, though not even a blip on Ed Dennis's ethical screen, is the troubling fact that cohorts of the Zappala family keep running to Justice Zappala for these emergency, all-powerful maneuvers.

Our attention next is drawn to Zappala's intervention in the Philadelphia King's Bench case. In his recusal petitions Larsen alleged that Zappala had met with "representatives" of the city of Philadelphia to guide the case. Larsen explained to the grand jury that, following his filing of the recusal petitions, Philadelphia attorney James Schwartzman had given him more information. Larsen testified that Schwartzman had been told by state Senator Vincent Fumo that "the city specially leased a plane" for a meeting of the great minds "to get (the case) taken care of on behalf of the city."

So Ed Dennis travels some more around the state. He asks why the mayor's office secured a plane for Senator Fumo to fly up to Lake Erie to see Justice Zappala. The plane ride occurred the week before Zappala interjected himself in the case the city of Philadelphia filed involving the Pennsylvania Labor Relations Board (PLRB). Fumo tells Ed Dennis he was just making nice with Zappala over a terrible blood feud the two'd been having over the court budget. Ed Rendell was merely a facilitator to the male bonding.

Even Dennis as he signs off on this nonsense can't bring himself to believe it. You can make Ed Dennis chew, but sometimes there's trouble swallowing.

Almost whimsically, Ed Dennis's report reads: "On July 2, 1992, Senator Vincent Fumo called David Cohen, Chief of Staff to Philadelphia Mayor Edward G. Rendell, and asked Cohen's assistance in obtaining the use of an airplane. Senator Fumo did not explain the reason for his request, other than to say he would consider it to be a favor to him. Even though Senator Fumo's reasons were unexplained, Cohen thought it was in the city's interest to accommodate the Senator.

"Accordingly, Cohen called Philadelphia attorney Robert Brobyn, who had politically supported Mayor Rendell and whose law firm at the time, Brobyn & Forceno, owned an airplane*." (Footnote reads: *"Brobyn & Forceno has since disbanded. Brobyn now has his own law practice. In addition, Brobyn also holds a position with the law firm of Dilworth, Paxson, Kalish & Kauffman, where Senator Fumo also works.") "Cohen asked Brobyn for the use of the airplane, telling him that it was for 'a matter important to the city.' Carl Lambert, the administrator for Brobyn & Forceno, was with Brobyn when Cohen called. According to Lambert, Brobyn consulted with state Senator Joe Rocks, who had been hired by Brobyn's law firm to help generate business. According to Lambert, Rocks encouraged Brobyn to go along with Cohen's request, as it would be to the overall good of the law firm. Brobyn also consulted with his law partner, Raymond P. Forceno. Forceno told Brobyn that if he wanted to be involved in political matters, he would be expected to do these kinds of favors.

"At Brobyn's direction, secretary Patricia Hand directed a subordinate to prepare an Aircraft Request and Approval Form. This form was completed with information Hand obtained by telephone from Cohen. The form reflects that the airplane was requested on July 2, 1992, and that the passengers would be Senator Fumo and an individual named Tom Myers. During the discussions surrounding the completion of the form, Cohen told Hand that the use of the airplane was a favor to him.

"The flight manifest and maintenance log reflects that the airplane left the Philadelphia Northeast Airport on the morning of July 3, 1992 and traveled to the Atlantic City International Airport in Pamona, New Jersey, to pick up two passengers. The airplane left the Atlantic City Airport at 10:20 a.m. and arrived in Erie, Pennsylvania at 11:35 a.m. The airplane then left Erie at 2:45 p.m. and returned to Atlantic City at 4:25 p.m. The total flying time was 3.4 hours.

"By letter dated August 13, 1992, Brobyn and Forceno sent Cohen a $3,009 bill for the use of the plane. In an interview, Cohen stated that when he asked Brobyn for the use of the airplane, he expected that the service would be free. He did not recall receiving any bill from Brobyn. In any event, this bill has never been paid*." (Footnote reads: *"Later in the summer of 1992, Mayor Rendell appointed Brobyn to the Philadelphia Gas Commission. Brobyn has stated that he does not accept any compensation for this position, and denies that he received the appointment in return for the use of the airplane.")

"In the same interview, Cohen acknowledged that the airplane trip occurred five days before the city filed the PLRB case. He also acknowledged that the city regularly briefed Senator Fumo and other key legislative figures during the course of the labor dispute which gave rise to the PLRB case, and that these briefings may have included the city's litigation strategy. However, Cohen denied that there was any connection between the case and Senator Fumo's trip to Erie. Cohen stated that Senator Fumo called him and asked him to get the Senator an airplane for a quick trip, which Cohen thought was to Pittsburgh. Cohen further stated that he did not ask Senator Fumo why he wanted to make the flight, but that he obtained the use of the airplane for Senator Fumo because he is a powerful public figure and it was in the city's interest to accommodate him."

Ed Dennis spends pages giving the principals the space to knit their unlikely story that this strange plane ride was all about Fumo smoothing Justice Zappala's ruffled feathers over a decreased Supreme Court budget. He notes there was indeed a flap over the budget. During the July 1992 meeting "Senator Fumo assured Justice Zappala that he would arrange for the court system to receive the extra funds Justice Zappala was seeking, telling Justice Zappala that he would 'get it done.'" Indeed, Ed Dennis tells us, in *May 1993* "the court system received a substantial supplemental appropriation." Even though he himself is a lawyer, Fumo tells Ed Dennis, he's never even heard of the King's Bench maneuver. As in the Allegheny County case, an attorney working for the city of Philadelphia, Howard Scher, says it was his idea, not Justice Zappala's, to employ the King's Bench.

But back to the airplane ride. Fumo, the narrative picks up, "called Cohen and asked him to get an airplane so the senator could go to Erie. Senator Fumo stated that he called Mayor Rendell's office because Mayor Rendell 'knows everyone.' Senator Fumo also acknowledged that he sometimes calls on the city for perks, because the city has 'a wealth of perks.' While this was the first time Senator Fumo had obtained the use of an airplane from the city, he recalled that he may have previously obtained the use of a helicopter and other forms of transportation.

For our $125 we even get some narrative about Vince and Tom's excellent adventure. "Senator Fumo acknowledged that (Tom) Myers accompanied him on the trip. Senator Fumo identified Myers as a close friend whom he has known for fifteen years. Myers rents a dock from Senator Fumo and lives on a boat during summer weekends.

"Senator Fumo stated that Justice Zappala picked him and Myers up at the airport in Erie. Justice Zappala gave them a tour of Erie and Conneaut, and then took them to his home on Lake Erie. Senator Fumo stated that Justice Zappala and his wife served lunch, and that he and Myers left later that afternoon....

"Tom Myers, the other passenger on the flight, was also interviewed," Ed Dennis tells us. Under Ed Dennis's deft investigatory technique Tom Myers takes on all the observatory powers of the block of wood that makes up Charlie McCarthy's head. The report continues: "Myers stated that he is a self-employed carpenter, and that he met Senator Fumo approximately 10 to 12 years ago when he rented a boat slip at the shore from the Senator's mother. Myers stated that he has developed a friendship with the Senator since that time. Myers' recollection of the circumstances under which he ended up traveling to Erie with Senator Fumo was unclear, but he believes the Senator may have asked him if he wanted to make the trip when they had dinner together the night before. Senator Fumo told Myers he was going to Erie to see a friend, and gave no indication that the trip was anything other than a social occasion.

"Myers stated that Justice Zappala, whom he referred to as Senator Fumo's 'buddy,' picked them up in Erie. After a short sight-seeing trip through Erie, Justice Zappala drove Senator Fumo and Myers to Justice Zappala's home in Conneaut. Myers recalls that he and Senator Fumo stayed for a few hours, during which Justice Zappala and his wife served lunch. Myers stated that he recalls only general social conversation during the visit, and has no recollection of any conversation involving the state budget or any matters related to the Philadelphia labor situation. However, contrary to Senator Fumo, Myers stated that the Senator and Justice Zappala never left the company of the others and engaged in a private conversation."

What's going on in this report is politics. It's about embarrassing Mayor Ed Rendell. Ed Dennis, the Republican Philadelphia prosecutor, is making light of Ed Rendell, the Democrat Philadelphia prosecutor (he's a former D.A.). I've noted in several encounters with Republican prosecutors that they dislike Ed Rendell. They think he's a phony, with a trumped up record for efficiency and honesty. I've yet to meet a Republican prosecutor who, upon mentioning Rendell's name, doesn't look heavenward and issue a gagging sound. Here Ed Dennis is laughing at Rendell. The sarcasm drips from the page. The unspoken gag — the in-joke — is that Dennis has caught them all in an implausible situation. Why did honest, efficient Mayor Rendell's chief administrator waste public time securing a plane for Vince Fumo to fly to Erie to discuss Supreme Court business? Maybe honest, efficient Ed Rendell can expend additional city resources ferrying the pope to break the baseball deadlock. But stick to this ridiculous story they all must do. Here we find Democrats Rendell, Fumo, Zappala all in bed together, and Ed Dennis allows them to say they were merely manipulating each other's spines. Very curious.

Not content with this scrumptious main course, Ed Dennis brings in more delectables. Ed Dennis notes, and correctly so, the flow of the largess around this unlikely story. He notes, almost with glee, Fumo's explanation that Rendell "knows everyone," and that the city has "a wealth of perks." He notes that Brobyn, the man with the plane and the unpaid bill, not only now "holds a position" in Fumo's law firm but shortly after the incident gets appointed by Rendell to the gas commission. And masters of gas is indeed what we have here. He notes that Brobyn denies the appointment was a tit for tat for the plane, and his cooperation. While yukking it up Ed Dennis reminds us that we should consider, and weigh, the trail of money, appointments and largess surrounding this most laughable and embarrassing story. The unspoken, and correct, implication Ed Dennis makes here is that we should naturally suspect the actions, and the reports, of those who end up in each other's employ, washing each other's backs, taking money from each other. Such as the money Ed Dennis has taken from Ernie Preate, and the money Preate has taken from the Zappalas.

Yes, it's all very amusing. Trouble is, Ed Dennis isn't being paid more money than the president of the United States to make light of these goombas. He's been invested with the public trust to ensure the integrity and impartiality of Pennsylvania courts. Here we have an implausible situation that cries out for real G-Men, not a front-office whitewash man. When he began his "investigation" Ed Dennis said he thought the intervention of the feds might be advisable. For some reason he never calls in the feds, whom he knows, more than any of these characters, won't sit idly listening to this rubbish. Instead, Ed Dennis travels around the state allowing these guys months to get their ridiculous story straight, months to allow the trail to cool, and then shovels this nonsense over the terrain to ensure it will never again see the light of day. In the parlance of real investigators, what Ed Dennis is doing here is obstructing justice. But again, this is pure politics, not criminal justice. As Dennis himself notes, since he wants to be involved in politics, he's expected to do these kinds of things.

Though Ed Dennis laughs it up over Ed Rendell, it would be Rendell who gets the last laugh at Ed Dennis.

Throughout Ed Dennis's report he takes Larsen to task for the exact language of the justice's recusal petitions. "The language of the allegations in Justice Larsen's Petition for Recusal is inconsistent with the testimony he offered in support of the allegations," we read, in various forms, again and again. Ed Dennis would have us believe it's a matter of semantics. He questions Larsen's credibility because he misstates the number of people involved in the plane ride. So what if all these people seeking emergency relief from Justice Zappala are doing lucrative bond business with brother Charles Zappala? So what if the justice's sons are helping to sell bonds at Uncle Charlie's shop? Ed Dennis tries to reassure us that Justice Zappala personally does not have an interest in any of this. Yet, most people would agree, if a man's sons are benefiting, the man is benefiting. Larsen's accusation will be measured by the precise meaning of his accusations that Justice Zappala was receiving indirect kickbacks from layered corporations. We begin to see that Larsen will be judged by his exact words.

Ed Dennis also makes much hay that Larsen didn't blow the whistle earlier on any of this. "Justice Larsen was unable to explain why he did not plead the specific information he claimed to know when he made his allegations. This adds to our view that his testimony about these allegations lacks credibility.*" (Footnote reads, *"We also note that, during his testimony, Justice Larsen agreed that any meeting between Justice Zappala and Senator Fumo about the PLRB case would have been improper and should have been reported to the [Judicial Inquiry and Review Board]. Rather than do so, however, Justice Larsen held the information for use in a pleading designed to further only his own interests.")

Ed Dennis is beginning to knit together a rationale that, if employed, would keep any whistleblower from coming forward. You better get it exactly right, and you better hit the fire alarm immediately, or we're coming after *you*.

This sudden emphasis on exact semantics becomes important to understand ostensibly why Ed Dennis never bothered to ask anyone about Justice Zappala's emergency intervention in the turnpike's Wagman case, or other cases. It wasn't part of Larsen's complaint. Even though we were told at the start of this million dollar investigation everything was fair game, that the integrity of Pennsylvania courts was the important thing, and would be ensured by these gentlemen, the scope has suddenly, inexplicably narrowed. Suddenly the scope of the investigation is limited to the exact wording of Larsen's original complaints. "...We are satisfied that the investigation has been comprehensive and complete," we're assured. Then, conversely, at the very end of the report, on page 246 of 249 pages, we read: "This grand jury has not sought to conduct a comprehensive investigation of the Pennsylvania Supreme Court as an institution. Nevertheless, it is appropriate to note that we have found that suspicion and mistrust exists throughout the Court." We're told again, on page 248 of 249 pages: "...We have not attempted to conduct a comprehensive investigation of the Court...."

"The grand jury has found that there is no credible evidence supporting any of the allegations of criminal conduct set forth in Justice Larsen's petitions," the report concludes. What about things not mentioned in the petitions? What about *unethical* conduct? The people of our state, after all, don't care about Larsen's recusal petitions. They only care about getting a fair shake with the fellow on the other side of the room when they go to court. It's here that Ed Dennis has failed, by omission, the people of Pennsylvania. Yet it's only one aspect of his breach of trust with powers entrusted him by the people.

There would be one sobering, frightening exception to Ed Dennis's myopic focus on Larsen's petitions. He was about to smear Larsen for unauthorized use of prescription drugs which, or course, has nothing to do with the petitions. But we're a little ahead of the story. The point I'd like to make here is that Ed Dennis and Co. appear to have abused the grand jury system. And that's not all.

You knock on this empty box built by Ed Dennis and you hear some pretty hollow sounds rattling around. What about the Wagman case that the turnpike's attorneys had expressed so much concern about? The story gets odder. I would learn, months after Dennis issued his whitewash, that Larsen had after all purchased a copy of my book and submitted the chapter on Wagman to the grand jury. Transcripts of Larsen's grand jury testimony from September 9, 1993, read, as he's turning supporting material over to the jury, "And there's a chapter from a book called When the Levy (sic) Breaks. It's only about 20 pages."

Larsen gives the grand jury other items, including a

September 5, 1993, New York Times article that, he summarizes, "gives you an intricate explanation on the problem with
competitive/non-competitive bond awards." The article,
"Bond Buyers' Gain, Taxpayers' Loss," appeared in the Sunday
Money section's Wall Street column and was written by Allen
R. Myerson. The article explains how non-competitive bond
underwriting creates huge hidden interest costs to taxpayers.

"All the uproar over the generous fees awarded to municipal bond underwriters who are in turn so generous to campaigning politicians may be missing the point," Myerson writes.
"The fees are a one-time hit, but higher interest costs on these
bonds can grind away at taxpayers for decades. These bonds
have a higher interest cost than they might have because they
are sold for less than buyers would pay. The surest sign of that
is when major buyers can get only a fraction of the bonds they
want. As a result, investment bankers and bond buyers, not taxpayers, get bargains. By selling bonds too cheaply — at high
yields — underwriters can avoid having the paper languish in
their own accounts should the market turn against them."

The article quotes one of the nation's largest municipal
bond buyers as saying that non-competitive bond underwriters
are "earning an underwriting fee, but they're not taking an
underwriting risk." Myerson describes a $1.8 billion New Jersey
bond issue which market watchers said was undervalued by a
fraction of a percentage point, creating too great a demand.
"But the strong demand suggests the state could have done
better," he writes. In a bond issue of this size the numbers add
up. "A seemingly narrow savings of a tenth of a percentage
point on such a huge issue would free $18 million a year —
enough to pay 300 more teachers. Over the life of the bonds,
the total expense could reach hundreds of millions of dollars."

"Citizens who scream at the threat of higher taxes never
march into city halls or state capitals to complain about bonds
being sold ten basis points to cheaply," Myerson observes. "It's
not just New Jersey," he writes. "Comparing negotiated and
competitive deals in the Pittsburgh area, the Government
Finance Officers Association found that half the negotiated but

none of the competitive deals were sold below the market." Myerson notes, "Several states are introducing greater competition," such as New Jersey, which was stung by bond scandals.

This *Times* critique demonstrates the growing national concern with no-bid bond awards. It also shows the extent to which the Philadelphia Inquirer, an apologist for Russell, Rea, Zappala & Gomulka in particular, and the awarding of corrupting no-bid bonds in general, is out of step with better newspapers, and the times.

My book's chapter on Wagman is assigned grand jury evidence number 316. But it's a dead number with Ed Dennis. He never pursues the lead. (In theory we could have a "runaway" grand jury, intent on its own investigation, but in Pennsylvania such an aberration would have no subpoena power.) It's Ed Dennis who was empowered, had the opportunity, and the public trust to ensure honest and fair courts in Pennsylvania. Without the guidance and cooperation of an honest prosecutor, a grand jury can do nothing but rubber-stamp the whims of dangerous men. Ed Dennis has become a tool for the mob, which wants nothing more thoughtful than Larsen's scalp.

Dennis obviously feels he can't completely ignore the turnpike and its relationship with the Zappalas. "Additional interviews were also conducted as part of this investigation, aside from the above-described interviews of Charles Zappala, Gregory Zappala and Stephen Zappala, Jr. The Turnpike Commission, being one of RRZ's largest customers, was chosen for this purpose." Nowhere does he tell readers that he's been alerted to concerns about Justice Zappala's intervention in a turnpike case, but that he's refused to interview those most knowledgeable of the incident — the turnpike attorneys who'd called in Justice Zappala.

Instead, for no apparent reason, Dennis picks two, and only two, turnpike financial representatives to question. And he asks them an inane question. He asks John Fogarty, the turnpike's deputy executive director for finance, whether Fogarty knew of "involvement by Justice Zappala in RRZ's bonding business with the Turnpike Commission." He asks James Cavanaugh, an independent bond advisor to the turnpike, whether Cavanaugh knew of "involvement by Justice Zappala in the Turnpike Commission's decision to use RRZ for its bonding work."

The public was told that Ed Dennis has been given public funds to look into the independence and integrity of the judiciary; suddenly, at the one state agency where he's been warned to look into a case involving Justice Zappala, he doesn't ask the right people about it, then he asks the wrong questions about, not the judiciary, but the bonding business.

Why would Ed Dennis ignore warnings that turnpike attorneys were concerned about an instance of case-fixing involving Justice Zappala? Here's where Philadelphia Mayor Ed Rendell comes back into the story.

I happened to mention to a Philadelphia attorney that I couldn't understand why Ed Dennis would be ignoring evidence. "Don't you realize Ed Dennis has undisclosed conflicts?" my conversant laughed.

He explained he'd been speaking to a Philadelphia Inquirer reporter Fred Cusick, who'd expressed dismay that his editors had declined to publish articles about Ed Dennis's conflicts of interest in his Supreme Court investigation. What were the conflicts covered-up by the Inquirer? Conflict one: Ed Dennis had been billed as an "independent" prosecutor by Attorney General Preate, yet Dennis was involved in political fund raising for Preate. Conflict two: Ed Dennis, at the time he was empowered by Preate, had been defending a Philadelphia nursing home attendant who was under investigation by Preate; Ed Dennis had left the nursing home client he'd been defending *from* Preate to go to work *for* Preate in the Supreme Court investigation. Three: The law firm in which Ed Dennis is a senior partner, Morgan, Lewis & Bockius, had signed on as co-bond counsel for a city of Philadelphia Water Department bond issue. Dennis now was a senior partner in a firm receiving large sums of money to opine that Rendell's administration was breaking no laws. This at the same time Ed Dennis was supposedly investigating whether Mayor Rendell had broken laws by arranging a plane to fly Senator Fumo to see Justice Zappala.

Inquirer reporter Cusick, I learned, was upset at his editors' mysterious lack of criticism of Ed Dennis in these matters. This speaks volumes. That information had to be leaked from a newspaper speaks volumes. Things were getting so bad the newspapers were leaking.

I called the Philadelphia Water Department. One of Rendell's men quickly sent me a copy of the bond prospectus. It was an offering of $1.1 billion city of Philadelphia Water and Wastewater Revenue Bonds, Series 1993. There they all were, their names printed together in prospectus black ink. The Honorable Edward G. Rendell, Mayor. The offering, the prospectus reports, is subject to the legal opinion of Morgan, Lewis & Bockius. Listed among the many underwriters on the front page, we see "RRZ Public Markets, Inc." Here we have the same familiar characters, all happily doing business together.

The unspoken, and correct, implication made in the grand jury report prepared under Ed Dennis's supervision is that we should naturally suspect the actions, and the reports, of those who end up in each other's employ, washing each other's backs, taking money from each other.

The date, incidentally, listed on the prospectus is August 5, 1993 — the day before I had written Ed Dennis on August 6, 1993, asking our independent special prosecutor to look into the turnpike's Wagman case. God knows what other cases Ed Dennis didn't look into. He also never disclosed his conflicts.

If Ed Dennis wants to be involved in political matters, as his report notes, perhaps he imagines he's expected to do these kinds of favors. While overseeing all this, I should note, Ed Dennis in the summer of 1993 was selected by the U.S. Justice Department to head the investigation of the federal siege, armed attack, fire and deaths of children at the Branch Davidian compound in Waco, Texas. In his report, Dennis would end up criticizing low-level investigators. Dennis wouldn't criticize U.S. Attorney General Janet Reno or President Bill Clinton, who, after all, had ordered a needless armed attack that ended with the deaths of children.

CHAPTER 10

Drugs in the Meat

Ed Dennis, his firm involved in the bonding business with the Zappalas, naturally wants us to forget the bonding business, and the Zappalas. It's Rolf Larsen's drug usage that melts Ed Dennis's butter. "(T)he grand jury has recently obtained evidence of other areas that are *appropriate* for investigation," the grand jury report tells us (emphasis mine).

As early as 1981, the report concludes, Justice Larsen had a Pittsburgh physician conceal that Larsen was taking anti-depressant drugs, like Valium, by prescribing the drugs to Larsen's employees. "The physician involved in this scheme," Dennis's report tells us, "was Earl Humphreys, M.D. Dr. Humphreys and Larsen are close friends." Their relationship dates back to the 1960s, Dennis tells us, when Larsen would perform legal work for the doctor, and Humphreys would treat Larsen. "Dr. Humphreys has treated Justice Larsen for various medical problems," Dennis writes. "However, Dr. Humphreys testified that the 'main thing' for which he treated Justice Larsen was 'anxiety and depression.'"

Ed Dennis and Ernie Preate are telling us that not only was Larsen lying about case-fixing, he was a nut on drugs.

Larsen, for his part, testified before the grand jury that one of his employees came up with the idea of placing his prescriptions in others' names. His employee suggested, "'Hey, why don't we put them in somebody else's name so you don't get this adverse publicity,'" Larsen testified.

"What adverse publicity were you receiving that would have given rise to such a suggestion?" Larsen was asked.

"Well," Larsen replied, "at that time the Post-Gazette and

the Inquirer were writing stories about me, and they were investigating the cause of my sister's death, trying to make it up as a suicide, and they were investigating the cause of my mother's death, which was not suicide.

"And they had gone down to the high school where my daughter had or was, I forgot when she graduated, matriculated, and gotten out of her files, out of her confidential files, a photograph, which is the only place the photograph existed. They had interviewed her grandparents, who were in their seventies, and misquoted her and attempted to make her out like a dolt, just nasty, pejorative false reporting and a gross invasion of privacy."

"These articles all appeared in the Pittsburgh paper and the Philadelphia paper around the time (your employee) made the suggestion you have told us about?" Larsen was asked.

"Yeah. Yeah.... (O)nce you become an object of a newspaper's obsession, then you're more talked about," Larsen explained.

The Inquirer and Post-Gazette gave the drug charges lots of play, as could be expected. Neither newspaper mentioned Larsen's explanation that he had been hiding his prescriptions from, and because of, *them*.

The bottom line of Ed Dennis's grand jury report was this: no evidence of case-fixing, and Larsen is on illegal drugs. The conclusions: "The grand jury strongly recommends that the legislature and the Judicial Conduct Board review our findings and take appropriate action, including possible removal of Justice Larsen from the Pennsylvania Supreme Court."

A few days after the grand jury report was issued I had dinner with one of our state's civic leaders. This person remarked that the drug charges seemed particularly onerous and low, and had adverse implications for others who may need treatment for depression or drug dependence. Ed Dennis's bully-boy charges seemed to set back the treatment of mental illness two decades, to a time when depression was a dark secret, not discussed, and those suffering from it lived alone with their black pain. There was a smell of the worst sort of smear about all this. "There's such a thing as prosecutorial discretion," my dinner companion said. "The prosecutor should have overlooked the drugs. How can Larsen be impeached in the legislature over this? I can't see it."

My dinner companion, I must say, had a higher opinion of the legislature's moral imperative than did I.

CHAPTER 11

Seating at the Scaffold

Before the drug charges were filed against Larsen, before the curious grand jury report was issued, the legislature was already off and running on a course for impeachment. In the fall of 1993 comrades in the committees took it upon themselves to conduct a "legal and historical analysis of impeachments in Pennsylvania." This "analysis" was reviewed in a meeting of the state house judiciary committee on September 25, 1993, a full month before the filing of drug charges against Larsen.

The state House adopted Resolution 205 on November 23, 1993, authorizing the judiciary committee to "investigate" Larsen's actions and determine whether the justice should be impeached for misbehavior in office. Under the resolution committee members designated their comrades in the subcommittee on courts to conduct the investigation. The minority and majority parties each hired an outside counsel at considerable expense to assist with festivities. These outside attorneys, like Ed Dennis, would end up being paid more money in a year's time than the president of the United States. Each attorney and their comrades in the committees would whole-heartedly embrace Ed Dennis's report. As I would later discover, they would also refuse to collect additional evidence concerning Justice Zappala in particular, and the fairness and impartiality of Pennsylvania courts in general.

For many months, through the winter of 1993 and into the spring of 1994, the comrades in the committees and their lawyers would fade from public view as they prepared their scaffolding of nastiness, omission and deceit.

By now, going into the winter of 1993-4, it began to sink into my thick skull that the leadership of our political parties did not want to investigate Justice Zappala's strange handling of the turnpike's Wagman case. Or, for that matter, any case involving Zappala. The state's two major newspapers also didn't seem to be falling over themselves to stroll over to the court-house to dig up records that might suggest Larsen might after all be right — if not in the letter of his complaint, certainly in spirit.

I decided it might be fun and perhaps enlightening to press the case. I began contacting a few citizens' groups. In early December 1993 I was asked to say a few words at a statewide meeting of Common Cause, a good government group. Common Cause has an old, steep hill to climb in Pennsylvania. One member told me he would be happy if Pennsylvania's laws regarding ethics, political fundraising and lobbying were merely brought up to the abysmally low standards of Washington DC. Despite glacial inertia against political reform in Pennsylvania, I found Common Cause members always willing to try, and cheerful in the attempt. Like sherpas who had yet to reach the mountaintop, they seemed ready for someone to come along and make the attempt.

Government and editorial boards should work so well. When I arrived the group was considering a public call for Justice Larsen to resign. I explained the Wagman case, and the concern of the attorneys who had handled it. I pointed out that issuing a call for Larsen's resignation merely played into the hands of those who refused to conduct a proper investigation. The group's chair of the judicial committee, Susan Mitchell, a social worker from western Pennsylvania, expressed eagerness to learn more. From that moment no citizens' group in our state called on Larsen to resign, or for that matter would support the impeachment proceedings.

Common Cause convened its meeting around a large table in an education association building in Harrisburg. There were about two dozen people in attendance. They were mostly members of the group's governing board and statewide officers. Also in attendance was the group's executive director, Barry Kauffman, who handles the group's day to day business and lobbying from a small office in Harrisburg. He greets all comers with a critical eye, a reflective bearing, an air of propriety, but ends up welcoming and helpful. Kauffman has a broad, dark, moustached face, and an expansive knowledge of the intricacies of Pennsylvania government. In his years as the group's Harrisburg lobbyist he'd developed many contacts around the capitol. Kauffman told me he'd for years been hearing some of the same stories found in Larsen's recusal petitions. He recalled for instance hearing stories around the capitol that Justice Zappala was wired for sound.

The state chairman was Hart Stotter, from Philadelphia, who'd served on the horse racing commission in the Thornburgh administration. Having seen the monster from the inside he'd thrown in with the reformers. He shared several stories with me about his experiences trying to bring reform to the state. It would seem easier to lecture to the stones in the street than to reform our increasingly insular Republicans and Democrats. He and Kauffman had endless stories of betrayals at the hands of state lawmakers, who always seemed to put off reform until the next session.

It was at this meeting that I first met Robert Surrick, the attorney from suburban Philadelphia who'd once served on the Judicial Inquiry and Review Board. Surrick has a long, hound dog's face, set off with bright eyes and a quick, toothy grin. He had served on the Judicial Inquiry and Review Board when it had conducted its initial investigation of Larsen in the early 1980s. In the election cycle before we met he had tried to win a seat on the state Supreme Court. He'd run on the Patriot ticket, a spin-off of the Perot party. I gather he spent considerable sums traveling the state but in the end the grip of the two parties was too strong and he hadn't brought in many votes. Now he was traveling around the state plugging his idea of district elections for the high court, complaining that high judges in Pennsylvania are elected statewide. These days, he explained to the group, the bench is controlled by the party machines of Philadelphia and Pittsburgh, with no representation from the rest of the state. Surrick had brought to the meeting a chart that displayed his proposal for carving the state into seven or eight judicial districts, each electing its own justice.

Surrick had been unhappy with Rolf Larsen for years. When he'd served on the Judicial Inquiry and Review Board Surrick had pushed, with no success, for a real disciplining of Larsen. In Surrick's mind Larsen had spent two decades mixing politics and justice. Larsen, apparently in retribution, had once filed a complaint against Surrick with the state attorneys' disciplinary board. With all this bad water over the dam you might expect Surrick to be happy about the justice's scheduled fall on drug charges. But happy he was not. "It's a lynching," he'd wave dismissively. In the current stampede against Larsen, Surrick saw the same unappetizing mix of politics and injustice he'd always seen in our state. He hated it, hated the bullying he was now watching, and hated the half-truths he was now hearing. Bob Surrick, I would come to see over the next few months, really had superior temperament, an innate sense of fairness, and was not too concerned with the politics of a thing — ideal qualities in a judge. The same qualities that kept him from getting elected.

Surrick, like the others, listened patiently to my story about Justice Zappala's handling of the turnpike's Wagman case, and my inability to get anyone to look at it. Surrick was not surprised at all to hear the current investigation of Larsen had been phony. There seems to be nothing official in Pennsylvania that is not phony. If it's not phony, it's not official. That wouldn't stop Bob Surrick from protesting. For years Bob Surrick had swum against the stream. For some reason, like the others at the meeting, he was willing to try one more time.

I left the Common Cause meeting that day with a promise that the group would join me at a press conference in the rotunda of the state capitol building sometime over the winter, or in the spring, when the fancies of our legislators turned to impeachment. We'd make a public call for an independent, federal investigation of the court. For what it was worth. Someone suggested we could also try filing a complaint against Zappala with the Judicial Conduct Board, the supposed watchdog of Pennsylvania courts which had assumed the responsibilities of the Judicial Inquiry and Review Board. If nothing else we'd see just how badly the system was broken.

I came away from the meeting with a positive impression of these people. They did not seem at all shrill, as you might expect from people who'd been ignored year in, year out. These Common Causers displayed endless patience and even humor in the face of a bi-partisan legislative leadership not at all receptive to reform. There was a resolve about them. They seemed to suspect that eventually they would have their day, if only because they recognized that big-money American politics could scarcely get much worse. If things could scarcely get worse, they'd have to get better, wouldn't they?

It would seem to me, the more I studied the subject, that it was the legislative leaders and their expensive lawyers who seemed shrill and vindictive. Our legislature seemed inordinately composed of white, male lawyers, overpaid specimens who had long since disconnected from the public. They'd long ago learned to shut their carved doors and be nowhere in sight. The party leaders might write our laws, they might control our purse strings. But who was listening to them? The public had long since tuned out the lawmakers. Perhaps that was why the legislative leaders had gotten away with unending decades of mischief.

So much the better, I thought, for an impending impeachment. A lynching is meant for the dark.

CHAPTER 12

A Chance Chat With a Judge

That winter I attended several book signings to autograph my new book. One Saturday morning, February 18, 1994, found me at the Plymouth Meeting Mall, outside Philadelphia. I was seated at a table at the front of a bookstore, signing copies of my book, when a woman came up and introduced herself as Commonwealth Court Judge Doris Smith.

She was a slight-built woman, I'd say around forty. That she was indeed Judge Smith I had no doubt. Her photograph that day had been printed on the front page of the Philadelphia Inquirer. Philadelphia city schools were in crisis, not providing the minimum education prescribed by law, and Judge Smith had recently been involved in court efforts to right the district. Running into her at the mall, on a Saturday morning when we had an idle moment to chat, was a serendipitous event.

Judge Smith, says I, weren't you the Commonwealth Court judge who was overruled by Justice Zappala in the *Wagman* v. *the Pennsylvania Turnpike* case?

Yes, she tells me. She said she thought Justice Zappala's emergency intervention in *Wagman* had been outrageous. She said several months ago Pittsburgh Post-Gazette reporter Bill Moushey had telephoned her office about the Wagman case. He'd left a message that he wanted to talk to her about *Wagman*, Smith said, but she hadn't returned his call, believing, she said, that her role as a judge prevented her from that sort of thing. She said she was glad "they're finally looking into the Wagman case."

Judge, I told her, they aren't looking into the Wagman case, because no one would talk publicly about it. The two big newspapers wouldn't write about it, so the investigators didn't feel prodded to look into it. I mentioned that Common Cause and I were considering filing a complaint with the Judicial Conduct Board.

Judge Smith laughed and said it was hopeless to expect the conduct board to investigate Zappala. Justice Zappala controls the conduct board, she said. Its chairman, Judge Joseph Del Sole, she said, was an ally of Zappala's. For that matter, she said, no one in state government would investigate Justice Zappala. The federal government would have to be involved, she said. Had we considered asking the U.S. Attorney, or the U.S. Justice Department in Washington to intervene? As for the state newspapers, she suggested I try calling David Boldt, the one-time editor of the Inquirer's editorial page. She stood holding the newspaper, her picture on the front page.

If nothing else came of Larsen's impeachment, Judge Smith said, at last the public was focusing on Zappala's antics. She expressed fear of Justice Zappala and his sway over the justice system. When she had run unsuccessfully for state Supreme Court in 1993, she told me, one of Justice Zappala's cronies in the courts had warned her that "they" would decertify her election if she'd won.

I said that didn't surprise me. I told her my brother had been campaign manager for Supreme Court candidate Allen Ertel. Ertel, a former Democratic congressman from Williamsport, was a political maverick who had almost upset Governor Dick Thornburgh's reelection bid in 1982. He'd later run for state Supreme Court. Ertel won the primary, but the court voted to nullify the primary and called for another election, which Ertel ultimately lost. He'd been robbed.

I sat talking with Judge Smith for some time. Book store employees came over and shared a laugh with us about our justice system. It was a Saturday in a mall in Pennsylvania.

The next Monday I called Bill Moushey at the Post-Gazette. Had he tried calling Judge Doris Smith about the Wagman case? I asked him. Yes, he said, several months ago, after I'd spoken with him. He said Judge Smith had worked in Pittsburgh earlier in her career, and he thought she might be willing to talk to him. He'd put in a phone call, but the judge never called back.

I told him I ran into Judge Smith over the weekend, and she'd told me about his call. It seemed I was in a strange cat-bird's seat. I was hearing distressful things about the Wagman case from turnpike attorneys, from Wagman representatives, even from the judge who'd been overruled by Zappala, but I couldn't get anyone else to talk to them.

Not long afterward I spoke with Barry Kauffman, the Common Cause executive director. I told him of my chance meeting with Judge Smith. Kauffman expressed surprise. "You're not supposed to have an idle chat with a judge about case-fixing," Kauffman told me. "She's duty bound to report allegations of impropriety." He said it seemed now up to Judge Smith to file a complaint against Justice Zappala.

I called Judge Smith at her office. She sounded nervous, and spoke more guardedly than she had in our chance encounter. I said I found myself in a difficult spot, having heard from three sides — turnpike attorneys, the Wagman people, and Judge Smith — that Justice Zappala's handling of the case had been suspect.

Judge Smith said I was mistaken, that she had said nothing to me indicating any wrongdoing in *Wagman*.

I asked her if it was true whether it was her responsibility to file a complaint with the conduct board when a member of the public came to her with concerns of improper conduct in a case.

Who has told me anything like that? she asked.

"Me!" I told her.

She ruffled up and made as if she was taking notes.

I told her she had to file the complaint, but she'd have no part of it. I must have sounded like Broderick Crawford in *All The King's Men*, barking Huey Long Kingfish orders over the phone: "Listen, judge, you're gonna do it! You're gonna take the walk on this one, judge!" It was totally ridiculous.

HE·FELT·THE·POWER OF GOD
WHO·FORMED·THE·DEEP
SOON·THE·STORM·ABATED·

Part Two

It isn't an instinct or a need — being in a crowd isn't necessary to our being complete human beings — but, for most of us, the crowd holds out certain essential attractions. It is, like an appetite, something in which dark satisfactions can be found.

Bill Buford
Among the Thugs

CHAPTER 13

Investigator is Investigated

The winter of 1994 was particularly nasty, and so were the politics in Pennsylvania. The snow piled up, and so did the various nasty little reports compiled by a growing number of nasty little committees and commissions. By late spring the snow would finally melt, but the reports would remain, lasting scars of an unhappy season.

There would be a flurry of reports hinting at criminal conduct involving not only Rolf Larsen, but his investigator, Attorney General Ernie Preate. This flurry of bureaucratic activity is understandable when you realize that the spring of '94 began the gubernatorial primary election season in Pennsylvania. This flurry of bureaucratic activity was really about elective politics. Governor Bob Casey, among the last of the state's old guard, had undergone a heart/liver transplant the summer before. Weakened physically, Casey also was a political lame duck, constitutionally unable to seek a third term.

Ernie Preate was and had been running for governor. He had been running for governor for some time. Over the years there had been a steady stream of criticism that his handling of high-profile cases amounted to little more than politicking for the governor's office. So it was when he first selected Ed Dennis to investigate Larsen's charges. A serious house cleaning of our long-running joke of a high court would certainly have been a leg up for anyone contemplating higher office. The goop that finally was squeezed through the tube ultimately displayed Preate and Dennis's desire to play to course public opinion without touching the underlying disease.

Running for governor though he was, Preate had serious

problems of his own. On April 8, 1994, a month before the gubernatorial primary, the Pennsylvania Crime Commission released the conclusions of a two-year investigation of Preate. The commission's 189-page report, titled "An Investigation into the Conduct of Lackawanna County District Attorney / Attorney General Ernest D. Preate Jr.," was obviously designed and timed to sink Preate's chances for the governor's office.

The Crime Commission itself was about to go out of business, and it was obviously hoping to go out with a bang, if not with vengeance. Preate had been instrumental in convincing the legislature the previous year that the Crime Commission should be abolished. His motives for seeking the commission's demise, and the moribund commission's motives for releasing its report against Preate, would be part of one of our state's darkest seasons. A look at what happened between Preate and the Crime Commission sheds much light not only on Preate, but also the handling of Larsen's case, and provides a measure of the venom in our body politic, and a sobering look at the breakdown of our system as whole.

The Pennsylvania Crime Commission for decades was an odd appendage to state government. Its mission was to investigate organized crime and public corruption, and to issue reports of its investigations. It reports were invariably thick (and mostly unreadable) tomes containing vignettes of some of our state's most illustrious gangsters. Those fingered by the Crime Commission often had close ties to our political leaders, which no doubt quickened the day of the commission's demise. Some complained that the commission tarred with a wide and indiscriminate brush, sometimes tying honest citizens to supposed "gangsters" via tenuous and questionable connections. The running joke was that the commission's reports often fingered men with Italian-sounding names who ate lunch together.

That said, over the years I've spoken with many civic leaders who could not understand what the commission was about, and why its job couldn't be conducted by the State Police. The commission's charter, for example, was limited: though it could issue subpoenas, it had no law enforcement authority. The State Police, the argument ran, could yield a big stick. (The argument for the Crime Commission was that the commission could issue public reports to the legislature, while State Police investigations could languish in the dark. The State Police also wasn't immune to political pressures.)

The Crime Commission probably deserved to be whacked. Trouble was, Ernie Preate wasn't clean enough to do the whacking. More alarming, perhaps no survivor of our state's electoral process was clean enough to do a job that should be done.

By the Crime Commission's own reckoning it's hard to say precisely when its investigation of Preate had begun. As part of a "proactive program to monitor organized crime trends," the commission reports, it began an investigation of "gambling markets" in May 1991, including the legalized bingo industry and illegal video poker gambling. "For several years, the commission has investigated the illegal video poker industry...." the report explains. "(I)t has determined that participants in this industry are involved in other rackets, particularly loan sharking and, to a lesser extent, narcotic activity....

"The illegal video poker industry in Pennsylvania permeates the organized crime subculture. Across the commonwealth, video poker machines are located in taverns and private social clubs, and State Police have seized thousands of these machines as illegal gambling devices. In Pittsburgh, for example, state troopers seized 339 machines in a single raid. Some establishments had as many as 15 video poker machines operating at one time. In central Pennsylvania, 189 machines were seized during the course of one evening. In April 1988, State Police seized 349 machines in four northeastern counties.

"Because of the time and resources involved in investigating this form of illegal gambling as well as the sophistication of the electronic technology, many police departments have taken the position that gambling does not warrant police attention. As a result, this form of illegal gambling represents an avenue for official corruption, that ultimately undermines the confidence of the community in its legitimate institutions of government."

"Soon after the start of the gambling markets investigative project," the report reads, "the commission received information alleging questionable conduct in regard to video gambling by the Attorney General, Ernest D. Preate."

On January 15, 1992, two commission investigators interviewed Elmo Baldassari, a Scranton video poker operator who was at the time in prison on extortion charges. "The commission regularly conducts prison interviews with criminals, such as organized crime members and associates, significant racket figures, and potential criminal informants," the report explains. Baldassari and his three brothers, Joseph Chester, Elio Joseph "Al," and Henry Jr., were "well-known to law enforcement officers as local gambling figures" with convictions and gambling associations dating back at least to the early 1950s. The Baldassari brothers were machine operators in a market that would reap "$500 to $1,000 in gambling revenues per week per machine." The report also notes that Elmo Baldassari had been "convicted of maintaining gambling devices in 1960. An investigation by the Crime Commission resulted in the arrest of Baldassari by the Federal Bureau of Investigation in 1990 and his conviction for extortion in 1991."

Commission officials would say that Baldassari, in the January 1992 interview, told the "astonished" agents, "I made Ernie Preate Attorney General."

Baldassari's story, according to the report, was that "when (Preate) was seeking the office of Lackawanna County District Attorney (in the 1980s), Preate approached Elmo for help. Help, according to Baldassari, consisted of fund raising and other types of events in support of (Preate) at the Bellfonte Apartment complex in Scranton, owned at the time by Elmo Baldassari, as well as solicitations for votes and campaign donations from acquaintances and contacts of Baldassari." When Preate decided to run for Attorney General in 1988, "Mr.

Preate again approached Baldassari and requested his help....
Mr. Baldassari was asked if he had contacts throughout the state
that could help Ernest Preate. According to Mr. Baldassari, Mr.
Preate then told him that in exchange for his assistance and the
help of other vendors, he (Preate) would not enforce the laws
against illegal video poker machines."

The commission notes, "These allegations were consistent
with information which the commission had previously received
from other sources. Mr. Baldassari's allegations were based
upon his personal knowledge of events." Because Baldassari was
a convicted felon, we're told, "corroboration was necessary to
ascertain the validity of his allegations," which was provided by
"numerous other witnesses and sources."

From this start the Crime Commission would come to
make five specific allegations:

First, "Preate, while D.A., approached Baldassari to seek his
help in obtaining campaign contributions from Northeastern
Pennsylvania video poker machine operators. According to
Baldassari, Mr. Preate stated to him that, in return, he would
not enforce the laws against illegal video poker gambling.
Through this contributions arrangement, Mr. Preate received
contributions from video poker operators which included unreported cash."

Second, "Mr. Preate, with the assistance of Elmo
Baldassari's business partner, the late Joseph Kovach, attempted
to replicate this contributions arrangement statewide, when he
sought the Office of Attorney General in 1988."

Third, "Video poker machine operators were forewarned of
the April 6, 1988 Pennsylvania State Police raids after
Lackawanna County District Attorney Preate and member of
his staff were informed of the raids." (The report also found
that "Mr. Preate was hostile towards Pennsylvania State Police
efforts to conduct video poker raids in Lackawanna County.")

Fourth, "After Mr. Preate assumed office as Attorney
General, investigation by the sixth Statewide Grand Jury into
allegations that he improperly received campaign contributions
from video poker operators was terminated."

Fifth, "The Sixth Statewide Grand Jury recommended that certain video poker operators be charged with felonies. The operators were subsequently able to have the recommended felony charges reduced to minor gambling offenses. Further, the operators succeeded in negotiating the substitution of corporate defendants for themselves. One of the defendants, Joseph Kovach, obtained plea agreements for himself and the other video poker operators after threatening to expose the contributions arrangement with Preate."

At the center of the allegations is Joseph Kovach, who died in June 1991. Baldassari is described as a long-time friend and business partner of Kovach; Baldassari was a silent partner in Active Amusement Machines, Co., of Scranton, which Kovach operated. The company distributed music and vending machines, including video poker machines, throughout the state. The report states that Baldassari at some point (it doesn't seem to be clear when) referred Preate to Kovach.

Preate, in a 1994 press conference, characterized a meeting he'd had with Baldassari as a chance encounter. The attorney general said he'd jokingly asked Baldassari to buy tickets to campaign events, and Baldassari had referred him to Kovach. (The crime commission report, meanwhile, quotes Baldassari as saying that Preate, when running for attorney general in 1988, again "requested Baldassari's assistance" and that Kovach again provided help.)

"On behalf of Mr. Preate," the report relates, "Joseph Kovach solicited campaign contributions from video poker operators. Because of Kovach's statewide contacts, these contributions came not only from operators located in the northeast region but also from other areas of the commonwealth. Baldassari told the commission's agents that Mr. Kovach subsequently took Ernest Preate to vending companies throughout the state that Active Amusements dealt with for cash campaign contributions."

The report states that the video poker operators contributed almost $23,000 in 1987 to retire a campaign debt of

$80,914 incurred from Preate's successful 1986 district attorney re-election bid. Numerous video poker operators gave sworn testimony to the commission that Kovach and, to a lesser extant, Joseph C. Baldassari, solicited cash and check contributions for Preate, and also kept a list of which vendors were contributing, and which were not. Many of the vendors were solicited for numerous contributions. Larger operators were expected to give more than smaller operators. Contributions were also given to members of Preate's campaign committee. "In most instances," the report reads, "the operators acknowledged making contributions to District Attorney Preate during May and June 1987 as reported in the campaign expense records of the Ernie Preate DA Committee."

Among those who testified was one "Mary Lou" Salerno, described as having "lived with Elmo Baldassari for approximately 18 years." Salerno testified that Baldassari became involved with Preate "because of the poker machines," that Baldassari had told Kovach they needed Preate "because of the machines.... You know, he wouldn't bother them.... (Elmo) said that Ernie wouldn't have them bother with the poker machines because they were using them (for) gambling.... They wouldn't get the machines kicked out of the locations. They wouldn't pick them up."

Salerno told investigators about campaign money collected for Preate. "The operators all got together for campaigning. They gave Ernie money. Joe (Kovach) was the one that collected all the money ... Joe had contact with them. He called them and got so much money from each person that owned vending businesses. And he got it all for Ernie in cash. Went to Ernie and gave it to him."

"How do you know that?" she was asked.

"... Because Joe Kovach was up at the house."

"Would Joe Kovach discuss this in front of you?"

"Yes."

Selerno's daughter, Mary Kasper, also testified about interesting household conversations. Kasper is described as having "lived with her mother and Elmo Baldassari and, for a period of time, functioned as Baldassari's bookkeeper.... (D)uring late 1986 and early 1987, she overheard numerous conversations between Joseph Kovach and Elmo Baldassari. During one conversation, Baldassari told Kovach, 'I don't care if you don't pay bills. Make sure Ernie gets his money.'"

As for the list of contributors, Salerno told the commission that Kovach would show the list to Baldassari and read off the names. The list, said Salerno, was kept at the office of Active Amusements. "The list was written on a white sheet of paper attached to a clipboard.... Ms. Salerno stated that she accompanied Elmo Baldassari when he took $3,000 cash to Joe Kovach at the offices of Active Amusements. According to Ms. Salerno, Baldassari laid the $3,000 cash on the desk and said to Joe Kovach, 'Here's the money for Ernie.'"

Joseph O. "Jo Jo" Baldassari, Elmo's nephew, would testify that his only concern about the list, apparently, was that his name might not appear on it. He said Kovach showed him the list and "I was really concerned (because) this was cash I gave ... so I can remember actually (calling) Ernie up on the phone and saying Ernie I had given Joe Kovach x-amount of dollars towards your campaign. I want to make sure you got (it). I want to make sure you know it came from me."

"So you talked to him (Preate) personally about that?" he was asked.

"On that particular instance, yeah.... (Preate) said, I saw your name on there. So he evidently saw the list."

Other operators testified about the list. One Eugene Caljean testified that Kovach "showed everybody the list....He showed me the list." One William McGraw, operator of McGraw Amusements, testified that he asked Kovach what would happen if he didn't "contribute."

"'If you give $1,000,' McGraw said Kovach told him, "'I have your name there.'" McGraw asked, "Supposing I don't give then you don't have my name. (Kovach) says, 'Well, then, you're put on the other side of the paper there. And he knows who gave and who didn't.'"

"Who knows?"

"Meaning Preate."

Gordon Potratz, operator of Maple City Amusement Company, testified that "other, bigger operators were paying more than I was. I was a very small operator and (Joseph C. Baldassari told me) 'you shouldn't pay that much. You're just a small guy. Pay that much or whatever you feel is right.'"

One William Ferrario testified that Joseph C. Baldassari asked him for $250 for Preate's campaign.

"You gave Joe two-fifty cash?" Ferrario was asked.

"Yeah," Ferrario said, "because he says, Bill, you got a small route, you shouldn't even be putting in this. The rest of the fellows will give more who have bigger routes. I wanted to give five hundred, and he (Joseph C. Baldassari) said, 'No, you don't have a big enough route. You only got a few machines out, give them two-fifty.'"

Jo Jo Baldassari testified, "If I remember correctly, the little guys, — didn't have to give (as much) — little guys, five hundred, and the big guys a thousand (dollars)."

Contributions by the machine operators in May and June 1987 to Preate's campaign were tendered, as mentioned, in cash and by check, and by money order. The commission heard testimony that contributions from the operators were given to Kovach, "members" of the Baldassari family, as well as direct contributions to Preate's committees. This confused disorganization made for disorganized campaign reports. Several operators would testify that they had given cash contributions to one of the Baldassaris, yet no record would be found in Preate's campaign reports of the donations. Making matters worse the Crime Commission's report on all this is confusing. It's not clear who gave what to whom, and when.

Of this period in mid-1987 the Crime Commission would conclude, "The Ernie Preate DA Committee declared that $22,875 had been contributed by the video poker operators which paid off approximately 28 percent of then District Attorney Preate's debt of $80,914. Campaign bank loans were retired on June 10 and June 30, 1987, respectively. No video poker machine operators were identified by Mr. Preate's campaign committees as such. In most instances, video poker operators were identified in the campaign reports as either a 'businessman' or 'self-employed,' while others were incorrectly identified as 'retired.' In some cases, operators contributed to Ernest Preate using bank cashier's checks or personal money orders."

All along Preate would maintain he'd done nothing wrong. If mistakes were made they were innocent clerical errors. At an unusual 1993 press conference, held while the commission was still working on its report, Attorney General Preate would characterize the legal status of video poker machines in 1987 and '88 as a gray area. He'd say he considered the video poker operators to be legitimate businessmen, and that their contributions were legal and reported properly.

This clash of opinion as to the legality (and, one senses, perhaps the morality) of video poker machines, and political contributions from their operators, would, from the early days on, be at the heart of the controversy.

In 1987, in Scranton, District Attorney Preate would have his first brush with outside opinion. He'd have what the commission would describe as "disagreements" with the Pennsylvania State Police. "In July 1987, the Pennsylvania State Police held a regional seminar on video poker gambling sponsored by State Police Area 2 Commander, Major Michael Jordon, to which all local county district attorneys and chiefs of police had been invited," the Crime Commission report relates. "(D.A.) Preate expressed opposition to the focus of this conference and to video poker enforcement in Lackawanna County." State Police corporal Peter Tonetti, who headed the video poker investigation in the northeast region, was asked by the commission about a discussion he'd had with Preate about the conference.

"...Somewhere between the ... 8th of July and ... 28th of July (1987), I was approached by District Attorney Preate on Washington Avenue (in Scranton)...," Tonetti testified.

"(Preate) said, 'What's going on with this video poker seminar?' ... He proceeded to advise me that he didn't want any enforcement action in Lackawanna County relative to video poker machines, that he would not attend or have anybody from his office attend, and that he didn't have any problems with these machines in the bar(s). And he wanted (the) support of the bar owners, and he didn't want them bothered ... I thought to myself, what's Ernie up to now? He's always closing the bars. He certainly doesn't have the support of the bar owners. He was a crusader against the bars being opened after 2 a.m. It (struck) me ... he wouldn't have any enforcement action. I told him we have to do what we have to do."

"You understood him to be serious?" the commission asked Tonetti.

"Oh, sure."

"He didn't say it in a joking manner?"

"He was very serious."

Within six months Lackawanna County D.A. Ernie Preate would be running for the office of state attorney general. The Crime Commission would come to allege that: "Mr. Preate, with the assistance of Elmo Baldassari's business partner, the late Joseph Kovach, attempted to replicate the contributions arrangement statewide, when he sought the office of attorney general in 1988."

The report explains that Kovach arranged a meeting between Preate and members of a state amusement machine association at the Hotel Hershey in January 1988. "Joseph Kovach, in his attempts to contact video poker operators in other areas of the (state) on behalf of (Preate)," reads the report, "called an old friend, Philip Eisenberg, former manager and co-owner of Consolidated Vending Company, Johnstown. Eisenberg had been in the vending business since the 1940's. He was one of the founding members of the Pennsylvania Amusement & Music Machine Association (hereafter 'PAMMA'), created in 1982. He was a director of PAMMA, was a Chairman of the Board, and was on its Board of Directors

from approximately 1985 until his resignation in June 1992.*"
(Footnote reads: *"Mr. Eisenberg's company, Consolidated
Vending, was one of the largest distributors and operators of
illegal video poker gambling machines in the Johns-
town/Cambria County area in the 1980's until approximately
1992, when the Pennsylvania State Police seized 157 of its illegal video poker machines on June 16, 1992. Eisenberg pled
guilty to one charge of money-laundering on September 15,
1993, stemming from the June 1992 State Police raid. The case
was developed by the Pennsylvania State Police and prosecuted
by the office of attorney general....")

The report states Eisenberg testified "that he organized a
retreat for the Board of Directors of PAMMA in January 1988,
which was held in Hershey. Prior to the retreat, Mr. Eisenberg
received a request by telephone from his long-time friend
Joseph Kovach, asking Eisenberg if Kovach could bring attorney general candidate Ernest Preate Jr. to meet some of the
directors of PAMMA. Mr. Eisenberg arranged for several members of the PAMMA board to attend a dinner at the conclusion
of the retreat, at which Mr. Preate gave a talk." Eisenberg and
several other PAMMA board members testified that Preate
stood up at the end of dinner and said a few words, asking for
support, and stressing his priority as attorney general would be
drug prosecutions, and not video poker machines. "At the dinner," the report summarizes, "Mr. Preate solicited the support
of those in attendance for his bid for the office of attorney general, and indicated his priority, if elected attorney general,
would be drug enforcement. Mr. Preate left the impression that
video gambling would not be a priority."

Preate, in his news conference following the issuance of the
report in 1994, agreed he had attended the meeting, saying
that he told the members his priority as attorney general would
be to prosecute drug dealers and violent criminals. (In a news
conference in 1993, before the report had been issued, the
Inquirer's Fred Cusick and Robert Zausner reported, "Preate
said he *might* have attended a meeting of state video poker
dealers with Kovach during the 1988 campaign." Emphasis

added.)

Eisenberg testified about some of what Kovach had told him while trying to arrange the meeting. "He told me Ernie Preate was running for the office of attorney general of Pennsylvania," Eisenberg said. "...He told me he was district attorney in the area which Mr. Kovach lived.... He told me Mr. Preate was not interested in poker machines — for the prosecution of anybody in the poker machine business, that his main thrust was always drugs and that's what it would continue to be."

"Did Mr. Kovach discuss with you at any time any enforcement efforts or lack of enforcement efforts that may have taken place in his home area?" Eisenberg was asked.

"He said that they haven't had any problems up in that area in many years."

Henry Baldassari Sr., the brother of Elmo, was asked by the commission about the purpose of contributions to Preate:

"Well, you know," Henry Baldassari testified, "the guy (Preate) is running for office. He needs money. I guess everybody was under the impression he wouldn't bother nobody, and he didn't bother nobody in Lackawanna County."

"Who didn't?" commission investigators asked.

"Ernie Preate."

"What do you mean?"

"He never raided no poker machines while he was in office."

"Why?"

"They were contributing him good money.... I don't mind giving him a couple hundred dollars."

"And hope that he would continue not to enforce gambling laws?"

"Certainly."

Testimony revealed that nine people attended the meeting at the Hershey Hotel. One of the PAMMA members, William James Shay Jr., operator of Shay's Vending Service of Lebanon, offered testimony about the reputation of Preate's sponsors,

Kovach and Baldassari.

"Did you know if Mr. Kovach was a member of your organization?" the commission asked Shay.

"I don't believe he was and I don't think so today...." Shay said. "I mean, I heard, you hear through the rumor... that he just wasn't a... fair player... I heard nasty things about Joe Kovach that we didn't want him to — that he was connected with that Baldassari. PAMMA isn't that kind of group.... I heard this already in the '60s, '70s... I remember hearing names like that from my father...."

The report notes that Shay and his father, William James Shay Sr., had both been arrested by the State Police for "charges relating to illegal video poker gambling." Charges against the junior Shay were dismissed, while his father received "probation, a $10,000 fine and costs."

Accompanying Preate and Kovach to the dinner at the Hershey Hotel was Gabriel Horvath, of Rex Vending, in Hazleton, the report tells us. At the time of the January dinner Horvath was facing prosecution in Schuylkill County. In two raids in January and March 1987, twenty-eight video poker machines were confiscated from Horvath. In 1987, Horvath would be charged with various counts involving the gambling machines.

This dinner in Hershey, the commission tells us, wasn't Horvath's only breaking of bread with Preate. The report adds that Horvath "acknowledged meeting with Mr. Preate, Joseph Kovach, and Henry Baldassari Sr. at a Scranton-area restaurant. During this meeting, Mr. Preate advised Mr. Horvath to retain attorney Richard Guida* to represent him on the video poker charges he faced in Schuylkill County. Additionally, Mr. Horvath acknowledged his role with Joseph Kovach in the collection and solicitation of campaign contributions from video poker operators." (Footnote reads: *"Richard Guida was interviewed by the Crime Commission staff on June 8, 1993. During this interview, Mr. Guida stated that Gabriel Horvath told Guida that Horvath was referred to him by then

Lackawanna County (DA) Ernest Preate. Mr. Guida stated that he began representing Mr. Horvath before charges were filed and shortly after the State Police raids.")

For those unfamiliar with notable Pennsylvania law enforcement scandals, I wrote extensively about Harrisburg attorney Richard Guida in my 1991 book *Maybe Four Steps*. Guida had been the state's chief drug prosecutor under AG LeRoy Zimmerman. In late 1986, Guida left the office under a cloud of public accusations that he himself used cocaine. In 1990 Guida was finally prosecuted for drug usage, but not before he'd also implicated another law enforcement official, Henry Barr, as having also used cocaine. Barr was an assistant to U.S. Attorney General Dick Thornburgh. This hadn't been Guida's only brush with outrageous law enforcement. Guida, in 1986, when he was still in the state AG's office, had headed the prosecution of Jay Smith for the murder of school teacher Susan Reinert. Jay Smith was released from death row in 1992, after it came to light that evidence had been concealed or fabricated by prosecutors, and that novelist Joseph Wambaugh had given $45,000 to State Police Trooper Joseph Van Nort for the trooper's cooperation in Wambaugh's best-selling yet phony reconstruction of the Reinert murder titled *Echoes in the Darkness*. Guida isn't exactly known as an upstanding contact in the law enforcement community.

Anyway, about the Hershey dinner, and Horvath. The report goes on to note, "Pursuant to a joint investigation of Gabriel Horvath's illegal video poker gambling activity by the Crime Commission, State Police and the Internal Revenue Service raids were conducted on January 25, 1994. During these raids, authorities seized 36 video poker machines belonging to Horvath's business, Rex Vending. Over one million dollars in currency and securities (over $900,000 cash and approximately $250,000 in securities) were subsequently seized from Gabriel Horvath by the Internal Revenue Service, on his person, at his residence, and at his safety deposit boxes."

Another of those in attendance at the Hershey meeting,

Albert Medved, testified about Preate's after-dinner comments. "Medved testified that there was a lobbying effort within PAMMA for the legalization of video gambling, and Mr. Medved felt that candidate Preate would be supportive of this effort," the report tells us. Though Medved was introduced to Preate at the meeting, "Medved also testified that he subsequently invited Mr. Preate to two political functions in Lancaster County in 1988."

"I was there having dinner and discussions and I think (Preate) spoke for a few moments," Medved told the commission, "and the thing that I recall that impressed me the most was that he was covering the state trying to get votes and he was out to get druggies.... (H)e just did not like to have these drug runners on the street and drunken drivers, and that was going to be his campaign and he wanted our support individually.... And I was impressed."

"Did he indicate what type of support that he wanted?" Medved was asked.

"Like any candidate, I guess whatever it takes — which I have supported him. Financial, whatever.... He also said that I will visit your town, make speeches, introduce you to people. Which I did to. ...I am a past president of the Lancaster Kiwanis Club. I had (Preate) come to our Kiwanis Club and give a talk. George Bush came into Lancaster and I invited (Preate) down into Lancaster and did a breakfast. It was more than money. It was just the opportunity of exposure.

"...I thought ... I am a Republican, he's a Republican and he indicated that he was out, he just gave me his spiel, that I am somebody that's out there that's willing to go out to bat. I am aware of the drug problem and whatnot and I said hey, fine."

Medved pointed out that Preate testified before a legislative committee to legalize video poker. "(H)e said I'd rather see them legalized than illegal out there because it's not a good thing, which I support. And he has my support. That's somebody who said I'd rather have them legalized. I'd rather him than Governor Casey. I figure we can go through the house and senate, we have somebody that could support it."

The report goes on to tell us that Eisenberg "stated that Joseph Kovach and Mr. Preate wanted video poker operators affiliated with PAMMA to raise $100,000 for Mr. Preate's election campaign, but the request was turned down.*" (Footnote reads *"In testimony, Philip Eisenberg refused to discuss this issue on the record, because of the ongoing criminal proceedings....")

Testimony was developed about plans to raise Preate campaign donations through the sale of breakfast tickets.

"After the meeting between Mr. Preate and the directors of PAMMA," we read in the report, "Mr. Eisenberg was telephoned by Joseph Kovach who asked him if he could sell tickets for a fund raiser breakfast for Mr. Preate, which cost $200 or $250 each.*" (Footnote reads: *"It appears, from subsequent testimony, that the tickets costs $200 each.") "Mr. Eisenberg testified he requested 100 tickets and sent either five or ten tickets each to his friends and the directors of PAMMA, along with a letter asking them to try and sell the tickets."

Several problems prevented the sale of many tickets. For one thing, the tickets cost too much. William Shay Jr., one of those who received tickets from Eisenberg, testified, "I know they were real salty. I said I am sure, Phil, I can't move any of those tickets for you."

"Salty?" he was asked.

"Maybe $100.00."

"Could they (have been) about 250?"

"That could have been...."

"You do remember an expensive ticket?"

"That I do remember."

Meanwhile, unknown to DA Preate, video poker machines in northeastern Pennsylvania had caught the attention of State Police in Troop R sometime, apparently, in the spring of 1987. State Police Corporal Peter Tonetti later would testify, "We went around to all the bars. I saw that the (machines in the) bars, in our opinion, were *per se* devices.*" (Footnote reads

*"Seizing a video poker machine as a *per se* gambling device means law enforcement officials no longer have to prove players have received pay-outs for winning games." Elsewhere in the report another footnote explains, "In 1985, Russell Warner, operator of Warner's Coin Machine Company, Erie, had approximately 59 illegal video poker machines seized by federal authorities.... This case was the source of the July 20, 1989, video gambling device decision by U.S. District Court Justice Gerald Weber which established that video poker machines [in the Western District of Pennsylvania] are illegal gambling devices *per se* for federal purposes, and that seizures by law enforcement authorities may be made without observing pay-outs...." In yet another footnote we read, "Video poker vendor Alfred Pelicci, operator of C&A Vending, Inc., testified before the commission that in 1988 poker machines were not used for amusement only because 'they [customers] wouldn't play them.'" In other words, without gambling, there was no business.)

Corporal Tonetti's testimony continues, "Almost every machine that we found seemed to be *per se*. So at this point ... I said, we're going to survey every bar in the Troop R Area, which is the Lackawanna, Wayne, Susquehanna, and Pike Counties, to see what machines we have where and take them all. And then we'll target these, have the specific bar owners come in and testify against the vendors. And that's pretty much how the investigation went. We had identified over 400 machines in the four-(county) area. And we made plans to conduct our raids." Several amusement companies operated by members of the Baldassari family were the "initial targets," Tonetti added. (An early footnote in the report reads, "A statewide assessment of illegal gambling in the Commonwealth, prepared by the Pennsylvania State Police Vice-Intelligence Division in September 1967, reported that, for Lackawanna County, 'All gambling is controlled in this area by the Elio Joseph Baldassari faction.' Pennsylvania State Police Sergeant Albert Broscius, a 35-year veteran, who was in charge of State Police Corporal Peter Tonetti's video poker gambling investigation in northeastern Pennsylvania, testified that he became involved in vice work in 1963. The Baldassari name was familiar to him then because of their involvement in gambling and other activities. Sergeant Broscius testified that this was 'common knowledge.'")

In September 1987, Tonetti and State Police Trooper Thomas Taylor approached the appropriate officials in the state Attorney General's office, under then-Attorney General LeRoy Zimmerman. The two policemen indicated, according to testimony of then-deputy Attorney General Nels Taber, that "they had been investigating video poker operators in the northeast section of Pennsylvania. They were interested in putting it before the grand jury (for) possible corrupt organizations investigations."

A raid was finally scheduled for early April 1988. A few days before the raid, on April 1, 1988, a meeting unrelated to the poker machine investigation was held at DA Preate's private residence. State Police trooper Walter Carlson, Preate, and two other attorneys attended. Carlson later testified, "(Preate) was angry that he was not being told what was going on. ...(T)he following day I was on the second floor of the barracks. Peter Tonetti went by ... I said, Peter, are you having a raid? And at that time he closed the door and said, yes, why? ...I said (these) exact words ... 'Pete, Ernie is pissed. he knows about this raid that's coming down. And he's pissed that nobody talked to him about it. He was quite vocal about it yesterday. I was in a meeting with him.' Peter came back and said, 'How about doing a G.I. (General Investigative Report) on that, what occurred with Ernie?' I said, 'Sure.'"

In the report, dated April 25, 1988, Carlson wrote, "...Upon arrival at the residence, Atty Preate asked the undersigned what was going on in connection with (the) upcoming video poker machine raid ... stated he had just learned of the raid on 3/31/88 ... subject (Preate) was angry and upset as to (the raid) and was verbalizing loudly...."

Corporal Tonetti later would testify about what Carlson told him. "Carlson's description to me was that in all his

(Carlson's) years, he never saw Preate so upset," Tonetti said. "He was violently upset in his apartment, throwing things around, cursing and screaming. I wasn't getting the search warrants and I wasn't picking the machines up.... It wasn't going to happen, not in Lackawanna County."

Another trooper, Salvatore A. Burruano, filed a G.I. report dated April 11, 1988. Burruano stated that on April 1, 1988, the county magistrate coordinator, James Doherty, told Burruano that Doherty had been approached by an assistant DA and a county detective with the instructions that "...should he receive a call from Cpl. Tonetti concerning assigning a special magistrate for the up and coming poker machine raids on Wednesday, 4/6/88. ... any such request should be denied and to have Tonetti call his office."

Tonetti testified he asked the county detective in question about this, who acknowledged the conversation with Doherty. "He told me he was told by Preate to do exactly what he did," Tonetti recollected. "...He told me, 'Ernie told me to do it.'"

On April 5, 1988, the day before the raid, Tonetti and his supervisor, Sergeant Albert Broscius, met with Preate in the DA's office to discuss search warrant approval. "Mr. Preate reacted in a hostile manner with regard to his approving the search warrants," the report tells us. Broscius would testify, "...Preate came in and got pretty boisterous toward us about doing machines, picking up machines in his county.... One thing that stuck in my mind was (Preate saying), 'you want to pick up all the machines in my county? And there are other crimes, more serious crimes... happening, murder and rapes'... the type of argument you get from your bar owners, your machine owners....'"

"Were you surprised at the reaction that you received?" he was asked.

"Yes."

"Why?"

"Well, I thought ... we'd get cooperation from him like we did the other counties, not any verbal abuse or resistance ... from him. That surprised the hell out of me."

The report continues, "Assistant District Attorney Andrew Jarbola recalled that when the State Police met with Mr. Preate for approval of the search warrants, an argument ensued in Preate's office, which was at the other section of the building from where Jarbola's office was located. Jarbola stated he could hear Mr. Preate arguing with the State Police about the video poker raids and believes that everyone in the office could hear the argument.

"The search warrants prepared by Corporal Tonetti were for video poker operators' records, not for the video poker machines, since the machines were regarded as *per se* gambling devices by the State Police, and would be seized as such without any warrants."

Tonetti testified, "I sensed a change in things when I told (Preate) no matter what he was doing with the search warrants, they (the machines) were all going. I wasn't getting search warrants for the machines. He was surprised. He thought I was coming to get search warrants to pick up machines at the individual bars. I was not. I was seizing them on view as *per se* gambling device. The only search warrants I was coming in for were for records from different vendors ... I think ... he realized he can't stop this no matter what."

Preate, in a press conference following the release of the Crime Commission report, said he had been angry with what he described as "fatal inadequacies" in the drafting of Tonetti's warrants.

The report continues, "According to Corporal Tonetti, District Attorney Ernest Preate Jr. asked Cosmo J. Mustacchio, an attorney in the District Attorney's Office, to review the affidavit of probable cause. Mustacchio resisted, telling Mr. Preate he had once represented the Baldassaris and that there might be a conflict of interest on Mustacchio's part. District Attorney Preate demanded that Mustacchio read the affidavit which Mustacchio did."

"What happened at the point?" Tonetti was asked by investigators. "...He reviewed them?"

"Yes he did."

"And did he approve them?"

"There (were) some changes that Preate made, nothing substantial to the warrant ... And that was basically it. I got the changes done and what he wanted in the probable cause, and then the search warrants were approved."

On the evening of April 5, 1988, the same day Tonetti and Broscius met with DA Preate to get search warrants, reads the report, "the State Police got word that machines were being pulled out of some of the bars in the area."

"We got out," Broscius would testify, "got people on the street and were able to get some of ... the machines that we had target(ed). We had a total of about 400 lined up ... and we wound up with about 300. So we missed a hundred machines.*" (Footnote reads: *"In 1988, a video poker machine cost(s), on average, $2,500. The April 6, 1988, raid resulted in the seizure of 349 machines.")

"Tonetti testified that on April 5, 1988," the report tells us, "he received a telephone call around 5:00 p.m. from an informant that Biff's Restaurant, Cedar Avenue, Scranton, and 'Barbara' at the VIP Lounge, Scranton, had been tipped off about the raids."

"I had several guys working for me," Tonetti testified. "I sent them out. I said you go ... on the streets and see what's going on out there. The guys were immediately calling back. The machines were flying out of bars all around town."

Trooper Taylor testified that, "(W)e went out on the streets and started surveillance and did see vendors' trucks flying around the city picking up machines, taking them out of the bar(s) and putting them in trucks and taking them to ware-house(s)."

Several people would later give testimony about the supposed tip-off of the raid. Barbara Passaniti, operator of the VIP Lounge in Scranton, testified that Jo Jo Baldassari had supplied her bar with a poker machine, and that he'd also tipped her off about the raids.

"When were you first advised that there was going to be a State Police raid?" she was asked.

"A few days before, I'd say."

"Who advised you?"

"Jo Jo."

"Did Jo Jo Baldassari tell you how he heard about the raids?"

"No."

Passaniti went on to say that an employee at the bar, Barbara Evans, received a call about 3:00 p.m., the same day Jo Jo Baldassari had called, from a woman warning of the upcoming raid. "(Evans) did get a phone call and she came out and told me about it," Passaniti told investigators. "And I told her I already knew. So it was old news to me."

William McGraw, operator of McGraw amusements, later told investigators, "(T)he rumor had been going around for like two weeks. If anybody had any information on the leak it would have been Joe (Joseph C.) Baldassari and he's deceased now.... Because Joe always had information that nobody else did."

As in much of this legal case, verification would become problematic. Joseph C. Baldassari died before he could be questioned by authorities, and much of the rest of the testimony would be second-, even third-hand.

Henry "Hank" Baldassari Sr. testified, "(at) 3:00 p.m. - 4:00 p.m. in the afternoon ... there was a message on my answering service to call my brother Joe (Joseph C. Baldassari). And I called my brother Joe and he said get your machines out. There is going to be a raid today, tonight...."

Henry Baldassari Jr. told investigators, "...I got a message on my beeper to call my uncle.... Joe Baldassari ... I returned the call and he said there was going to be a raid, move your machines. Just like that."

Corporal Tonetti would testify that, on the day of the raid, Jo Jo Baldassari said that his uncle, Joseph C. Baldassari, had been the source of information about the raid. Tonetti testified, "(Jo Jo) told me he received a call to remove his machines from his Uncle Joe (Joseph C. Baldassari) who had Baldassari Amusements. He said that his Uncle Joe told him that he got a call from Zangardi, his insurance man. And they had gotten the information about all the raids for years from Zangardi. That was their main source of information...."

"Who was this Mr. Zangardi, this insurance agent, that he would get any kind of information from the District Attorney's Office?" Tonetti was asked.

"(Jo Jo) told me it was Pat Zangardi's husband ... (Pat Zangardi) was Ernie's personal secretary, Mr. Preate's," Tonetti replied.

"(Jo Jo) specifically told you ... an insurance guy who was Pat Zangardi's husband?"

"Yes he did," said Tonetti. "...Baldassari Amusement had their insurance with them. And for years, they were the providers of information about different raids that were going to occur."

Mary Lou Salerno, who lived with Elmo Baldassari, told investigators, "(T)he day that they went in and raided them, Annie Stack called Elmo and said, Pat Zangardi called her and they were going to raid them." Salerno said the Stacks had been friends with Elmo "for a long, long time," that the Stacks "had a bowling (alley). ...And they had Elmo's machines. They had (James) Judges' machines in there."

"The Stacks were close to the Zangardis?" Salerno was asked.

"Yeah, very close. ...Annie had a lot (of) parties for Ernie (Preate)."

One Gerald Mancus had what the report describes as a "personal relationship" with Mary Lou Salerno. Mancus also had various business ventures with Elmo Baldassari, which included, the report reads, "Baldassari financing a rice exportation deal for him." Mancus told investigators, "Elmo gets a call from Annie Stack, Frank Stack's wife, who owned a bowling alley in Dunmore ... Annie Stack had gotten a call from Ernie Preate's secretary because, just prior to the raid, Preate was informed by the Pennsylvania State Police that they were going to (be) rounding these people up."

"Do you know the secretary that Annie Stack referred to?" he was asked.

"...Pat Zangardi. ...She called Annie Stack. She is a very personal friend of the Stacks, and she let them know because Frank Stack ... was Elmo's friend. ...So Pat called Annie Stack. Annie called Elmo."

Ann Stack, for her part, told investigators she had known Elmo Baldassari for years. "I've known him about 25 years," she testified. "...It was mostly social. My son — my oldest son bought a piece of land from him and we bought a piece of land from him. ...There were three condominiums (owned) by my husband and Mr. Baldassari."

She said she knew Pat Zangardi for twenty years. But she denied having advance knowledge of the police raid, and denied placing any calls.

"No," Stack said. "If it came, it didn't come from me."

Armond V. Zangardi, the husband of Preate's secretary, and said by police to be Elmo Baldassari's insurance agent, also denied having advance knowledge of the raid, and denied warning anyone.

Patricia Zangardi, who was Ernie Preate's secretary, as well denied prior knowledge of the raid, and denied warning anyone.

Had she become aware that there was to be a raid? she was asked by investigators.

"Yes, I did when I read the paper," she said.

The shit had hit the fan. Several repercussions arose from the Wednesday, April 6, 1988, raid. Preate seems to have undergone at least a partial yet sudden change of opinion as to the legality of video poker machines and the probity of receiving political contributions from their operators. The following Monday, April 11, Preate's campaign refunded eight contributions to seven of the operators who'd kicked in to his campaign. Our report notes that at least one of the operators, Ronald Sompel, received the following letter from Preate's campaign manager, Patrick Meehan, dated April 11, 1988:

"Enclosed please find a check in the amount of $260.00 which represents a refund of your contribution to the Friends of Ernie Preate Committee.

"Because of the present situation involving the seizure of video machines by law enforcement agencies, we think it is only proper and prudent that we refund your contribution to the Committee, even though your contribution to the Committee was made long before this situation arose."

It may have been prudent and proper to refund the operators' contributions, but the commission notes that of the eighteen contributions tendered from seventeen operators in 1988, only eight contributions were returned to seven of the contributors. Of the $6,060 received from the operators, only $2,970, or 49 percent, made its way back. And none of the money was refunded from the $22,875 donated the previous year to retired the '86 campaign debt.

Jo Jo Baldassari, for one, seemed to complain about his partial refund. Campaign reports list Jo Jo as contributing $1,000 to pay off the debt in 1987, and another $260 in January 1988. He'd only get $260 back. He'd later tell investigators that he had given much more than $1,260 — thousands more, much of it, the commission would say, in unreported cash contributions.

"(W)e're talking roughly you wound up kicking in a total of around $3,500, $4,000?" Jo Jo was asked.

"Yes. ...And the poker raids came. And then the stink. Do you remember that little stink about Ernie, and he gave the contributions back. ...I got a check back. It wasn't anywhere near what I gave (Preate). I was hoping I was going to get that all back."

"How much did he give back?"

"It was only a hundred and some dollars to make it look like he gave campaign contributions back, but it was none near (sic)."

(Records indicate Jo Jo in fact received a refund of $260.)

Henry Baldassari Sr. was asked about his $250 refund.

Why'd you get it back? he was asked.

"Well, there was some trouble after the raid," Hank testified, "and I guess Ernie didn't want to get in no trouble getting money from the operators, so he made it look —"

"Made it look what?"

"That it was clean, you know."

If the Baldassaris seemed philosophical, maybe even humored in their own confused way, about what had happened, Elmo Baldassari's partner, Joe Kovach, acted like a man betrayed. Shortly after the raids Kovach began contacting poker machine vendors to return contributions meant for Preate and to ask them to no longer solicit money for the attorney general candidate.

Among those contacted by Kovach were vendors who'd lost machines in the raid. One Eugene Caljean, of Caljean vending, lost thirteen machines. Caljean told investigators that Kovach returned a cash contribution after the raids.

"Did (Kovach) ever request cash from you?" Caljean was asked.

"Just the one time."

"...And you believe he gave it back to you?"

"I know he did," Caljean testified.

"...Was this around the time the raids had taken place?"

"It was after."

"...He gets the money before the raids. After the raids occur, you get a call to come and pick your money up?"

Caljean explained, "We were going to contribute to the campaign and then when he raided Lackawanna County, Mr. Kovach didn't think that he should get the money."

"And he gave it back?"

"Mr. Kovach did."

Kovach also contacted others around the state whose help he'd enlisted for Preate. At the same time machines were impounded and contributions refunded in Scranton, Philip Eisenberg, the Pennsylvania Amusement & Music Machine

Association board member, was still trying to sell the $250 tickets for Preate's campaign.

Eisenberg, for his part, remembered collecting money for the sale of only a few tickets. "I collected two, four, five, six — I collected for six tickets," he told the commission. "But there was an incident that took place after that that stopped the sale of the tickets."

"What was the incident that took place?" he was asked.

"There was a raid on machines up in the northeast; that is on poker machines," Eisenberg explained. "And some time — it was within a day or two after that, Joe Kovach called me up. He sounded very excited on the phone. He asked me to call him on a different number, which I presume was a pay phone number. I called him and he said 'Phil, do me a big favor. Get all those tickets back and return the money.'"

"Did he indicate why he wanted you to do that?"

"No."

Eisenberg dutifully returned a $1,000 check to a New Jersey machine distributor, SMS Manufacturing, which the commission tells us in the report "has been involved with members and associates of traditional organized crime in New Jersey." Other distributors told Eisenberg to keep the money and donate to Preate anyway.

As the campaign wore on Preate made an appearance at a breakfast fundraiser in Johnstown, where Eisenberg sought out the candidate.

"At that particular breakfast meeting, did you have an opportunity to talk to Mr. Preate?" investigators asked Eisenberg.

"No, I did not.... I wanted to talk to Ernie, but there were so many people around him because he was accompanied by (former Philadelphia police chief and mayor) Frank Rizzo at the time.... I saw a fellow outside with a Preate badge on and I started talking to him and he introduced himself as Ernie's brother," Eisenberg testified.

He continued, "I had two checks with me from the sale of

tickets and when I returned the tickets the people said, make the donation to Ernie, anyway. So, I handed him two checks. I believe one was from Seder Vending and one from (Bittner) Vending Company. And I also handed him $200 cash as a donation for myself."

Eisenberg testified that he believed he gave the checks and the cash to Robert Preate, Ernie's brother. Robert Preate would deny this, testifying, "No, I did not receive cash from Mr. Eisenberg or any individual in Johnstown."

The report notes that Preate's "Campaign expense records indicate only a $100 contribution, entered October 28, 1988, in the name of 'Philip Esenberg.'" (Sic.)

There's also some confusion about the two checks from operators that Eisenberg says he gave to Robert Preate. One of the checks was returned to its donor, Walter Seder, owner of Seder Vending. Handwritten on the check's back was this inscription, "For obvious reasons check is returned. Tell you next time I see you." Eisenberg told investigators he thought this message "was most probably" written by him.

Eisenberg went on to tell investigators he finally got to talk to candidate Preate sometime before the election.

"The only thing discussed was the situation up in the northeast," Eisenberg said. "Some of the operators like ... (Gabriel) Horvath—were having problems. And Ernie said they could probably get out of it without too much problem because it was the state's intention to go after the manufacturers of the machine(s) rather than the operators."

"He said this to you?"

"Yes."

"This was at the point prior to his actually being elected, though?"

"Yes...."

Despite the "little stink" of the raid, and the returned contributions, and the resulting fallout in the newspapers in Scranton, Ernie Preate was elected attorney general of the commonwealth of Pennsylvania.

CHAPTER 14

It Pays to be the Boss

After the raids Ernie Preate had to worry about a growing list of unhappy associates. The miffed video poker machine operators, the miffed State Police, a gathering swarm of outside investigators and, to a lesser extent, the press.

The current grand jury, called the Sixth Statewide Grand Jury, working with prosecutors from the office of outgoing state Attorney General LeRoy Zimmerman, began investigating allegations that Preate had improperly received contributions from the operators. The scope of the probe seemed ever-widening. Soon the grand jury would be looking into allegations that the operators had been forewarned by a leak from DA Preate's office. Among those testifying was Jo Jo Baldassari, who shared with the grand jury his opinion that he thought he'd been paying for the privilege of operating the machines, yet had been raided. In his mind we seem to have a consumer protection issue.

Frances Hamacher was the grand jury's administrative officer. Her duties, she testified, including taking "care of all logistics concerning the grand jury ... housing jurors, paying the jurors, paying witnesses, subpoenaing witnesses, scheduling them into the grand jury, preparing various pleadings, anything that had to do with running the operation of the grand jury." She was the gatekeeper and her testimony would give the report what would become its most widely quoted line. Investigators asked for her recollections.

"As this thing progressed in the Sixth Grand Jury," she remembered, "...they were quite honestly shocked at that time of the investigation in what they were hearing. I'm not sure all of what they heard in there but they were quite shocked and I can remember many of them coming out of the grand jury and saying, 'My God, he's a crook....'"

The sledding was getting rough, the natives were getting restless, and when the mob starts to get unruly it pays to be the boss. Now Ernie Preate found himself state attorney general-elect. But what could those grand jurors be hearing?

Francis Hamacher, the grand jury administrator, was surprised one day to receive a phone call from a member of the attorney general-elect's transition team, Lois Lichtenwalner. Lichtenwalner had been an assistant DA under Preate in Scranton, and now she was slated to be a new deputy attorney general, following Preate's inauguration.

Preate's transition team, Hamacher recalled to investigators, "set up an office in the city of Harrisburg and they interviewed the heads of the various units ... and this was so they could get a good picture of the office."

"Did you have to undergo that type of interview?" she was asked.

"No— well," she said, "I was very shocked that I was called by Lois Lichtenwalner and asked— she asked if she could come over to talk to me. As a matter of fact, I mentioned it to Mr. Gracci." Gracci was a higher-up who was chief deputy attorney general in charge of the appeals and legal services section. "I said I really don't understand why she's coming over because she said on the phone that she wanted to talk about the grand jury. ...It was apparent immediately that what she wanted was information on the video poker case that was currently running in the grand jury."

"How did that become apparent?"

"She asked— she asked me if the case was in the grand jury and I said I was not at liberty to tell her anything. She asked if I had the list of witnesses and I told her that we kept a log of people who went in and out of the grand jury. And she asked if she could see this log and I said, no, that she was not under disclosure. This went on for quite a while and finally I guess she understood that she just was not going to get any information and she said, 'I can tell you quite frankly that Mr. Preate is very concerned about this investigation.' So when she left the office, I immediately went to Mr. Gracci and related this. He was furious. He went to Paul Yatron" (first deputy attorney general under AG Zimmerman) "who told Mr. Zimmerman and a memo came down that after that no one was to disclose anything to the team that after all they were not at that point in power ... I think at that point when this happened it pointed out that he really was concerned about the investigation. And from what all we know about the investigation," Hamacher added, "he had every right to be."

LeRoy Zimmerman, our state's first elected attorney general and Preate's immediate predecessor, himself had been an object of a federal investigation, involving a bribery conspiracy that ended in the suicide of state Treasurer Budd Dwyer. On Zimmerman's watch there had also been the aforementioned scandals involving Jay Smith and Richard Guida. Republican Zimmerman's staff apparently had no stomach for doing favors for Republican Preate.

Unable to get anything from Hamacher, Lois Lichtenwalner went to the office of the case's lead prosecutor, Deputy Attorney General Nels Taber. "Mr. Preate felt the only reason the State Police conducted the raids and were conducting the investigation was to embarrass him (Preate)," Taber later recalled Lichtenwalner telling him. "And he (Preate) indicated that he was very interested in the case."

"(W)e knew before ... the swearing in ... that Preate had an interest in that case," former senior deputy AG Michael Kane told investigators, "obviously since he was probably at least one of the subjects in the investigation.

"And I also knew and everybody in the office knew that he had Lois Lichtenwalner snooping around to see what she could find out about that investigation. And we were all of the opinion back then that he shouldn't have anything to do with that case.

"And, in fact, Lois was trying to pump information out of Fran Hamacher. ...And Nels told everybody that she planted herself in his office and started drilling him on what was going on.

"So we were all aware of this and we all knew what was going on was wrong and Paul Yatron put a memo out saying don't disclose any grand jury information to the transition team ... we all knew there was an interest there. And we knew that he shouldn't have had anything to do with it. But there were discussions about that ... what's this guy (Preate) doing coming in and sending in his former assistant DA. It was clear what he was trying to do. He wanted to find out who was testifying and what they were saying."

Lichtenwalner, for her part, later would tell investigators that, as a member of the transition team, she had spoken with Hamacher, but suggested that Hamacher had perhaps been the one who had brought up the subject of the video poker investigation.

Following Preate's swearing in as state attorney general, the report notes, Preate's aide Lois Lichtenwalner was sworn in before the grand jury and granted access to grand jury material. Nels Taber would say, "...at that point there was no basis on (which) she could have been denied access." Elective politics is a wonderful thing.

Taber would go on to say that he had been told by the director of the criminal law division, Anthony Sarcione, that Preate wanted Lichtenwalner assigned to the case.

"Assigned is a very bad word," Lichtenwalner later told investigators. "...(T)here (had) been this general education in the office about how a grand jury can assist you. ...(W)e were even given ... a little mini-seminar on grand jury practice. And I do recall going down on my own in this respect. No one assigned me."

Many of Preate's peers in the law enforcement community began expressing concern over contributions (some hidden or unaccounted) tendered to the DA. There would also soon be plenty of professional concern that Preate, once showered by some $20,000, failed to properly prosecute the donors, and even stood in the way of a proper investigation. Once Preate was installed as state attorney general there was an added and roundly vocalized concern that Preate and his hirelings tampered with or manipulated grand jury proceedings or abused prosecutorial discretion to protect themselves. What happened next underlines the dangers of placing the grand jury system in the hands of untrustworthy individuals. The allegations that would come to be leveled against AG Preate and his staff raise serious questions about other matters entrusted to them, the most obvious being the grand jury investigation of Pennsylvania's state Supreme Court.

Several developments in early 1989 affect our story. Ernie Preate would be sworn in as attorney general in January 1989. Following his assumption of office there would be a gradual changeover in staff at the AG's office as Preate hired his own people. Some attorneys would leave, others would stay on, at the pleasure of the AG. Meanwhile, the term of the Sixth Statewide Grand Jury would be coming to an end, leading to the writing of its investigative findings, called its presentment or indictment.

A grand jury's presentment is normally written by the prosecutor in charge. It's then reviewed and approved by higher-ups, including the front office, and lastly is submitted to and voted upon by the grand jury. A great deal of public trust is therefore placed in the hands of the prosecutor and his supervisors.

In the case of the video poker investigation, language in the presentment early on became a hot topic. A controversy would rage up and down the chain of command. Higher-ups ultimately would delete language mentioning contributions Preate received from the operators. Language also would be removed that implicated Preate's former county DA's office as a source of leaks that tipped operators off to the raid. Ernie Preate's exact role in these changes are not known, as he refused to be interviewed by the Crime Commission. It is clear though that Preate did not recuse himself from this issue.

The Crime Commission report notes, "Nels Taber, the Deputy Attorney General assigned to the Sixth Statewide Grand Jury's video poker probe, prepared a draft presentment for the Grand Jury sometime after Mr. Preate became Attorney General in January 1989.... Prior to a draft of the presentment going to the *front office,* Mr. Taber discussed with Chief Deputy Attorney General Robert Graci* whether or not it would be appropriate to include the material concerning Mr. Preate's receipt of contributions from the video poker operators." (Footnote reads: *"Graci has held the position of Chief Attorney General for the Appeals and Legal Services Section since 1987. One of Graci's duties was reviewing grand jury presentments.") Gary Reinhardt, the chief deputy attorney general in charge of the Prosecutions Section, also participated in the discussions. "Mr. Graci had reservations about the legal relevance of the contributions material, while Mr. Reinhardt indicated that the material was within the scope of the original Grand Jury Notice," the report tells us.

The exact law (42 Pa. C.S.A. 4550 [a] States) reads, "Before submitting an investigation to the investigating grand jury the attorney for the Commonwealth shall submit a notice to the supervising judge. This notice shall allege that the matter in question should be brought to the attention of the investigating grand jury because the investigative resources of the grand jury are necessary for proper investigating. The notice shall allege that one or more of the investigative resources of the grand jury are required in order to adequately investigate the matter."

Taber, in charge of the investigation before Preate took over, came away with the opinion that the grand jury felt it appropriate to look into Preate's involvement with the operators. Had the grand jurors expressed an interest in pursuing the contributions issue? Taber was asked by investigators. "It was expressed to me from Fran Hamacher who was the administrator for the grand jury that they were interested in that, yes," Taber testified.

Despite the grand jurors' interest, Graci told Taber he

didn't think it would be within the scope of the grand jury's original orders to mention campaign contributions to Preate. Graci's high-up, Anthony Sarcione, took a different view. In this controversy we see the chariot and charioteer workings of a grand jury and its prosecutor.

"Grand jury notices, however, were not always interpreted so restrictively," the report tells us at one point. "The Director of the Criminal Law Division at the time, Anthony Sarcione, in his testimony before the commission, implied there was some latitude granted to investigative attorneys in determining the subject matter of presentment. For example, during the Sixth Statewide Grand Jury, Nels Taber conducted an extensive inquiry into whether or not different operators had been solicited by Joseph Kovach for campaign contributions to Mr. Preate. Mr, Sarcione testified he told Taber '...Wherever it goes, go with it.'"

Not only had Taber felt it proper to include language involving Preate in the presentment, he'd wanted to continue the investigation by granting immunity to Kovach, Elmo Baldassari and other vendors. Immunity would have compelled these people to testify, without fear of prosecution. The change in administration ended that plan.

"Did you ever discuss with anyone your desire to obtain or attempt to obtain immunity orders for those witnesses; Mr. Kovach and Mr. Baldassari?" investigators asked Taber.

Taber explained, "...what happened was there were other vendors I believe that I wanted to call first and when I attempted to get grants of immunity for those vendors, I was informed that they were—the Attorney General was not going to allow grants of immunity to be given any longer for persons testifying before the grand jury in this case."

As for the matter of writing the draft of the presentment, Taber received help, as was a normal practice, from Deputy Attorney General Brain Gottlieb of the Appeals and Legal Services Section. Gottlieb would testify, "After Nels (Taber) and I finished working on the document, I had the expectation that it was pretty much in finished form. Usually after the appeals and legal services lawyer (Gottlieb) and the prosecution's attorney (Taber) reviewed the document, there might be some changes made ... but once it got beyond Bob's (Taber's supervisor, Robert Graci) level ... I don't recall instances where it was routine for there to be substantive changes in the document. So in this case we reviewed it, we sent it through Bob. I don't recall Bob having any specific concerns with it and it then went up for further approval."

Former Senior Deputy Attorney General Michael Kane would describe the normal links in the chain of command. "...It would normally go from the deputy that did the case (Taber) to Bob Graci, who's chief of Legal Appeals and Services... who would ... send it up to Anthony Sarcione (director of the criminal law division) and then it would go up to the front office to Preate or Cohen." Walter Cohen was Preate's first deputy attorney general. Kane added, "...No doubt in my mind that it went to Preate. Any presentment went to Preate and then came back down and .... I don't believe I have had one that got changed. I mean, this is the only one ... I can think of right now that got changed."

The presentment came back down to the prosecuting attorney with all mention of Preate's office deleted. Brian Gottlieb, who'd helped Taber write the altered draft, picks up the story:

"Nels Taber came to me one morning," Gottlieb testified, "and he said that ... Walter Cohen, the first deputy attorney general, had made some changes in the document. And I believe this happened over a weekend. ...And I said to him (Taber) 'Well, what changes were made.' And he referred to a part in the presentment that discussed testimony regarding a leak of information about a State Police raid on establishments that had video poker machines. And he said that Mr. Cohen had removed the section that discussed the leak.

"...I immediately went to Mr. Gracci," Gottlieb went on, "and ... explained to him that I felt that it was inappropriate to remove the section of the presentment. ...I felt that under the circumstances ... there had been testimony taken during the

Grand Jury investigation regarding the Attorney General's relationship with ... some of the subjects of the investigation. (I)t
was especially inappropriate for someone in the executive office
to have made that kind of change in the document."

Graci tried to reassure Gottlieb. Graci "told me that he had
been assured that there was going to be a continuing investigation into the issue of the leak," Gottlieb said. "And that as a
result of receiving those assurances, you know, that made him
feel comfortable that this matter was satisfactorily resolved."
Later, before he was to testify about all this, Gottlieb would
speak to Graci about the "matter of the assurance he said had
been given to him" but that, "He (Graci) said that he didn't
remember saying that to me."

Removed from the document, as mentioned, was a section
having to do with leaks in DA Preate's office. Walter Cohen
later would provide the commission a document which, the
report tells us, "on its face, appears to be pages 15 and 16 of
the un-edited version of the presentment. The un-edited version contained specific mention of the Lackawanna County
District Attorney's Office:

"These 'leaks' had been attributed to several sources,
including the Lackawanna County District Attorney's Office ...
Corporal Tonetti had brought several search warrants to the
district attorney's office for approval a day or two before the
scheduled raids ... Joseph Baldassari testified that he had been
informed of the raid a week before the raid. Such a 'leak' would
have occurred before the search warrants were brought to the
district attorney's office ... there was no identifiable source for
the release of any information concerning the raid.*"

(The footnote in the commission's report reads: *"This un-
edited version, however, was inaccurate insofar as it implied that
the district attorney's office was not an 'identifiable source' of
the leak merely because news of the raids had circulated prior to
the search warrants being brought to Mr. Preate's office. As
mentioned in ... this report, Mr. Preate knew of the impending
raid at least as early as March 31, 1988. Mr. Preate met with

Trooper Walter Carlson on April 1, 1988, and told him that he learned of the raid one day prior. Mr. Preate therefore knew of the raid at least six days prior to the raid's occurrence.")

There would be a continuing controversy as to who made the changes, and whether Preate recused himself from the matter.

Michael Kane, the former senior deputy attorney general, testified, "Brian (Gottlieb) told me that Walter Cohen was the one who redacted it, that he was told by Bob Graci that it was Walter Cohen who read it over the weekend... (and) Walter Cohen did whatever Ernie wanted ... I never knew of anything that did not go to Preate. I never knew of a case that didn't go; a plea bargain, a request interview ... a presentment it all went to him (Mr. Preate)."

Sarcione, director of the criminal law division, gave what can only be described as contradictory testimony about Preate's involvement in all this. Sarcione, the report tells us, "testified that Mr. Preate never formally recused himself from any involvement in the video poker investigation and prosecution. Mr. Preate discussed developments in the video poker case with his subordinates."

Besides discussing the presentment with Preate, had there been any general discussion with the AG concerning this investigation? Sarcione was asked by investigators.

"I am quite certain that I probably informed—I informed him of—that the thing was going on," Sarcione testified. Did Preate indicate that he thought he should recuse himself? Sarcione was asked.

"...(T)here was," Sarcione recalled, "I remember, one discussion about that, whether he should or shouldn't. And basically it was left that, you know, I (Sarcione) would dispose of it as a way I felt appropriate and I don't believe he ever did formally recuse himself."

"When was that?"

"...(I)t was probably sometime shortly after the presentments," Sarcione said.

The report goes on, "Although Attorney General Preate had never officially recused himself from the investigation, there were those from the Attorney General's Office who testified that they were told that Mr. Preate had informally removed himself from the case."

Investigators would ask Sarcione the central question: "Did it ever occur to you that the issue of the possible improper or perhaps criminal behavior of the Attorney General should be explored?"

Here loyalty, position, and public and private trust all seem to intersect. Sarcione replied, "I will be frank. ...(T)he Attorney General hired me. I didn't know him. He showed a lot of faith in giving me such a position ... I didn't see him as a potential criminal.

"...I did not at the time have any belief ... that that was possible. That's my statement ... I didn't know either all these details from '87 and '88 either, you know, that obviously everyone has brought to light ... I didn't have all this stuff from Scranton that you have," Sarcione told the Crime Commission.

The Crime Commission report sums up: "The final version of the presentment for the Sixth Statewide Grand Jury dated July 27, 1989 and handed down on July 31, 1989 does not mention the Lackawanna County District Attorney's Office, nor does it make any mention of the alleged improper contributions from video poker operators." The grand jury recommended felony gambling and/or corrupt organization charges against twenty-five operators, including Joe Kovach and Elmo Baldassari. The charges against all but one of the individuals would never be brought, and several other funny things would happen on the way to justice.

The Sixth Statewide Grand Jury would vote not to extend itself, basically ending its investigation, unless the inquiry was picked up by the Seventh Statewide Grand Jury.

The presentment, once handed down, would be sealed until late February 1990. State Police Corporal Peter Tonetti, the officer behind the original investigation and the raid, wouldn't see a copy of the presentment for some six months after it was handed down, until January 1990. Tonetti would testify that the AG's office hadn't even alerted him to the presentment's existence. (Graci, head of the Appeals and Legal Services Section, told investigators it was unusual to exclude the State Police. "When you prepare a presentment, you've been working with a particular trooper or agent, depending on where the case comes from," Graci said. "(I) have them review it before it comes to me to make sure that they think it's accurate because ultimately they're going to be the ones signing a criminal complaint if this is to be used as an affidavit of probable cause.")

The cops might have been out of the loop, but in the last six months of 1989 there were several interesting contacts between the AG's office and the accused video poker operators. There was even a contact *before* the issuance of the presentment by the grand jury. On July 21, 1989, ten days before the presentment was handed down, Anthony Sarcione, head of the Criminal Law Division, met in Wilkes-Barre with three defense attorneys representing various operators. The attorneys would be identified by the commission only by their initials: "S.C.," "R.I.," and "J.M." Corporal Tonetti might not have seen the presentment, but there is speculation that at the July 21 meeting Sarcione showed a copy to the defense attorneys.

Sarcione himself would say he didn't recollect taking the presentment to the meeting. But one of the defense attorneys made notes entitled "Meeting Wilkes-Barre 7/21/89, Anthony Sarcione" in which businesses and individuals were listed in an order that the report calls "identical to the final version of the presentment."

"The defense attorney's list," the report adds, "also included the names of individuals who were not represented by any of the three attorneys present at the Wilkes-Barre meeting."

The first item on the first page of the defense attorney's notes read, "Grand jury voted not to extend." Sarcione, for his part, did not recall informing the attorneys that the grand jury had voted itself out of business. "My recollection of that (July

21, 1989) meeting was simply them trying to bully me and tell me: 'What are you doing here? This is horse-shit...'" The defense attorney's notes tell a different story. The notes detail the negotiating positions of both the AG's office and that of the defense. The defense, among other things, wanted corporations or partnerships charged, not individuals. The notes regarding the position of the AG's office also mentioned corporations, and wanted fines yet no jail time; the notes indicate Sarcione sought the cooperation of the operators in an investigation of the machine manufacturers, and offered immunity.

Sarcione would testify that he later spoke with Preate about this meeting. "(H)e laughed at it," Sarcione recalled Preate's reaction. "He said, 'Don't worry about it ... You can deal with them' ... Because I guess he knew, being from Scranton, he knew (two of the attorneys, identified in the report as 'S.C.' and 'J.M.')."

The report notes, "Mr. Sarcione stated that after the July meeting Mr. Preate met or talked with Mr. S.C.*" (Footnote reads, *"Mr. S.C. represented video poker operator Anthony Rinaldi who, although recommended to be charged in the grand jury presentment, was not arrested. Three of Rinaldi's employees ... were not only named in the presentment, but were also arrested. These three employees testified before the Crime Commission that they learned of their impending arrest from Anthony Rinaldi, their employer. They also testified that Anthony Rinaldi paid for their legal counsel, Mr. S.C. The Crime Commission received sworn testimony (from the employees) that Anthony Rinaldi and (his son) Elmo Rinaldi were directly involved in a video gambling enterprise. ...(Two of the employees) testified that Anthony Rinaldi's son, Elmo Rinaldi, besides being their immediate supervisor, would do collections when the collectors were on vacation or sick.")

"Did (Mr. Preate) indicate he met with (S.C.) ... or Mr. (J.M.)?" Sarcione was asked by investigators.

"(Preate) may have indicated to me that during this time from presentment to disposition that they called him or (he) spoke to them...."

"...He may have or he did?"

"...I believe he did," Sarcione said. "He did. ...they go back a long way. I don't know what the heck they talked about ... I know they had contact. I know (J.M.) was friendly with (Preate). I mean from being in Scranton. So was (R.I., another involved defense attorney)."

The report summarizes what was to happen: "The Sixth Statewide Grand Jury recommended that certain video poker operators be charged with felonies. The operators were subsequently able to have the recommended felony charges reduced to minor gambling offenses. Further, the operators succeeded in negotiating the substitution of corporate defendants for themselves."

That corporations, and not individuals, would come to be charged is mystery enough. Thickening the mystery is that several of these corporation didn't even exist until after Sarcione met with the three defense attorneys on July 21, 1989.

"Four of the nine corporations ultimately charged were formed after the April 6, 1988 raids but prior to the unsealing of the grand jury presentment," the report tells us. "Moreover, the principals of these four corporations were each represented by an attorney who participated in the July 21, 1989, Wilkes-Barre meeting.*" (Footnote reads, *"S.C. represented, among others, Joseph Gustin, operator of Joseph G. Amusements and Vending, Inc., which was incorporated on July 26, 1989. R.I. represented C&A Vending, Inc., incorporated on November 22, 1988, and HLJ Amusements, Inc., incorporated on September 29, 1989. Finally, J&R Amusements, represented by J.M., filed for incorporation on July 31, 1989 — the same day the presentment was issued — and was incorporated on August 18, 1989.")

The deputy AG who would ultimately handle the plea arrangement, Dennis Reinaker, would testify that he was under the impression that the substitution of corporations for the individuals hadn't even been broached until a meeting Reinaker had had with the defense attorneys in October 1989. "I assumed it (the October meeting) was the first time the corporate plea was raised because in my conversations with Mr. Sarcione afterward it seemed as though that was something new to him that was being brought into this," Reinaker testified.

Something screwy appears to be going on here, and the commission doesn't pull punches about what its investigators think happened. The report alleges that Joseph Kovach "obtained plea agreements for himself and the other video poker operators after threatening to expose the contributions arrangement with Mr. Preate." These conclusions aren't what can be called airtight, since the main player, Joe Kovach, died in June 1991, before all this could be investigated.

So, for example, the chronology of the late Kovach's supposed threat against Preate isn't clear in the report. There was lots of second-hand testimony concerning stories Kovach supposedly told others.

"Elmo Baldassari," the Crime Commission report tells us, "in an interview by the commission, stated that Joseph Kovach told him 'he (Kovach) had spoken with Preate's top assistant, whose name Baldassari could not recall, and told this individual that if he (Kovach) went to jail, so would Ernie, as he had records of the money given and the individuals who gave money to Preate's campaign." Two other operators testified Kovach had told them as much, too. Operator Eugene Caljean told investigators Kovach "wanted to get even with Ernie Preate for what he did to Joe personally. And the arresting (of) him ...."

Kovach "felt betrayed because of that?" Caljean was asked.

"Oh definitely...."

"So it was his understanding that he wouldn't be prosecuted in exchange for his contribution?"

"(H)is understanding (was) that Ernie Preate would not raid the poker games," Caljean explained.

Mary Lou Salerno, the woman who lived with Elmo Baldassari, was asked by investigators, "Before Joe Kovach died, do you know if he made any efforts, if Joe Kovach made any efforts to contact or do anything with these people?"

Salerno replied, "Joe was really upset because they were indicting him ... And Kovach said to Elmo, 'I'm involved.' He said, 'If ... this happens, if I get in trouble,' he said, 'I'm going to fix Ernie too. He'll never get away with this.' ...(H)e said that he would go after Ernie if they didn't drop whatever they were doing to him and all the other operators."

"Joe Kovach said that?" she was asked.

"Yeah. He said, 'Ernie won't screw with me.'"

Salerno went on to tell investigators about "an angry exchange of words between Elmo Baldassari and Mr. Preate during a fund raiser at the St. Mary's Center in Scranton," the report tells us. Salerno testified, "Ernie was there and Elmo walked up to him. And there were people standing there. And he said to Ernie, 'You're a f—-ing bum.' And Ernie said, 'I don't know what you mean.' (Elmo Baldassari) says, 'You know what you did. You know what you did to me.' ...It was a reference to the machines."

AG Preate held a press conference on February 23, 1990, to announce that certain individuals would soon be arrested on video poker machine charges as a result of an investigation by the Sixth Statewide Grand Jury. Preate's typically fork-tongued comments were as follows:

"We are not going to stand idly by and permit Pennsylvania to become a *de facto* gambling state," Preate told reporters. "...In the past, (bar owners and distributors) knew that even if they were convicted of illegal gambling, the only punishment they were likely to get was a modest fine ... our goal is nothing less than driving every video poker machine out of Pennsylvania ... we're clamping down because blatant illegal activity and sporadic enforcement breed contempt for the law ... and we're clamping down evenly, on the entire industry, top to bottom ... all the distributors, all the bars and clubs."

Yeah, right. Preate made no mention of returning contributions he'd received from video poker operators he was about to let off the hook. Preate's *modus operandi* was to do whatever sort of poor, unfair, irresponsible job he wanted, make a high-horse, bombastic and bullying speech about justice, and hope that the press or the public (or outside agencies) don't look too far into the matter.

On February 26, 1990, the grand jury presentment was unsealed and charges were filed against individuals and corporations. "Twenty-five individuals involved with video poker were recommended to be charged with first degree felony charges of corrupt organizations," the report tells us. "Within two months, the pleas were settled, rendering the individual operators free of criminal penalties."

The report goes on to summarize the outcome of the cases: "Of the 25 individuals recommended for prosecution by the Sixth Statewide Grand Jury on charges of Corrupt Organizations, Criminal Conspiracy and Gambling, Gambling Devices etc., seven were never arrested. The eighteen remaining individuals were arrested in February 1990. Sixteen either had their arrest records expunged and/or the charges were withdrawn. Only two operators received dispositions: Frank Brozzetti pled *nolo contendere* and paid a $12,250 fine; and Henry Baldassari Sr. was sentenced to Accelerated Rehabilitative Disposition (ARD), 25 hours of community service and court costs.* The nine corporations ultimately charged (yet not recommended for prosecution by the grand jury) on the same day as the eighteen individual video poker operators, pled *nolo contendere* to one count of gambling devices. Eight of the nine corporations charged paid fines ranging from $7,500 to $14,750. Corporation fines totaled $74,500 while individual operator fines totaled $12,250." (Footnote reads, *"Mr. Brozzetti did not file for incorporation of his business. His attorney, Charles Volpe, was not a party to the private negotiations with representatives of the Office of Attorney General. As for Henry Baldassari Sr. Common Pleas Judge (Robert) Conway refused to accept a plea by Mr. Baldassari's newly formed corporation.")

The report notes that on July 21, 1990, Judge Robert Conway of Wayne County asked deputy AG Reinaker to explain the plea agreement that allowed Baldassari to personally get off scot-free while his newly formed corporation pled *nolo contendere*. Reinaker replied that although some of the corporations had been formed after the April '88 raid, the AG's office was satisfied that the gambling "activity continued after the time that the corporation was chartered." This twisted thinking meant that Preate's office was satisfied these guys were still gaming, so he was letting them off.

Judge Conway then told Reinaker, "All right. I don't agree with you at all. I think that this is so much garbage ... I think it is a fraud on the Court, sir, and I am not going to be any part of it."

Henry Baldassari Sr. explained his hard luck to the commission.

Baldassari was asked, "Your plea was for — a corporation was supposed to enter a plea. Is that correct?"

"Right," Baldassari explained.

"And the judge indicated that he was not satisfied because the corporation—"

"Was formed after the raid," Baldassari said.

"After the raid?" investigators asked. "Who advised you to do that (form a corporation?)"

"My attorney." The report notes that Baldassari's attorney, referred to only as "R.I.," was present during the Wilkes-Barre meeting on July 21, 1989.

"He advised you to form a corporation?" Baldassari was asked.

"Yeah."

"Subsequent to the—"

"After the raid."

"After the raid?"

"Because," Baldassari explained, "...the other operators did the same thing and Judge Walsh accepted it."

"He accepted it with all the others but with you —."

"Well, I didn't go before Judge Walsh I went before Judge Conway in Wayne County and he wouldn't accept it."

Judge Conway not only refused the plea, the report tells us, but he also said he was forwarding the information to the Wayne County DA for possible "criminal sanction regarding obstruction of justice." The judge suggested that the State Police ought to re-arrest Baldassari.

In the end, Baldassari told the commission, he went through "a lot of red tape" to get his case sent to Lackawanna County. He agreed to be re-arrested; he then accepted the ARD probation, court costs and twenty-four hours of community service.

Explaining the reasoning behind the plea agreements, Sarcione implicated the judiciary, Judge Conway notwithstanding. "What I considered was do I want to tie up one of the few experienced trial lawyers that I had on my staff at that time on video poker prosecutions in the northeast from whence these people came from? And we all know how judges (rule) who know the locals guys. I see it in any county I go to...."

Judge Conway was not the only one to express disbelief over the inequity of the arrests and subsequent plea agreements. The State Police, the prosecutor handling the grand jury investigation, even the video operators themselves and a defense attorney expressed incredulity.

Joe Kovach was arrested on February 27, 1990, several days after the indictment was unsealed. The investigating officer, Corporal Peter Tonetti of the State Police, told of an odd encounter he'd had while booking Kovach.

"I was fingerprinting Joe Kovach at the barracks," Tonetti told investigators. "... Kovach was quite irate over the fact that (Anthony Rinaldi) that had (Automatic Vending) wasn't arrested ... and I turned to Sarcione and Reinaker because I didn't understand it myself. And I told Sarcione and Reinaker to give me a warrant, and I'll go down and arrest Rinaldi because I think he should have been arrested too.... I thought some people were missing that should have been involved. ...It was a hostile situation at the barracks between myself, Sarcione, Reinaker, and Joe Kovach."

There was another dispute between Tonetti's supervisor,

Sgt. Albert Broscius, and Sarcione. "When representatives of the (AG's office) decided on the pleas that would be accepted they then met with the State Police and sought their concurrence," the report tells us.

Broscius told investigators that trying to get information from the AG's office about the presentment before the arrests was almost like pulling teeth. "We had to coax them to give us the Grand Jury findings...," Broscius recalled. Coax whom? he was asked. "Coax Tony Sarcione ... I'm sure there were phone calls made and personal visits made for the presentment. After we got that settled with them, they then wanted not to arrest the individuals. They wanted to arrest the corporations."

Broscius told investigators he was unhappy with charging corporations. "...We did not want it. And I specifically told him (Sarcione) that this wasn't the way we did business. And it was a bad judgment. I can remember telling him that if you arrest those corporations, the next day the corporations are going to go in and reincorporate under a new fictitious name and there's no record. The only way is to have an arrest record on the individual...."

Trooper Tom Taylor recalled Broscius's adamant opposition. "If you charge this corporation," Taylor told investigators, "...charge a non-person with a criminal violation, then the company can be dissolved. Then there's really no record ... (for example) it used to be Star Vending. Now it doesn't exist. I'm now Ace Vending, and they don't have a record. (Sgt. Broscius) foresaw that."

Deputy AG Taber, who'd handled the grand jury investigation before Preate took office, told investigators it had always been his intention to charge the individuals, as described in the presentment. "The individuals were the ones who were responsible for the various activities that took place," Taber explained. "...I didn't see where it would be appropriate for the criminal penalties to fall upon the corporations to shield various individuals from their criminal responsibility."

Charles Volpe Jr., an attorney for two of the Baldassaris, told investigators he too was surprised that operators were allowed lenient pleas. His clients were initially looking at much worse. Before Preate's office cut the deals, Volpe testified, "...(I)t was made clear to me ... what they were after was a first degree felony for corrupt organizations which, naturally, I relayed to my clients. It caused a great deal of concern. That felony carries a ten-year prison sentence and some stiff fines. So at that point what I understand ... from Mr. Taber was that was their intent."

Volpe went on to describe the evidence against his clients as "voluminous." Volpe said, "The odds of my clients winning a trial would have been negligible. ...They would inevitably be facing a corrupt organizations charge. Nels Taber had pretty well indicated that to me in so many words." Volpe said Taber had tentatively agreed on the individuals pleading guilty to a lesser misdemeanor charge.

Taber never got the chance. The Sixth Statewide Grand Jury, having voted not to extend, was dissolved. Preate apparently made good on his promise to vendors that any investigation would shift to the manufacturers. "After Mr. Preate had been elected," the report tells us, "the Office of Attorney General issued a new grand jury notice to investigate the manufacturers of video poker machines. The Office of Attorney General, however, chose not to issue a notice to pursue the allegations against Mr. Preate that had surfaced in the Sixth Statewide Grand Jury, specifically the contributions arrangement and the issue of the forewarning. The Seventh Statewide Grand Jury was located in Harrisburg and consisted of new jurors who were not privy to the testimony of the Sixth Statewide Grand Jury. In addition, in August 1989 a new Deputy Attorney general, Dennis Reinaker, was assigned to the Grand Jury video poker cases. He did not begin working on the video poker cases until after Mr. Preate was elected and after the Sixth Statewide Grand Jury had issued its presentment."

Investigators asked Reinaker whether there had been any effort to follow up on testimony developed before the previous grand jury, particularly allegations concerning contributions to

Preate and talk of a tip-off. "There was not any effort made by me," Reinaker said. "I mean, when I got the case, it basically was finished from an investigative standpoint. The grand jury presentment was prepared...." This contradicts Taber, who said not only had he thought there were avenues to explore, but that he'd been told that Preate had refused his request to grant immunity to Kovach, Elmo Baldassari and other vendors.

So Taber and Sixth Statewide Grand Jury were gone. A fresh grand jury was convened under new marching orders to look into only the manufacturers. Suddenly immunity was offered to Joe Kovach and other vendors. Under immunity Kovach, the commission notes, was never asked about his primary role in the contributions arrangement with Preate.

"At the point where (Kovach) testified," Reinaker explained, "there had been a new grand jury impaneled and a new notice submitted. And the focus of that was to look at the manufacturers of these machines to see if, in fact, we could do anything at that level to try and deal with the problem on a statewide basis."

The report notes, "Mr. Reinaker testified before the commission that Attorney General Preate would have had to sign the petition for Mr. Kovach's immunity. The immunizing of Kovach and others, however, contradicted Mr. Preate's general stance on grants of immunity. In an August 7, 1989 letter from Attorney General Preate to the Crime Commission, Mr. Preate refused to grant an Allentown video poker operator immunity. Preate wrote, 'I personally frown on giving immunity to persons who have violated the criminal statutes of Pennsylvania. I am of the belief that immunity is warranted only when it is a case of last resort.'"

Preate suddenly was throwing around immunity left and right. Video poker operator Arnold "Arnie" Taksen, who with his wife Pat had attended the early 1989 amusement association meeting with Preate and Kovach at the Hotel Hershey, received an unexpected grant of immunity. Taksen told investigators "he was subpoenaed before the Seventh Statewide Grand Jury in 1990 and given immunity without requesting it."

The operators were left off the hook, their newly formed corporations charged, and now the AG's office expunged their records. Reinaker testified it was his and Sarcione's decision to immediately clear the operators' records. Sarcione defended the expungement by saying, "Well, under the law, under the law as it is right now on expungement in this commonwealth I believe if you are not convicted personally, if you are charged and it doesn't happen, I believe you are entitled to expungement."

The commission countered, "If there is no disposition within a three-year period you may move for expungement. Even if the charges are dismissed and there has been no new arrest and you weren't convicted on those after ten years you may move for expungement. These expungements took place at the same time that the corporations pled guilty, without keeping any records on these individuals to see if they were ever to repeat again."

And that's the way the game was played. The operators were off the hook, and the state attorney general's office no longer pursued an investigation of former Lackawanna County District Attorney Ernie Preate, who was now the state attorney general.

"It was finished," Reinaker told investigators. "...(Y)ou guys have been involved in law enforcement. It is just not realistic to think that we in this office were going to be asking questions about our boss. I mean, maybe it's something somebody else should have brought up."

The Crime Commission report notes, "After Mr. Preate was elected, a notice of investigation targeting video poker manufacturers was issued by the Office of Attorney General. The principal witnesses from the Sixth Statewide Grand Jury — including the key figure in the contributions arrangement, Joseph Kovach — were granted testimonial immunity at the request of the Office of Attorney General. Despite testimony before the new grand jury that the manufacturers had shipped illegally equipped video poker machines across state lines into Pennsylvania, the Office of Attorney General failed to follow-up on key aspects of the investigation. Former Director of the Criminal Law Division, Mr. Sarcione, testified:

"*Q: What ever happened to the probe of the manufacturers?*

"*A: It fizzled....*"

The report continues, "State Police Sergeant Albert Broscius testified similarly before the commission that Attorney General Preate had announced a *statewide crackdown on machines.* Sergeant Broscius testified:

"*Q: And it was a general consensus that the State Police would not participate in this crackdown?*

"*A: I don't think that there was a statement that we would not participate. I think our feeling was that we would cooperate once we found out what our game plan was. The game plan never seemed to mature or develop into anything.*"

In short, there was a growing body of evidence that Pennsylvania Attorney General Ernie Preate was a crook. But that's putting it too mildly. Throughout the report what the Crime Commission and various video poker operators were hinting at but didn't quite have the courage to say was that Preate had taken money from, and formed an alliance with, a faction of Pennsylvania's organized crime syndicate.

The vendor, for example, who says of Joe Kovach, "I mean, I heard, you hear through the rumor... that he just wasn't a... fair player... I heard nasty things about Joe Kovach that we didn't want him to — that he was connected with that Baldassari. PAMMA isn't that kind of group.... I heard this already in the '60s, '70s... I remember hearing names like that from my father," etc. And the 1967 State Police report that states, "All gambling is controlled in this area by the Elio Joseph Baldassari faction."

Once elected state attorney general Preate was threatened with exposure by member(s) of organized crime, and altered the course of official law enforcement business accordingly.

A mob-controlled public official not only was in charge of investigating himself, he'd soon be overseeing an investigation of Pennsylvania's highest court.

Preate had appointed a supposedly "independent prosecutor," Ed Dennis, to look into Larsen's charges of misbehavior on the court. Dennis would turn out to have serious conflicts and ethical problems of his own. As the criminal case against Ernie Preate progressed, Ed Dennis would be retained as Preate's personal attorney. He'd hardly be independent.

There is a close parallel between Ernie Preate's dishonest handling of the video poker case and his dishonest handling of the state Supreme Court case. Preate took campaign contributions from those whom he helped in the video poker case, as Preate accepted nearly twenty thousand dollars from interests connected to the Zappala bond firm. In both instances Preate refused to conduct a real investigation, and turned a blind eye to well-developed evidence. In the case of the video poker operators, Preate promised to look the other way and instead go after "drugs." This bears a striking resemblance to Preate's refusal to look into Justice Zappala's handling of all cases that have a connection to the Zappala bond firm. Instead the attorney general's office would come to smear Justice Rolf Larsen for Larsen's use of drugs. In both instances the grand jury system would be abused and selectively employed. In both cases guilty parties would not be charged. In both cases the people of Pennsylvania — those seeking fairness, equality and impartiality in their justice system — would be the ultimate losers.

I began to see that what we had here transcended Larsen, the Zappalas, Preate and Dennis. It transcended Pennsylvania. Here we see the dangers of overwhelming corruption in our justice system, and the mixing of politics with justice. Here we see a system in the dumper. Corrupt prosecutors, and diminished, big-city newspapers bent on vengeance, all more than willing to turn a blind eye.

Into this moral decay would step politicians aimed at advancing personal and political careers, and settling political scores, through the means of political impeachment. This would not be justice. It would be the thing our justice system was created to prevent. It would be mob rule.

HE·HATH·BROKEN THE·GATES·OF·BRASS

AND·BURST·THE·BARS·OF·IRON·ASUNDER

Part Three

The first step in any crowd, the essential a priori choice by the potential members of it, is this: will we, as individuals, choose to cease being individuals and become a crowd? It sounds contrived, put so explicitly, but the choice is always an intensely conscious one.

Bill Buford
Among the Thugs

CHAPTER 15

In Which I Make a Pest of Myself

The legislature was off and hopping on the impeachment trail even before the "independent prosecutor's" report had been released. The majority Democrats had appointed John P. Moses, an attorney from Wilkes Barre, as their "Special Counsel," while the Republicans picked J. Clayton Undercofler, of suburban Philadelphia. Both men would be scandalously overpaid. Both, theoretically, worked for the house judiciary committee's subcommittee on courts, though it would soon become apparent they were working for the leadership of our two political parties.

Moses and Undercofler prepared their "Preliminary Report" for release in the spring of 1994. It would more or less be a rehash of Ed Dennis's whitewash job — highly critical of Larsen and protective of Zappala. The two special counsel prepared to release their report on March 16, 1994, two weeks before Larsen was to go to trial and select a jury on his prescription drug charges. They also planned to release it more than a month before Larsen would have the opportunity to testify before the subcommittee, on April 21.

They planned to release their one-sided report with great media hype, certainly polluting the potential jury pool with negative publicity, making it all the more difficult for Larsen to get a fair trial on the drug charges.

I telephoned John Moses, the Democrats' counsel, and told him about Zappala's fixing of the Wagman case. He seemed surprised, and asked for the docket number of the case, and said it was distressing news. He added he was only empowered by House Resolution 205 to look into those cases investigated by Dennis and Preate, and so could not look into *Wagman*. "You'd do well to read House Resolution 205," he told me, a touch of condescension coloring his voice. John Moses would do well to read the transcripts of the Nuremberg Convention. Following morally corrupt orders is no excuse.

I told Moses the drug charges against Larsen were contemptible, that they had the potential to set back the cause of psychiatric care and drug treatment. Didn't Moses have any friends or family suffering from depression, or with a drug or alcohol problem? I asked him. I added that releasing his highly critical preliminary report before Larsen had a chance to select a jury seemed particularly low. Moses said he'd pass along my concerns. "I'll tell the Chairman," he told me, then he hung up. I assumed he meant he'd tell representative Thomas Caltagirone, chairman of the house judiciary committee. That was the last I head from Moses. Later, after the impeachment, Moses' hometown newspaper, the Wilkes-Barre Times Leader, reported that Moses received $213,000 for his work with the committee.

Next I called minority Special Counsel J. Clayton Undercofler, and told him about the Wagman case. Undercofler responded that Zappala's handling of *Wagman* sounded very troubling, took the docket numbers, and promised to look into it. I never head from Undercofler again. My sources at the turnpike later told me they had not been contacted by either Moses or Undercofler or, for that matter, anyone from the judiciary committees.

On March 11, 1994, I wrote both legislative special counsel, again telling them about *Wagman*. "Information was given to me by reputable citizens that Larsen was correct," I wrote Moses and Undercofler, "that Justice Zappala in fact did improperly intervene in the Wagman case. I am alarmed that Mr. Edward Dennis did not bother to investigate these charges, or even interview the Pennsylvania Turnpike attorneys who handled this case. My ongoing study of Dennis's grand jury report indicates to me that many leads were not pursued. I can only wonder what other cases were not investigated, and whether other concerned citizens were ignored." I went on, "It also seems highly unfair that you plan to release a preliminary report on the drug charges on March 16, 1994, only two weeks before Larsen must go to trial on these charges, before he must select a fair jury, and before he has had a chance to respond. History demands at this juncture that the legislature bend over backwards to exhibit fairness."

Somebody must have gotten through to the committee goons, because they suddenly backed off, and announced they'd withhold issuing the preliminary report until after Larsen's drug trial. After the trial they would still have all the time and resources in the world to be as nasty as they wanted to be.

CHAPTER 16

The Press Suppresses the Bad News

Spring approached, and so did the press conference I planned to hold with Common Cause. I wrote up a press advisory to summon the Fourth Estate. I hand delivered them, and made follow-up phone calls. Our state's large daily newspapers had degenerated into organs for the political parties, so I decided to bug them like I would any other government agency.

I called Emilie Lounsberry at the Philadelphia Inquirer and told her about our press conference. She didn't seem interested in citizens' complaints. Sounding bored, she said she wouldn't be there.

Following Judge Doris Smith's advice, I telephoned Inquirer editor David Boldt. He explained news was no longer his department, and said he didn't understand why I had been referred to him by Judge Smith. He'd met her only once, at a candidate's roundtable, he said. Nothing came of the call, though he was polite.

The next morning I visited the offices of the Harrisburg Patriot-News, a Newhouse-owned monopoly paper. In this period, the spring of 1994, the Patriot-News was performing PR work for gubernatorial candidate Tom Ridge, whom they portrayed as the second coming in a banker's suit, even as they endlessly dumped on Ernie Preate. This was primary election season, and the Patriot was giving Preate a pounding over the video-poker episode. The Patriot's unusual crusade against Preate struck many Pennsylvanians as somewhat of a puzzle, as the Patriot's usual idea of chasing corruption was to go after delinquent advertisers.

At the front desk I asked for reporter Peter Shelly, who was the Patriot's point man for making Preate's life miserable. The more the merrier, so I also summoned reporter Phil Galewitz. Shelly showed up first. He straightway expressed displeasure over comments I'd written about him in my book *When the Levee Breaks*. In the book I'd passed along the comments of one befuddled Democrat who couldn't fathom why the Patriot was picking on Preate. This Democrat had suggested that the Patriot and other Republicans objected to Preate's ethnicity.

As Shelly gave me the evil eye a confused Galewitz showed up. I told them about our press conference. Shelly said he didn't think they'd make it. Disappointed as I was, I still had my little job to do. I asked Shelly whether he was aware that Ed Dennis had conflicts that prevented an honest investigation of Zappala/Fumo/Rendell, Inc.

"*Which* conflict?" he asked. Now he was excited, his brow aflutter. "Geri-Med? You mean Geri-Med?"

"No," I said. "The Philadelphia Water Authority Bond Issue."

"Oh that." He gave a dismissive wave. So what, he was saying.

"If you know that Ed Dennis has conflicts which prevent him from doing an honest job why don't you write about it?" I asked. "Why don't you tell your readers?"

He shrugged. I took him to be telling me, We're Republican, Ed Dennis is Republican, and it's not for us to keep him honest.

We were standing in the lobby of the Patriot-News. People drifted by while we openly discussed corruption in the state's highest offices. Perhaps Shelly had a moment to continue our conversation in private? I suggested. He said, in not so many words, that he didn't have no stinking moment to discuss jack shit with me in private. It's always nice to keep the lines of communication open. I concluded our interesting encounter. Shelly stomped away, giving me one last look. Good thing I'm not the object of a gang attack, or on death row, or I'd have something to worry about.

Ah, that obscure object of Pete Shelly's desire, Geri-Med. Geriatric & Medical Centers, or Geri-Med, is the largest nursing home chain in the Philadelphia area. The company cares for more than 6,000 patients in southeastern Pennsylvania and south New Jersey. One of the largest nursing home chains in the country, the company is publicly owned and traded, and employs about 3,400 people. In the early 1990s two elderly patients under Geri-Med's care died horribly.

When she died in 1990, Elizabeth Ellis, 69, had been a resident for four years at Geri-Med's Cob Creek Nursing Center at 6900 Cobbs Creek Parkway in southwest Philadelphia. She was one of approximately 200 patients at the center. A state grand jury's affidavit of probable cause charged that Ellis's body, before her death, became "twisted and contorted," and "covered with large and infected decubiti (bedsores)" which poisoned her body. "The staff made her into a living cadaver," the affidavit charges.

Margaret White, 75, died in November 1991 at Geri-Med's Care Pavilion at Walnut Park. The grand jury charged she died of a preventable bed sore "so deep it penetrated the victim's internal organs and her bowels drained out of her hip," reads the affidavit.

Both homes were operated by GMS Management, a subsidiary of Geri-Med. Ernie Preate's AG's office would come to charge several employees, and the company, in the deaths. In actuality the deaths could more accurately be described (like the Larsen matter) as a total system failure. Where, one might well ask, was the government oversight that might have prevented such lingering deaths?

It would turn out that both Geri-Med nursing homes had been under government scrutiny in the years leading up to the deaths. State inspectors in 1989 reported six pages of deficiencies at the Care Pavilion. The state then temporarily suspended the home's license, and banned the admission of new patients. In 1990 the Care Pavilion found itself temporarily dropped from the Medicaid and Medicare programs following an inspection by the federal Health Care Finance

Administration. Also in 1990, the state cited Cobbs Creek Center for poor nursing care. The center was given a six-month provisional license, during which time the home was forbidden to admit more patients.

Two former GMS and Care Pavilion administrators told the grand jury that the company sent staff from corporate headquarters to address problems at the homes. After the feds resumed Medicare and Medicaid payments, the grand jury charged, Geri-Med "corporate officials directed that regular facility staff be reduced at Care Pavilion and Cobbs Creek."

One former Care Pavilion administrator, Ronald Deal, told the grand jury he protested the staff cuts, but his warnings were ignored. The grand jury affidavit states the staff reductions "followed a promise made to the federal inspectors that staff levels at the Care Pavilion would not be reduced after the federal government inspectors left the facility."

The grand jury hired a gerontic nurse consultant, Dolores Alford, to review the Care Pavilion's care of Margaret White. Alford concluded that records told "a story of a frail woman who went to Care Pavilion because she was in need of care and compassion. That she did not get. She was sorely abused physically and mentally by a most incompetent staff, who willfully and wantonly destroyed her body. Mrs. White had to die to get some relief."

This story is bad enough. Once the lawyers get into the act familiar patterns begin to emerge. Following the release of the grand jury findings, AG Preate held a news conference on September 1, 1992, to announce criminal charges against four Geri-Med officials, and the company. Preate's motives, and his handling of the case, came under immediate suspicion. Preate had received campaign contributions in 1989 and 1991 from Geri-Med's chairman, Daniel Veloric, a long-time fundraiser for state and Philadelphia-area politicians. Geri-Med had even named Preate "Man of the Year" in 1989.

Preate elected to charge two *staff members* from each home with misdemeanor charges of involuntary manslaughter and reckless endangerment. *The corporation* was also charged with felony welfare fraud, as well as involuntary manslaughter and reckless endangerment. Preate filed no charges against the *corporation's officers.*

As in the video poker case, we again see contributions to Preate, a corporation charged, and higher-ups let off.

What else did this case share with Larsen's impeachment? One of the four staff members charged, Molly Yates-Levy, an administrator at the Care Pavilion, selected as her attorney none other than Edward S.G. Dennis. This was in the fall and winter of 1992. In December 1992, Preate selected Dennis to persecute Larsen. Ed Dennis dropped Yates-Levy as a client and went to work for Preate, who was still prosecuting Yates-Levy.

The manslaughter and neglect case against the two administrators from Cobbs Creek went to court the following spring, in April 1993. After one week the judge threw out the case, citing lack of evidence. Several weeks later Preate dropped all charges against the two Care Pavilion employees, including Ed Dennis's former client, Yates-Levy. In November 1993, Preate accepted a plea bargain from Geri-Med. The company entered a plea of no contest to one misdemeanor count of involuntary manslaughter, paid a $20,000 fine as well as an additional $100,000 to cover the AG's costs. Preate then dropped the felony Medicaid fraud charge, and the reckless endangerment charge.

As bad as the festering wounds of the maltreated elderly patients must look to sensationalizing daily newspaper reporters, the Geri-Med case isn't as pertinent to Larsen's impeachment as the big-money bond conflicts involving the Philadelphia Water Authority.

I suppose Peter Shelly's point was that in Mary Yates-Levy we see yet another Pennsylvanian who'd placed trust in Ed Dennis, who goes off to work for the opposition. The rap against Ed Dennis is that you can't trust he's on your side because he'll jump ship for whoever offers the biggest bank roll or the brightest limelight. We'll unfortunately never know Peter Shelly's point, as his concerns for some reason never made it into print.

CHAPTER 17

The Problem With the Menu

Common Cause and I threw our press conference on April 13, 1994, at the capitol rotunda in Harrisburg. The entire capitol press corps, it seemed, turned out, along with a respectable number of interested citizens.

By this time the comrades on the house judiciary committee had released their preliminary report on Larsen (it was stamped "Confidential," yet everyone seemed to have a copy, though it was mostly unreadable). More importantly, the Pennsylvania Crime Commission released its long-awaited (and somewhat more readable) report, "An Investigation into the Conduct of Lackawanna County District Attorney / Attorney General Ernest D. Preate Jr," dated April 8, 1994. The Crime Commission dropped its bag of dimes on Preate just in time for the primary election season. Preate, crying partisan politics, quickly retaliated by appointing a special prosecutor to investigate house judiciary committee Democratic Chairman Thomas Caltagirone. Chairman Caltagirone played a role in releasing a draft of the Crime Commission report four days before the primary. Now Caltagirone found himself the target of a special prosecutor whose job was to investigate criminal charges of sexual harassment. Over the next year Preate's probe of Caltagirone would expand to include allegations that Caltagirone threatened a woman with a gun, and other charges involving the chairman's conduct going back ten years. These were Pennsylvania's political leaders. It was turning out to be a lively political season.

While waiting for our press conference to begin people stood around the rotunda reading the myriad of recently released nasty reports.

At my press conference I spoke out against Ed Dennis's aforementioned conflicts which, after all, I'd learned from newspaper reporters who oddly hadn't written about them. There were about thirty reporters present, and I made it a point to ask them to report on Dennis's conflicts. Larsen, I pointed out, was about to be impeached thanks to Dennis, and the people of Pennsylvanina deserved to know that Larsen might not have been given a fair shake.

I went on to spend a few moments on the turnpike's Wagman case. When I coupled the words "Zappala" and "fix" the reporters from the Associated Press, the Pittsburgh Post-Gazette and a few others flinched, like I was a dentist who'd struck a nerve. I said the word "fix" a few more times to see what would happen, and each time the reporters flinched. They looked on at me with an odd sort of concern, as if to say, "Don't you know you can get in trouble, young man, by saying Justice Zappala fixes cases, even if he does?" Here then were the mob rules of the day: One could say just about whatever one wanted concerning Larsen, that he took drugs and was insane, but you better not say anything about our beloved and party-protected comrade Justice Zappala.

I concluded my remarks by pointing out that Justice Larsen at times may have been unfair and unjust, but the proper way to respond was not to lynch him, but to show Larsen and the people the true meaning of fairness and justice. As things looked now, I said, we were heading for star-chamber justice, akin to committee injustices meted out by revolutionary France.

Many of the reporters overhearing my remarks, like the party leaders, were themselves going through the motions of the mob. They wanted to eat Rolf Larsen for lunch — Ed Dennis and Ernie Preate had served him up on a platter. The only options on the menu would be whether to eat Larsen with red or white wine. So what if Preate was a criminal, and Dennis was hobbled by outrageous conflicts?

Hart Stotter, state chairman of Common Cause, followed my remarks by calling on the U.S. Justice Department to investigate all the known and unknown cases fixed by Justice Zappala, as well as Ed Dennis's undisclosed conflicts of interests.

Though our press conference was well attended, not one newspaper in the state printed a word of it. Why delay dinner?

CHAPTER 18

His Honor Gets Bounced

The Philadelphia Inquirer said they'd bounce Larsen like a basketball, but to me it seemed more like a slow moving game of pinball. The game proceeded apace, month by month, bumper by bumper.

The criminal prescription trial against Larsen geared up in late March and sputtered into April '94. Now was the first that the public began to see live pictures of Larsen and his attorney walking into the courthouse in Pittsburgh. Before this we'd only seen still newspaper morgue shots. Dragged into court like a common drug fiend, we could drink in Larsen's elfin countenance, his jaunty step as he moved from bumper to bumper.

In sunny April Larsen was found guilty of conspiracy involving the prescription charges. In the merry month of May he was promptly and unanimously impeached by the state house. *Unanimously,* by some two hundred and fifty house members. Either they were all right, or they were all wrong.

In June, flowers were blooming, and the sentencing judge removed Larsen from office and gave him two years probation and two hundred and forty hours of community service. The state senate now prepared to formally remove Larsen from office. Seven charges of impeachment were drawn up. Article I: That Larsen kept a list of cases for special treatment. Article II: That Larsen met with Pittsburgh lawyer Richard Gilardi in 1988 and agreed to review two of Gilardi's cases. Article III: That Larsen lied before Dennis's grand jury about Gilardi's cases. Article the IV: That Larsen improperly discussed another case with Allegheny County Judge Eunice Ross. Article V: That Larsen misused the legal process by complaining that Justices

Zappala and Cappy fixed court cases (this, of course, was the most interesting article.) Article VI: That Larsen used his court employees to obtain prescription drugs. Article VII: That all the above undermined the public's "confidence in the judicial process."

Two thirds vote of the state senate would be needed on each count to convict. Before festivities could begin the full senate decided not to hear the impeachment trial, so that the lawyers in that body could go about the business of running their practices. The senate instead shoved the matter to its judiciary committee, which supposedly would take the "evidence," after which the full body would give thumbs up or thumbs down.

Larsen, ever litigious, appealed this and other matters (he pointed out he was already removed from office, so couldn't be impeached) to the state courts, asking that the trial be postponed or disallowed. The court demurred, saying the boys in the senate could do whatever they damn well pleased, that the judiciary had no business interjecting itself in legislative matters. The fellas in the senate were mindful that Larsen The Undead was appealing his drug conviction in the courts. Should his conviction be overturned, Larsen could find himself back on the bench. Wanting to make sure they'd drive their stake through the blood sucker's heart, they scheduled the public execution for a sultry Monday in August.

The game was a sham, run by the party lawyers, and the public was left with no levers with which to hit the ball. The Inky and the Post-Gazette were drooling to see Larsen go down, and so end Larsen's libel suits against them. The U.S. Justice Department was no where to be seen. The previous October the U.S. Justice Department had been given a clean bill of health by none other than Ed Dennis, who saw nothing wrong with Janet Reno and Co.'s handling of affairs in Waco, Texas. It was still a year and a half before someone would park a Ryder truck loaded with fertilizer and fuel oil in front of the federal building in Oklahoma City.

CHAPTER 19

Family Feud

One day in early August 1994 the doors to the splendiferously decorated state senate chambers were thrown open to a generally disinterested public. The chamber awaiting our mob justice was gilted in gold leaf. The walls boasted scenes depicting Lincoln at Gettysburg, Franklin and company deliberating in Philadelphia, even Christ in his passions, and other inspirational tableaus incongruous to the low-down, mean-spirited half-truths and out-right lies about to be vented to the people of the state.

The public, as I said, seemed disinterested (as usual of late in all things political), and stayed away in droves. In the mid-90s the public seemed resigned to a corrupt, overly expensive and detached political system in which they have no influence. In that sense Larsen's impeachment was tailor made for the 90s. A visitors' gallery open to the public overlooked the chambers, yet the seats throughout the weeks of proceedings would only be peppered with attendants. Mostly old folks, or sharp dressed men and women with legal pads whom I took to be lawyers, and your occasional bored tourists who wandered in from the capitol tour, staying for five or so minutes before bumping out.

The capitol reporters preferred not to sit among the public, and instead seated themselves out of sight in their own reporters' gallery. I sat with the public, where I could observe and chat with onlookers. The only time I saw a capitol news reporter was when one of them would break out of their separate gallery to hobnob on the floor with one of the participants of the proceedings.

I passed my time in the visitors' gallery reading Bill

Buford's book *Among the Thugs*. The book, on its surface, is about the violent life of British soccer fans. Buford, an American, is the editor of the Penguin Corp.'s Granta magazine, which is published in England and is probably the corporate world's preeminent slick "literary" magazine. Buford spent several years traveling around Europe with low-life British soccer hooligans, creating mayhem and rioting with them, supposedly so he could write a pseudo-intellectual account in his book. He writes of his delight in fitting in with the mob, participating in the senseless violence of the rabble. Experiencing the sensations of becoming invisible in a mob, Buford writes sentences like, "Everyone — including the police — is powerless against a large number of people who have decided not to obey any rules. Or put another way: with numbers there are no laws." He writes about the strange, light-headed sensations of being sucked into a mob at the moment of riot: "In the vernacular of the supporters, it had now 'gone off.' With that first violent exchange, some kind of threshold had been crossed, some notional boundary: on one side of that boundary had been a sense of limits, an ordinary understanding — even among this lot — of what you didn't do; we were now someplace where there would be few limits, where the sense that there were things you didn't do had ceased to exist. It became very violent."

Buford and his book in the early 1990s became the darlings of the corporate literary world. It's not too hard to understand why. In today's corporate and political world the wholesale mob is the target of marketing and advertising. The individual, today, is ignored, and considered small change not worth listening to, of trying to reach. In the last century people like Henry David Thoreau and Walt Whitman celebrated the individual and the importance to society of those who take the road less traveled. Buford's book is a corporate celebration of joining in with the dirty mob. To me the book summed up the gathering ugly atmosphere of Rolf Larsen's impeachment. So I read Buford's book as I sat in the visitors' gallery listening to the mob justice on the senate floor below. I'd found myself on a lonely road, out of step with the mob.

Not that I was so absorbed in the book that I was oblivious to the goings-on around me. Interesting people crossed my path in the visitors' gallery. During one recess in the hearings I struck up a conversation with an older gentleman, a Republican, who turned out to head a state military agency. He lamented the passing of party discipline. In the old days, he told me, party bosses called every shot, and now here essentially were the Democrats fighting it out with Larsen on the senate floor, for everyone to see. It never would've happened in the old days, he assured me. Did I know what it was like in the old days? It's like this. He played a trumpet. Once, he said, in the 1960s, the Republican women hosted some function, and a member of the all-lady orchestra had taken ill and couldn't perform. The Republican state chairman ordered him to dress up as a woman and play his trumpet in the ladies' orchestra. This he did. The military man said he showed up at the Hotel Hershey dressed as a woman, praying not to be spotted. *That was party discipline,* he winked at me.

Down below, in sight from the visitors' deck, the senate chamber had been pushed clear of its usual rows of ornate desks, replaced with two long tables. One table was reserved for the "people's prosecutors" — members from both parties of the state house judiciary committees and their overpaid "party counsels." The defense sat at the other table.

Members of the senate "evidentiary committee" sat front and center, at either side of the central rostrum, flanked on both sides by each party's permanent senate lawyer. The whole senate having voted not to hear the case, the chamber was notably devoid of legislators. To those unfamiliar with Pennsylvania politics the state senate chamber must have seemed strangely empty and museum-like. The emptiness was not unusual. The previous summer and fall, in 1993, the senators had voted themselves a six-month vacation, with pay, to avoid a special election that might have changed leadership. That year the senators went home to practice law, and nobody missed them.

The place, more than usual, stunk of overdressed lawyers. The charade of the day was that this was some sort of court proceeding, with a panel of judges, a prosecution table, and a defense. Seated at the defense table, looking all the world like Howdy Doody in a three-piece, sat the object of our legislative pique, Rolf Larsen. Larsen had succeeded in pressing his right to personally question witnesses. He'd stand, quite unruffled, at defense inquisitor's podium, at times confidently striding around the senate floor, handing around exhibits or documents. This drove the prosecutors nuts. They unceasingly complained that to allow Larsen to speak for his own defense was to allow him the benefit of testifying without taking the oath. They also complained unendingly about Larsen's walking around, and his personally handing out documents. The bullies at the prosecution table seemed to want him bound and gagged. Larsen certainly had their number.

Perched beside Larsen at the table was his attorney, William Costopoulos. Ever the showboat, Costopoulos's neatly trimmed, graying mustache rode herd above a mawkish grin. He favored cowboy boots — an affectation erupting beneath expensive court suits. Occasionally a pant leg would rise up and you'd get a blast of Costopoulos's brightly colored sock. Also at the defense table sat a second, younger man, presumably another lawyer from Costopoulos's firm.

The comrades from the house who were seated at the "prosecution" table included Democratic representative Frank Dermody, from Pittsburgh, the Zappalas' trotting ground. Dermody looked shifty eyed and sported a strange sculpted hair style that made him look like Dr. Smith in Lost in Space. Beside Dermody sat John Moses, corpulent, rumply, the Democrats' hired lawyer. Dermody and Moses would prove to be the real windbag bullies of the proceedings.

Dermody intoned in the opening session, "Our resolve is not a fine or imprisonment but to restore the public confidence in the institution of government." Yeah right, and thunder's caused by God bowling with Irish saints. They were impeaching

Larsen, Dermody added, because of Larsen's "fundamental lack of respect for the truth and a pattern of totally unacceptable conduct." Dermody ought to know, as he would time and again attempt to cover-up Zappala's case-fixing.

Moses, rumply and baggy, hollered incessantly that "the people" demanded clean courts, but he was as much or more guilty as the others of protecting judicial conflicts and misdeeds. He'd yell insistently about "the people." It sounded like he was yelling "the peep hole!"

The Republican side was much more buttoned down, favoring that empty-suit corporate look Republicans prefer. Representative Jeffrey Piccola sat bubble-headed at the table, waving hello to whoever gleaned his attention, looking light-weight and self-important. The Republican counsel, J. Clayton Undercofler, a former U.S. attorney, was so buttoned down and dull that he was a sure cure for any sleep disorder. Undercofler brought along a young assistant lawyer from his office who was so dull that his speech was unintelligible. This young Republican lawyer, an Undercofler clone, wheezed on and on, making any subject seem unimportant, sounding like a muted trumpet. He reminded me of Charlie Brown's teacher. "Wah wah wah. Wah wah wah wah wah."

The six state senators who composed the panel of judges presiding over the "evidentiary committee" sat at the head table looking like long-at-the-tooth muppets. The chairman, Senator Stewart Greenleaf, seemed continually uncertain, even frightened, about what Larsen and his lawyer might say or do next. Proceedings would halt as Larsen or his lawyer opened prickly lines of inquiry. Problem was, Larsen had been charged with besmirching the integrity of the judiciary, so whenever he set out to show he'd been telling the truth about inside dealings and case-fixings, the prosecution would be on their feet to silence the line of inquiry. Greenleaf and his comrades would fall into a huddle lasting for minutes, until an alarmed Greenleaf would lift his head to ask Larsen or his counsel, "What's the purpose of this line of inquiry?"

Larsen's response, time and again, would be something

like, "I've been accused of violating the procedures of the state Supreme Court, so we must demonstrate what those practices were to show that I have done nothing out of the ordinary." These responses would send the committee back into a long protective huddle.

By defending, protecting and covering-up the dirty system, the prosecutors and the evidentiary committee were prohibiting Larsen from defending himself.

There were continual conferences with the senate Republican counsel, thick-jowled Steve MacNett, who'd roll over to the trough of justice. MacNett would shake himself alive from his doghouse perch, and slowly trot over to the chairman's thrown, his nose slightly lifted as though he'd caught scent of some succulent morsel. He'd make his slow way to the rostrum, go in a huddle with Greenleaf and the others, and you knew some travesty of law or civility was about to be discussed under the watchful gaze of Lincoln, Franklin, Madison and Christ.

Republican senate counsel Steve MacNett's wife, Kathryn, was a lobbyist who, at the time of Larsen's traducement, enjoyed a large lobbying portfolio. The MacNetts had plenty of corporate sponsorship. While the impeachment investigations sputtered on, Kathryn Speaker MacNett listed her clients as Aetna Life and Casualty; American Cancer Society; Athletic Trainers Society; Beer Wholesalers Association; Browning Ferris Industries; Buchanan Ingersoll; CEO Venture Fund; Communications Alliance; Dow Elanco; Economic Development Association; Horticultural Society of PA; Hospital Association of PA; PA Society of Hospital Pharmacists; Marine Spill Response Corp.; National Medical Care, Inc.; Medical Society of PA; Mental Health/Mental Retardation Community Centers, Inc.; Motorcycle Industry Council; National Hemophilia Assoc.; Panhandle Eastern Corp.; Associated Pawnbrokers; Philadelphia Eagles; Philadelphia 76ers; Philadelphia Flyers; Philadelphia Phillies; Propane Gas Association; Rail Corporation; PA Association of Realtors; Rodale Press; Safe Buildings Alliance; The Spectrum;

Technology Council; Travelers Express; Video Lottery Technologies and West Publishing Company.

Not that the Republicans had a corner on inside lobbying and corporate sponsorship. Democrat house Speaker William DeWeese's wife, Holly Kinser, also works as a lobbyist, representing International Paper.

These proceedings were about economics and inside largess. The unspoken contention was that political families had a birthright to siphon as much moola as they could from the public trough. That's why they were going after Larsen, for reminding people about the overreach of the Zappala family.

One of Larsen's opening motions was a "Motion for Recusal of Certain Senators." "Under this motion," the record reads, Larsen "stated that he reserves the right to move for the recusal of certain Senators, especially Senators who appear as witnesses at trial" (read Vince Fumo) "or have received political contributions from prosecution witnesses or their immediate family members." This was a not-too-veiled reference to the hundreds of thousands of dollars the Zappalas had shared with their political friends over the years. This motion got nowhere.

Throughout the "trial" the house members representing the supposed "prosecution" would repeatedly succeed in having the "evidentiary committee" agree that no mention could be made of any cases not specifically addressed in the articles of impeachment (the PLRB and the Port Authority cases). The house managers of the case would fight unendingly to prevent the public airing of other suspicious cases handled by Zappala, such as the turnpike *Wagman* case. No use undermining the public trust. No use opening a floodgate of doubt by visiting any but the two cases that had been whitewashed, sanitized and given the good housekeeping seal by Ed Dennis. Zappala would be protected at all costs, as would the Zappala family money flowing into the legislature.

These tedious preliminaries out of the way, and the family largess duly protected, the comrades from the house committee proceeded to introduce their evidence. First came the slime about Larsen's prescription depression drugs, and from there it would slide downhill to such elevated and socially edifying smear topics as Larsen's jock strap and his jock-itch medicine, and whether the justice would send his secretaries out to buy pornography, cantaloupe and bananas.

Many of the prosecution's witnesses came off as, to put it mildly, dishonest rapscallions. Others seemed to be outright mentally disturbed. The prosecution did not bring the state's keenest minds to testify about the court. As bullies do, they brought out the dregs. One of Larsen's former office workers, with some unknown yet obvious ax to grind, said she would ask Larsen at the start of work, "How are you judge?" "'Just great,'" she said Larsen would reply, "'I just jerked off fifteen times.' All the time comments like that." Testimony like this seemed unbelievable. It was hard to understand why such incongruities were introduced. Unless, of course, these were bullies engaged in the lowest sort of smear.

The prosecution lawyers seemed fixated on this secretary's accounts of being sent on shopping sprees for Larsen's jock straps and his jock itch medicine. They seemed to want to disrobe Larsen literally and figuratively. This secretary also was repeatedly asked my Moses to detail the temperature and consistency of the fruit served to Larsen. This brought several salient objections from the defense.

"I just don't think the temperature of his bananas and his apples has any probative value to these proceedings," Costopoulos posited. The committee conferred privately (though the record does not state whether senate counsel MacNett oozed over to partake in this conference), then overruled the defense. The evidentiary committee didn't want to hear about Zappala's fixing of the Wagman case, but bananas and apples were something it wanted on the record.

And so it went. They collected the worst testimony they could peel off the biggest scoundrels they could find. At least one employee working in Larsen's office, and now testifying against the justice, admitted to practicing law on the side during business hours. Other office workers were sleeping around with each other like kittens. When Larsen's attorney tried to question one employee about his love affairs with other Larsen employees it spun the proceedings into a half hour recess as the comrades in the committees huddled, and the audience in the gallery chuckled.

Counsel MacNett would ooze over, Greenleaf would lift his frightened head from the huddle to ask Larsen's side why this line of inquiry was pertinent.

"Because intimate relations are breeding grounds for collaboration," Costopoulos would reply.

The prosecutors protested that questioning their questionable witness about his inner-office promiscuity was "inflammatory," "prejudicial," and the like. Undercofler would condescendingly tell Greenleaf that he'd be glad to explain to the chairman why such inquiries would never be permitted in a *real* courtroom. Amen. While Greenleaf and the comrades returned to their huddle the love-bird witness was supposed to talk to no one. Moses, embarrassed and surprised by these revelations involving the sleeping habits of his witness, couldn't resist trying to talk to the rascal, bringing a loud protest from Larsen's side that the house was defying the sequester.

All this brought howls of laughter from those in the public gallery. It was all downhill from here.

Soon it became apparent that this was a blood-letting between nesting Pittsburgh politicians. The unmistakable western-Pennsylvania twang of Larsen, his office staff, witnesses and the prosecution clapped jarringly around the chamber. Other regionals were only too happy to chirp in. Here were Pennsylvanians tearing into each other with their various warbles. Larsen and the others from the west. Names like "Papadakos" rolled from the tongues of the westerners sounding like Indian bird calls — pee-ap-ea-dackas. Moses's backward Scranton intonations made him sound all the more primitive. The smoothspeak of the Philadelphia lawyers belied their dishonesty. Costopoulos's course central Pennsylvania gravelly harangue — "Vince Fume-O," he'd caw. These were the things that caught my ear, when I wasn't reading Bill Buford's book about the fun and recreation of the mob.

CHAPTER 20

I Try Getting Into the Open House

From time to time over the next several weeks newspaper reporters would wander onto the senate floor to banter with the house bullies, or to seek insight and maybe a quote from Larsen's attorney. Several times I watched a reporter tenuously approach Larsen, which was touchy business. His former honor would invariably and curtly shoo the reporter away. Once Larsen wordlessly backed away an approaching reporter with a brisk motion of his extended arms, arching them around his place at the table and his papers as if to say, "This is what's left of my country. My remaining jurisdiction. Stay away." To the end he was at war with the world.

The reporters had to approach the participants while the impeachment proceedings were in session since the actors would disappear quicker than the inhabitants of Kafka's castle when they were not on the senate floor. It was impossible for a citizen to have a word with any of the players — house, defense or senate evidentiary committee member. These proceedings were conducted in a lawyer's vacuum — away from reality, input or feedback from the public at large. It all added to the detached, surreal atmosphere of the strange proceedings.

The players certainly seemed to think this is the way it should be. Following one session I noticed a small mob of television reporters, their cameras and lights ready, milling about an obscure senate doorway. A young senate page, alone and bored, sat in a nearby alcove. I asked her why the reporters waited in the other doorway.

"Oh they think Larsen might come out that door," she snickered. Why do they think that? "That's the way he left yesterday. But he's not going to come out there today. He'll probably come out from a door on the other side. Or in the garage. There's a thousand ways to slip out of this place. They're all real good at knowing how to slip out of here without anybody seeing them. They all disappear like smoke. That's the name of the game around here."

Me, I never tried to talk to Larsen directly. I didn't think it would be smart. I'd been trying, on my own, to piece together the story of a case fixed by Zappala, and I didn't want anybody to think I was in cahoots with Larsen. In the months leading up to the impeachment I'd had several telephone conversations with Larsen's attorney, Bill Costopoulos, who expressed interest not only in the Wagman case but also Ed Dennis's refusal to look into the case. Costopoulos, at one point, said he would call me as a witness at the senate impeachment trial. It never happened.

I was smart enough to realize that I, and the people of Pennsylvania, had different interests than Larsen. Larsen's interest was to avoid prosecution and impeachment. The people of Pennsylvania probably would be best served by Larsen's removal, as well as the removal of Zappala and one or two other justices. (The party leaders, conversely, had an interest in attempting to maintain the ridiculous notion that all would be well with Pennsylvania courts if only Larsen was removed.)

It came then as not a great surprise to me that, as the impeachment trial neared, I began to hear less and less from Bill Costopoulos. I began to detect a noticeable coolness from the defense team. Unreturned phone calls, a hesitancy to make specific commitments, etc. It didn't take a genius to see I could not depend on Costopoulos or his client to pursue Zappala's handling of the Wagman case. And why should they? It was probably Costopoulos's job to caution Larsen against throwing more gasoline on the fire.

I wasn't much saddened. I really didn't trust Larsen or Costopoulos. Why should I pursue the devil to do an angel's work? I came to the opinion that it was the job of the people's representatives — the members of the house team — to look into Zappala's handling of *Wagman,* and other cases. The more I thought about it, the more angered and indignant I became at the smear job conducted by the house team. I resolved to force the issue.

One afternoon, while the impeachment proceedings droned on, I walked through the capitol rotunda. Passing a table that held literature for tourists, I came across an expensively printed, four-color brochure entitled "An Open House." It was campaign literature printed with public money designed to puff incumbent legislators. Inside, beneath a full-page photo of the speaker of the state house, who leaned against a rotunda colonnade as if he usually hung out there, with the people, I read the caption, "The House of Representatives is truly an open house for all Pennsylvanians." Another page showed legislators amiably chatting amongst themselves beside the oversized, and open, door to the house chamber. "The door of the Hall of the House, by constitutional mandate, has been open since 1776," this caption read. It may be open, but the public can't get in, and there's nobody on the other side. Like most of the hokum of our government, the open door to the state house chamber is an empty gesture. Behind every ornate door is either emptiness, rot or malignancy.

I got it into my head to test the openness of the state house. For the next several days, while the impeachment proceedings filled the senate with talk of grapefruits, jockstraps and drug addictions, I made it a point to visit the offices of the house and senate managers. I went to the offices of comrades Caltagirone, Dermody, Piccola and Greenleaf.

At each office I told the secretary at the gate that I was aware of evidence that would disprove one of the articles of impeachment. (Though I did not say, I was referring to the article of impeachment that alleged Larsen had incorrectly accused Zappala of case-fixing.) What mechanism had been established for citizens to come forward with evidence pertinent to the impeachment proceedings? I asked at each office. Each

secretary shrugged, took my name and number, and said someone would get back to me.

No one got back to me. There was no mechanism, I realized. To say no one wanted to talk to me is putting it mildly.
They were all too busy crucifying Larsen to bother collecting
evidence that might disprove their rancid philosophy.

The offices of Messrs. Caltagirone and Dermody, in particular, buzzed with impeachment festivities. In Dermody's office
a secretary continually worked a large Xerox machine, popping
out page after page of dirt concerning the jockstraps and God
knows what else. Mountains of paper surrounded the copy
machine, the air was hot and reeked of ozone, and the secretary
looked worn out.

Each morning I would again visited Caltagirone, Dermody,
Piccola and Greenleaf's offices. What mechanism had been
established for citizens to come forward with evidence pertinent
to the impeachment proceedings? I politely asked each time.
No one bothered to call me back. By the third day I was starting to get to them. The secretaries began to get nasty. This is
supposed to be an open house, I told the secretaries. Still nothing.

Finally I got a call from someone identifying himself as
Gregg Warner, an aide to Senator Greenleaf. He as much told
me to flip off. He explained to me that the evidentiary committee wasn't collecting any evidence. They didn't have to take no
stinking evidence. This wasn't a public trial, he tried to explain,
like the kind we see in courtrooms. What was it then? I asked.
He replied, impatiently, that they were aware of my book, and
would I please go away.

I sat down and typed out the following letter to Larsen's
attorney. Dated August 12, 1994, it read:

"Dear Mr. Costopoulos,
"I am aware of the existence of evidence that seems to have
a direct bearing on one of the articles of impeachment brought
against former state Supreme Court Justice Rolf Larsen.
"On Monday, August 8, 1994, I visited the offices of house

members Thomas Caltagirone, Frank Dermody and state Senator Stewart Greenleaf to inquire about the mechanism for the public to come forward with evidence. I left my name and number, yet no one returned my call. On Wednesday, August 10, 1994, I visited the offices of these men again, as well as the office of house member Jeffrey Piccola. I left messages with the aides in those offices that I believed I was aware of evidence pertinent to the articles of impeachment. I was told in several offices that members and their aides had been too busy to speak with me. Again none of the house members' staff returned my call. An aide to Senator Greenleaf, who identified himself as Gregg Warner, telephoned on Thursday, August 11 to say that the senate had no control over the collection of evidence and that I should take up the matter with the house management. He made the troubling request that I (and I suppose other citizens) no longer visit the office of Senator Greenleaf in petition of grievance. He furthermore shared with me the interesting opinion that the proceedings were closed to the public, and were not like other trials, though he said Senator Greenleaf was very much concerned that the proceedings are perceived as fair.

"I am concerned that other Pennsylvanians may be unable to deliver evidence to the general assembly. I am disturbed that there is no simple and trustworthy mechanism for concerned citizens to come forward with evidence bearing on the fairness and thoroughness of these historic and public proceedings. Some legislators and their aides seem to hold the peculiar notion that the impeachment proceedings are some sort of bizarre inter-party disciplinary event, 'closed' to the public. Yet the Pennsylvania general assembly for centuries has prided itself as an open house. Justice Larsen is the public's duly elected official. The public, moreover, paid for the investigation that led to these impeachment hearings. These proceedings continue to be funded by the people of Pennsylvania. The hearings are held in the state senate chamber, open to the public. The public owns these buildings, and it is a government of the people. Why then is there no trustworthy mechanism for concerned citizenry to come forward? It is our house, so why are we treated as troublesome visitors? The people, not the collaborating parties, own this house. Do the two political parties propose to reduce the public to gagged guests in their own house?

"House members pressing these charges claim to be acting as prosecutors. Yet public prosecutors are held to a high standard of conduct, particularly in the collection and handling of evidence. This is fundamental to a fair system of justice. Here we seem to be witnessing the strange and deeply troubling phenomenon of prosecutors who are too busy, unwilling or unable to collect a full range of evidence. Only dishonest prosecutors act this way, and the public has a right and obligation to oppose them. In short, I am concerned that the general assembly's handling of these proceedings is unworthy of a free society.

"The senate of Pennsylvania has the great responsibility to ensure that evidence in this trial has not been tampered with, destroyed, distorted or suppressed. To do less is to preside over mob justice, or star-chamber justice, not a fair hearing in the American tradition."

I sent copies to Senator Greenleaf, Senator Craig Lewis, and representatives Caltagirone, Dermody and Piccola. For good measure I ran off thirty copies and dropped off the stack in the capitol newsroom.

The next morning I got a call from Dave Krantz, a Caltagirone staffer, who said I should bring by the evidence. I brought it by, and Krantz told me maybe they'd look into it.

I sat chatting with Krantz, whose title was executive director of the house judiciary committee. He said I had a well-known name "around this campus," and that the "chairman," having read my letter, expressed curiosity about why I had it in for Zappala. I said I didn't have it in for Zappala, simply that this after all was an impeachment proceeding supposedly designed to ensure the integrity and fairness of our high court, and several turnpike lawyers had expressed their concern to me about a case Zappala had fixed for them. It wouldn't do for me to simply ignore their informed concerns, would it? I asked Krantz. He smiled and said no, that wouldn't do. We spoke a bit about state politics. What was Krantz doing here, I asked him. He said he had run for the house himself a time or two, yet couldn't garner enough support, so now he was working for Caltagirone. "What happened?" I asked. "I lost," he said. He was somewhere in his fifties, I thought. He rocked back in his chair and said politics was a younger man's game. At least, he said, you must enter politics as a young man, younger than when he had started. "It's like any other club." "Indeed," I said. And now the boys in the club were looking out for their pal Steve Zappala.

Krantz took my folder about the Wagman case and again said maybe they'd look into it, "this fall, after the proceedings were over." He halted, "Of course, I can't promise anything," he said. "I understand," I told him.

Caltagirone's office never did a damn thing. Never even bothered to call the attorneys who handled the case. The meeting with Krantz, I knew even before I showed up, was Caltagirone's way of covering his butt.

I also got a call from representative Jeffrey Piccola, who sounded confused. He didn't understand what Zappala case-fixing had to do with Larsen's impeachment. These guys were already breathing hot and heavy down the impeachment pike, and they weren't going to let a few inconvenient facts get in the way. I told Piccola we were looking for honest leadership. All someone had to do was *pick up the phone and call the turnpike attorneys*. Piccola never bothered. The next year Piccola would be elected to the state senate.

Shortly after I hung up with Piccola I got a call from a reporter with the York Daily Record. He'd read my press release. The reporter asked for more information, as Wagman was a York construction company. He spent several weeks reviewing the case, making inquiries. His paper ended up publishing an article about Zappala's intervention in the turnpike case. The state senate Republican clipping service, in turn, circulated the Daily Record's Zappala/Wagman story among the senators.

No state senator bothered following up on the newspaper article. No turnpike attorney was even asked about the turnpike case.

CHAPTER 21

This Particular Political Dispute

By this time, mid August, the capital city found itself wrapped in heat and humidity. Distracted by pursuits of summer, the public largely tuned out the impeachment. At last the hearings turned from talk of underwear, fruit and prescription drugs, to the two 1992 court cases at the heart of the impeachment: the so-called *Port Authority* and *Pennsylvania Labor Relations Board,* or *PLRB* cases which Larsen accused Zappala of fixing, respectively, for the cities of Pittsburgh and Philadelphia.

Our special prosecutor Ed Dennis, in his whitewash report, provides the following bare bones description of Zappala's intervention in the Pittsburgh episode, *Sophie Masloff, etc., and the City of Pittsburgh* v. *the Port Authority of Allegheny County, et al,* referred to simply as the Port Authority case:

"On March 16, 1992," Dennis's report reads, "Amalgamated Transit Union Local 85 went on strike against the Port Authority of Allegheny County. Local 85 represented approximately 2,700 individuals employed by the Port Authority in connection with the operation of the county's regional transit system. The strike brought public transit service for the region, including the city of Pittsburgh, to a complete stop.

"The Port Authority Act, which governs labor relations between Local 85 and the Port Authority, provides that an injunction against a strike by the Port Authority's employees may only be issued if the strike 'creates a clear and present danger or threat to the health, safety or welfare of the public,' and that any injunction order must mandate that the parties submit to binding arbitration. The Act further provides that '(no) party, other than the (Port Authority), shall have any standing to seek relief in any court of this Commonwealth under this subsection.'

"On March 27, 1992, the city of Pittsburgh brought a 'King's Bench' petition directly to Justice Zappala, asking that the Supreme Court enjoin the strike."

Explaining the King's Bench maneuver, the report states, "The Port Authority and PLRB cases were brought before the Supreme Court under a state statute which provides as follows:

"Notwithstanding any other provision of law, the Supreme Court may, on its own motion or upon petition of any party, in any matter pending before any court or district justice of this Commonwealth involving an issue of immediate public importance, assume plenary jurisdiction of such matter at any stage thereof and enter a final order or otherwise cause right and justice to be done.

"This provision codifies what is sometimes referred to as the court's 'King's Bench' powers. In essence, 'King's Bench' is a mechanism which allows the court to take complete jurisdiction over and decide proceedings of public importance without the normal lower court proceedings. Accordingly, litigants who successfully invoke the court's 'King's Bench' powers are able to obtain more expeditious resolutions of their disputes.

"The Court's 'King's Bench' authority has its origins in English common law. (See 42 Pa. C.S. 502, which defines the general powers of the Supreme Court to include 'the powers vested in it by the Constitution of Pennsylvania, including the power generally to minister justice to all persons and to exercise the powers of the court, as fully and amply, to all intents and purposes, as the justices of the court of the King's Bench, Common Pleas and Exchequer, at Westminster, or any of them, could or might do on May 22, 1722.') While some maintain that this common law authority is distinct from the plenary jurisdiction 42 Pa. C.S. 726 makes available to the court, there is little practical difference. As Justice Zappala testified, the

'King's Bench' power, in whatever form, allows the court to 'reach down, take a particular issue and bring it right up so that the court can dispose of it.' As Justice Zappala explained it, the 'King's Bench' gives the court the 'power to do whatever they so please to do.'

"The 'King's Bench' is an extraordinary procedure which is not widely known or used. Justice Zappala testified that 'King's Bench' matters 'are very difficult and I don't think used that often. I don't know how many times while I've been on the bench that we either had King's Bench powers or plenary jurisdiction which was exercised.'

"The extraordinary nature of the 'King's Bench' mechanism extends to the way in which such matters may be initiated, and the way in which they are processed by the court. These procedures have developed according to custom rather than according to any formal, written directives. (In fact, the practices may vary between the western, middle and eastern districts of the state. Given the absence of formal, written procedures, Justice Zappala was unsure as to the practices in the districts outside the western district, where his chambers are located.) Litigants might file 'King's Bench' petitions with the prothonotary, or might approach an individual justice to hear the matter before actually filing it with the prothonotary. Thus, a litigant can essentially select the justice he or she wants to initially review the matter.

"There also may be differences in the way in which individual justices handle 'King's Bench' matters. According to Justice Zappala, any 'King's Bench' petitions which are brought to his chambers are immediately referred to his law clerk, who directs the litigant to file the petition with the prothonotary. The law clerk then analyzes the petition and reports to Justice Zappala regarding whether the petition merits review. If it is determined that the petition merits review, the opposing party is given the opportunity to file a response. After receiving the response, Justice Zappala meets with counsel for the parties to discuss the legal issues, preliminary to advising the rest of the court as to whether it should consider the matter.

"After this conference, Justice Zappala prepares a letter to the other justices, notifying them 'of when the petition was presented, essentially what the petition was about, what analysis was done in connection with the legal issue, and what, if any, recommendation we would make for the disposing of that particular petition.'

"Justice Zappala testified that this is his procedure for dealing with 'King's Bench' petitions. However, given the absence of internal operating rules, other justices may handle these petitions differently."

So with King's Bench the court is handed unlimited power, and each justice may handle this power as he sees fit. Great system. Dennis's bit about Zappala's clerk first reviewing each petition is an apologist's crock. At the heart of Larsen's charges involving the Port Authority and PLRB cases is Larsen's contention that Justice Zappala was first personally contacted by Democratic party power brokers, who asked Zappala to invoke King's Bench, and who were then advised by Zappala how to formally make the request through his clerks or the prothonotary. This jibed with the accounts I heard of Zappala's handling of the turnpike's Wagman case. Turnpike attorneys told me that Zappala first was contacted by turnpike Commissioner Dodaro, who then instructed the attorneys to telephone Zappala's office, where a clerk advised them how to *officially* make the request.

So the city of Pittsburgh, in March 1992, brought its King's Bench request directly to Zappala. "However," Dennis's report continues, "the city had not filed a complaint in the court of Common Pleas, which meant that there was no existing proceeding over which the court could take jurisdiction. With the knowledge of all the parties, Justice Zappala therefore dismissed the original petition with leave for the city to re-file it after filing a complaint in the lower court. (By letter dated April 1, 1992, Justice Zappala reported all these events to the rest of the court. During his [grand jury] testimony, Justice Larsen acknowledged that Justice Zappala took these actions in an 'official capacity,' and that they were not 'surreptitious.' Justice Larsen does not claim any impropriety by Justice Zappala with respect to these actions.)

"Accordingly, on March 31, 1992, the city of Pittsburgh filed a Complaint in Equity in the Allegheny County Court of Common Pleas. At the same time, the city filed a 'King's Bench' petition with the Supreme Court, asking the court to assume jurisdiction over the complaint and enjoin the strike. The Court agreed to assume jurisdiction over the city's complaint. The Court then remanded the case to Commonwealth Court for hearings on the city's request for an injunction. Judge Silvestri of the Commonwealth Court held such hearings and, on April 10, 1992, issued an order enjoining the strike.

"Local 85 appealed to the Supreme Court arguing, among other things, that the (Port Authority) act precluded the city from interfering in the strike and seeking an injunction.

"On July 29, 1992, in an opinion written by Justice Zappala, the Supreme Court affirmed Judge Silvestri's order. (On June 25, 1992, Chief Justice Nix had assigned the appeal to Justice Flaherty. On July 27, 1992, Justice Flaherty sent the Chief Justice a memorandum requesting that the case be reassigned to Justice Zappala, since, 'he handled the ancillary matter in the first instance and has explored the issues involved in this case.' By memorandum dated July 7, 1992, Chief Justice Nix reassigned the case to Justice Zappala.) The court ruled that the (Port Authority) Act was unconstitutional in restricting the city's access to the courts, and that the city had demonstrated that the strike posed a clear and present danger to the public. Justice Larsen dissented. While Justice Larsen agreed that the (Port Authority) Act was unconstitutional in restricting access to the courts, he disagreed that the city demonstrated a clear and present danger."

In any event, Zappala's intervention led to a favorable disposition of the case for the city of Pittsburgh, forcing the union back to work. Dennis's report next waxed romantic about Zappala's King Bench intervention in Philadelphia's PLRB case.

Dennis explains the case as follows:

"On June 5, 1991, the Pennsylvania Intergovernmental Cooperation Authority Act was enacted. The statute created the Pennsylvania Intergovernmental Cooperation Authority ('PICA') to help the city of Philadelphia solve its severe financial problems and to raise capital. Pursuant to the statute, the city and PICA entered into a cooperation agreement on January 8, 1992, which required the city to submit a five-year financial plan and corresponding city budgets to PICA for approval. In April 1992, PICA approved the city's financial plan and corresponding budget for that fiscal year. Among other things, the financial plans called for PICA to undertake a massive bond issue to raise capital for the city.*" (Footnote reads: *"PICA oversaw a $474 million bond issue on June 4, 1992. RRZ [Russell, Rea & Zappala] was one of numerous investment banks which acted as underwriters for the bond issue.")

"During this same time period, the city was engaged in negotiations with District Councils 33 and 47 of the American Federal of State, County and Municipal Employees (AFSCME). The collective bargaining agreements between the city and the unions were due to expire on June 30, 1992. During the negotiations, the city sought concessions from the unions which the city maintained were necessary to effectuate the PICA-approved financial plan and budget. These negotiations did not result in agreements. On June 17, 1992, the unions asked the Pennsylvania Labor Relations Board (PLRB) to appoint fact-finders, pursuant to the state's Public Employee Relations Act. The PLRB appointed fact-finders on June 26, 1992.*" (Footnote reads: *"[T]he Public Employee Relations Act ... sets forth timetables for bargaining and mediation. If these steps do not result in an agreement, the PLRB may appoint a fact-finder.")

"By law, during the fact-finding process the city had to continue paying the wages and benefits set forth in the existing collective bargaining agreements, which impeded the implementation of the PICA-approved budget and financial plan. Accordingly, on July 8, 1992, the city filed with the prothonotary of the Supreme Court a petition for extraordinary relief under the above-described 'King's Bench' powers, asking the court to assume jurisdiction over and overturn the PLRB's fact-finding order. The PLRB and the unions opposed the city's application. The court assumed jurisdiction on July 17, 1992, and on September 16, 1992, the court issued an opinion vacating the PLRB's fact-finding order.*" (Footnote reads: *"The court held that the PLRB appointed fact-finders beyond the deadline for such an appointment set forth in the Public Employee Relations Act.") " Justice Flaherty wrote the majority opinion, in which Justice Zappala joined. Chief Justice Nix and Justice Larsen dissented."

What becomes immediately noticeable about Dennis's report of these two cases is what he doesn't say about them. Most glaringly, we see no criticism of the archaic King's Bench maneuver, an all-powerful judicial device with great potential for abuse. And, as throughout his report, we see absolutely no mention of the appearance of impropriety when Justice Zappala rides to the rescue of Democratic allies, entities or institutions, which often are funded by the Zappala bonding firm. Ed Dennis, as always, seems to have a high threshold for abuse. What we do get from Ed Dennis, here and elsewhere in his report, is nit-picking and petty semantic hair-splitting — but only where Larsen is concerned. Dennis, for example, rakes Larsen over the coal for writing that Zappala met with "representatives" of Philadelphia City Hall. "Thus," the report complains, "Justice Larsen explicitly alleged that Justice Zappala met with more than a single representative ... (y)et in his testimony, Justice Larsen related a meeting between Justice Zappala and Senator Fumo alone." Dennis's microscope is reserved for Larsen alone.

Nowhere will the reader find a similarly sharp and critical eye cast on the obvious patterns of abuse found in the Port Authority and PLRB cases. (For the moment let's ignore Senator Fumo's strange plane ride to see Justice Zappala the week before the city of Philadelphia filed its King's Bench appeal involving the PLRB case.) Here we have two instances, within months of each other, where Democratically controlled city halls in a political pinch take a case directly to Justice Zappala by way of the King's Bench, even when, in both instances, there is no ongoing lower court proceedings by which the Supreme Court can take jurisdiction. In the Port Authority case, Zappala himself must instruct his supplicants to first file a case with a lower court, so that his bench can later take it up. If the Democrat pols seem quick to run to Zappala for help, Zappala is just as quick to help, always with the desired result. Ed Dennis, and later the impeachment managers, refuse to put words on the obvious: Zappala is the Democrats' house judge.

Dennis's report reads, "In an interview, Pittsburgh Mayor Sophie Masloff denied having any contact with Justice Zappala in connection with the case which was filed in her name. Similarly, every attorney in the Pittsburgh city solicitor's office who was involved in the Port Authority case was interviewed, including City Solicitor Mary K. Conturo.*" (Footnote reads: *"The other members of the city solicitor's staff who actively participated in the case were Robert Smith, Richard J. Joyce and April Marchese.") "All stated that Justice Zappala had no role in the development of the city's legal strategy, and that there had been no improper ex parte meetings between Justice Zappala and representatives of the city or the county.

"In fact, the evidence shows that the city's legal strategy was developed entirely independently of Justice Zappala. Two separate members of Mayor Masloff's administration suggested the filing of a 'King's Bench' application to city Solicitor Conturo. George R. Spector was a Deputy City Solicitor at the time of the Local 85 strike. Conturo asked Spector for advice as to how the city might expeditiously obtain a final resolution on a request for an injunction, so that the injunction would be final. Spector suggested the 'King's Bench' mechanism, and asked Marchese to research it. Marchese has confirmed that she did, in fact, research 'King's Bench' at Spector's request. In addition, Joseph Sabino Mistick, an attorney who was the

Mayor's executive assistant at the time of the strike, also suggested this procedural mechanism to Conturo. Mistick, who is now a professor at Duquesne University Law School, had used the mechanism in a prior criminal case."

The report goes on to say, "Even representatives of the county and the Port Authority, the losers in the case, offer nothing to support Justice Larsen's allegations.... Even counsel for Local 85 offered no support for Justice Larsen's allegations that Justice Zappala acted in the Port Authority case to further RRZ's interests." Here Dennis outright bends the truth. While the union attorney, Joseph J. Pass, did not speak to the issue of RRZ, evidence suggests Pass shared with Dennis's investigators his suspicions of improper behavior on the part of Zappala, and Pass would go on to voice those suspicions at the impeachment trial.

Dennis similarly attempts to whitewash the genesis of Zappala's handling of the *Philadelphia* v. *PLRB* case.

Dennis's report tells us, "(E)vidence shows that the idea (to employ the King's Bench maneuver) arose with an attorney at the law firm of Montgomery, McCracken, Walker and Rhoads which, together with the city solicitor's office, represented the city in the PLRB case. Kenneth Jarin, a labor lawyer with the Montgomery, McCracken firm, was interviewed. Jarin stated that Justice Zappala had no contact with city representatives in connection with the case. Rather, Jarin stated that the use of the 'King's Bench' mechanism was the idea of one of his partners, Howard Scher.

"During his own interview, Scher confirmed that it was his idea to proceed directly before the Supreme Court using the court's 'King's Bench' powers. Scher explained that the city's financial crisis made it necessary to have the case heard and resolved in the most expeditious fashion possible. Scher was familiar with the 'King's Bench' approach from a previous case, and therefore proposed it as the fastest way to proceed. Scher steadfastly maintains that the idea was his alone, and adamantly denies that Justice Zappala or Senator Fumo had any role in the matter whatsoever."

Dennis's report states that his investigators also interviewed one of the losers in the case, the PLRB's chief counsel, James Crawford. "Crawford had no evidence to suggest that Justice Zappala had any improper involvement in the case," the report tells us. Crawford's appearance at the impeachment proceedings would disclose that Ed Dennis again wasn't telling the truth.

Ed Dennis's grand jury report, which led directly to Larsen's impeachment, becomes the tyrants' friend. Where the tyrants' friend leaves off, the tyrants pick up. Now that the impeachment was in full swing the house of representatives impeachment managers were quick to call the same cast of see-no-evil/say-no-evil lawyers behind these two cases, who more or less repeated, with some interesting exceptions, the same stories scribed by Ed Dennis.

Mary K. Conturo, the solicitor for the city of Pittsburgh who was involved in the Port Authority case, found herself testifying as a witness at the impeachment trial in the state senate chamber on August 18, 1994. Conturo began by describing the gravity of the 1992 transit strike. The strike, she testified, "halted all the bus service, all the public transportation service to and from within the county and to and from the city of Pittsburgh.... The strike had been going on for ten, twelve, thirteen days, I'm not sure. There appeared to be no end in sight to the strike. The strike ... was doing severe economic hardship to the city and had severe impact on the citizens. And at that point the city determined that they should do what they could to end the strike."

The problem was that the Port Authority Act only gave standing to the Port Authority to take legal action, not the mayor's office. "Initially," Conturo testified, "because of the terms of the statute ... the city felt there wasn't anything that it could do. As the strike went on it wasn't being resolved and the hardship was getting greater on its citizens, the city, the law department, we kept thinking about what could be done. Could the city intervene, could the city ask for an injunction, despite what the statute said?" The city, Conturo said, "was looking for a means to end the strike without prolonging (the negotiations) in case they were not successful.

"...(T)he city's position," Conturo elaborated, "was that whatever they did, they didn't want to be prolonging the strike. So the initial thought was if we were going to do something, we would have to go to Common Pleas Court. That did not seem to be a viable alternative because the city believed that if we filed something in Commonwealth Court — or Common Pleas Court — no matter who won, there would be a long appeal process, and during that appeal process neither the union nor the Port Authority really would negotiate in good faith. They would probably wait to see what the ultimate resolution of the appeal process was. That, as you know, could go on for months. So that was not an alternative the city was interested in pursuing."

We begin to see that what made nervous Democrats beat a path to Zappala's bench was not bonds, but the search for a quick and tidy court resolution to a politically embarrassing tar baby. This is what the Port Authority case, and the PLRB case, and the Wagman case, all have in common. Zappala, for his part, seems time and again more than willing to help Democratic allies. That his brother's company sells bonds for many of these characters is only a happy sidelight.

Conturo testified about what happened next. "Well, during the period of time when the strike started until we did the filing, we were constantly every day trying to figure out what could be done, brainstorming generally. In speaking with Joe Mistick, who was the executive secretary to the mayor at the time, he recalled that he had participated in a case that used the King's Bench powers in a criminal matter, and that got us started in looking at the rules with that respect."

Why had the city selected Zappala to apply the King's Bench maneuver? she was asked.

"I think I ultimately made the determination," Conturo said. "It wasn't something that was discussed a lot. It made sense.... I knew that Justice Zappala had been a county solicitor, so he was aware of all the municipal issues and ramifications of the municipal issues, and I thought that was the most appropriate place to go, that I found that he was in town and so that's where I went."

(Under cross-examination Costopoulos would ask her, "When you petitioned pertaining to bench powers initially, were you aware that it took a majority of the court to handle or grant such an application?"

"I don't know if I was aware at that time," Conturo replied. "I became aware of that, and that is what, in fact, happened."

"But at the time you filed, why at that time did you take this application to a single justice?"

"Because there was a rule that provided that that was possible, and that's what I did."

"What rule under the King's Bench powers?'

"It's not specifically under the King's Bench powers," Conturo said, "but it's under the Rules of Procedure for the Supreme Court, the Rules of Appellate Procedure, perhaps.")

Once more, this time for the impeachment boys, the accelerated chronology of the case was hashed through. Conturo recalled that the city of Pittsburgh filed a motion with Zappala's office on Friday, March 27, 1992, asking the Supreme Court to take jurisdiction to end the strike, though the case was not before any lower court. Zappala's office asked all parties to decide on a date to discuss the issue. The following Tuesday, March 28, Conturo recalled, counsel for the city, the Port Authority, the union and the state attorney general's office met in Zappala's office. The house impeachment managers made it a point to establish that this was not a secret meeting, that the Pittsburgh media was "present and aware" of the request for Zappala's intervention. "I think they were outside every door that any meeting took place with respect to the strike," Conturo concurred.

At the March 31 meeting Zappala told the interested parties, Conturo recalled, "that the action was improperly filed and he was, therefore, dismissing it. He advised — he really referred to the rule and noted that the rule provided that two filings needed to be made. One filing needed to be made with Common Pleas Court, and the other filing made with the Supreme Court.... So the city then proceeded to refile on that basis, and the next day I believe an order was issued that the Supreme Court was taking jurisdiction." It certainly seems that Larsen was right, that Zappala was directing the case.

The next three days saw several hearings and rulings by both the Supreme and Commonwealth courts, including a Supreme Court ruling affirming the city's standing in the case. Following these three days of accelerated hearings, Conturo testified, on April 3, "Friday of that week, an order was issued ordering the workers to resume work, that the strike had been enjoined, and that the parties were to work with the court in terms of resolving the labor issues involved."

"It clearly was a very rapid process in the courts which resulted in the Supreme Court issuing the injunction which the city wanted, correct?" Larsen's attorney asked the witness during cross-examination.

"It was a matter of public importance affecting the citizens' daily (lives) and, yes, it was," Conturo replied.

"Were you aware of an IRS investigation allegedly involving Russell, Rea, Zappala and a subsidiary of RR&Z?" Costopoulos asked.

"I received a phone call from someone that represented themselves to be an IRS investigator or something along that line," Conturo replied. "I don't remember the time, or I don't remember the specific questions."

Conturo's testimony, to the chagrin of the house managers, whose witness she had been, didn't help the cause of impeachment. Larsen hadn't been too much off mark: Zappala had guided the Port Authority case, and the feds had been snooping around RRZ.

The clear-cut victim of Zappala's intervention in the Port Authority case was Local 85 of the Amalgamated Transit Union. Joseph J. Pass, the attorney representing the union dur-

ing the King's Bench maneuver, found himself a reluctant witness at the impeachment hearings. The impeachment lawyers
seemed to have difficulty attaining Pass's attendance. When he
finally appeared, as a decidedly reluctant witness for Larsen,
Pass seemed to want to tone things down. At one point he
expressed obvious concern that testifying (presumably against
Zappala) might down the road come to harm his clients or his
practice. Pass bolstered another of Larsen's charges, that
Zappala had met privately, or ex parte, with parties to the strike.

When he finally appeared Pass characterized his union's
strike by saying, "Some thought it was very inconvenient. Some
thought it was a clear and present danger. And it certainly was
disruptive."

Pass recalled that several weeks into the strike he'd been
summoned to Zappala's office with the other participants.

"Did you know what you were going there for?"
Costopoulos asked.

"Well, I knew because I had had a conversation with the
city solicitor indicating that she was going to present a motion
for an injunction."

"When you initially met, you were all there?" he was asked.

"Yes, sir."

"What happened after the initial meeting, Mr. Pass?"

"Well," Pass replied, "if you're referring to during the
meeting with the justice, there was a period where he spoke to
each litigant alone."

"That's what I'm referring to."

"Yes. He had spoken to me alone, yes."

"And when you say alone, for the purpose of explaining to
the senate impeachment committee what we're talking about,
the other litigants weren't there?"

"That's correct."

"Your client wasn't there, or a representative of your clients
weren't there?"

"That's correct also," Pass said. "But I want to put it — it
was in the same meeting. It was as if he had said, all right, I
want to talk to counsel. And he then brought me into cham-

bers. And I suppose he did it similarly with the other counsel, although I wasn't there so I don't know."

"Wasn't it a fact that even the law clerks were excused from these private meetings?"

"When I met with him, yes."

"Now, regarding that isolated meeting between the two of you, without the other litigants, without the parties, without the law clerks, did you express any concern about that isolated meeting?"

"Did I? No, I did not."

Costopoulos asked Pass whether he'd expressed concern about the private meeting to an investigating State Police trooper who'd been part of Ed Dennis's investigation. "When you were interviewed by Trooper John Kelly on January 26, 1993?"

"I think that what you are referring to," Pass replied, "is a statement which I was just recently shown. The context of that, I was concerned not so much with being alone as I was with the idea that Justice Zappala wanted a message carried, if you will, that he did not consider this case to be a frivolous lawsuit. And that the, there was a statement (carried in the press) made by (Allegheny) county Commissioner Tom Foerster then at the time, that he viewed this as a frivolous lawsuit. And Justice Zappala's comment to me was that I would like everyone to realize this is not a frivolous lawsuit and I would like for you to carry that message. I thought that was somewhat unusual."

(Ed Dennis, in his report, didn't mention much of Pass's illuminating and certainly pertinent eye-witness testimony. As usual, Dennis recognized only the petty, irrelevant [and characteristically personal] observations made by the witness. Dennis wrote that Pass "indicated that he believes Justice Zappala favored the city in the case because of a political dispute Zappala had with Foerster, who was chairman of the Allegheny County commissioners." Dennis went on to relate, "According to Pass, Justice Zappala commented to him that Pass should tell Foerster that the Court took the case seriously." Nowhere does Dennis mention the ex parte nature of this meeting.)

"And who were you to carry that message to?" asked Costopoulos.

"I suppose it was to the awaiting press," Pass answered, "because it was, as you can imagine, a rather heavily followed story."

"How soon after the lawsuit was filed (by the city), Mr. Pass, did this meeting take place, if you know?"

"I really don't remember when the lawsuit was filed, honestly. I haven't looked at the records. It certainly was within a very short time. Very short time."

"In addition to your being told to take this message to Foerster, did Justice Zappala make any reference to votes he had lined up regarding jurisdiction?"

"Yes," Pass said. "He indicated that he did not consider this a frivolous lawsuit and that he had the votes to prove it. I assumed that to mean that they were going to take jurisdiction of the case."

Hardly the impartial judge, Zappala, in this private meeting with Pass, sounds like a political boss throwing around his weight.

"Did you find that unusual?" Costopoulos asked.

"Well, having never been before a King's Bench proceeding, yeah, the whole proceeding was unusual."

"Now," Costopoulos went on, "the truth of the matter is, you live and practice law in the city of Pittsburgh, the County of Allegheny, the Commonwealth of Pennsylvania, is that correct?"

"Yes, sir."

"And as a practical matter, you have some concerns about giving the testimony you're giving today for that reason, isn't that correct?"

Here the house managers, attempting as usual to protect Zappala, objected, but were overruled.

"My concerns were the same as I expressed to Trooper Kelly, and they were that I didn't want to — it wasn't my dispute, if you will, and I didn't feel that I should be brought into the dispute. I was a litigant, and I might add, the injunction was issued against my client, and I just felt, and I still feel, that I was not a part of this, so whatever is going on, I didn't want to get involved."

Under questioning, Pass went on to say that he felt it was unusual for the Supreme Court to next remand the case down to Commonwealth Court Judge Silvestri Silvestri. "Well, I thought that the — and this is again, just my opinion — that the proper forum would have been the Court of Common Pleas, which generally takes testimony and conducts evidentiary hearings."

"If you know, do you know what the relationship was between (Silvestri) and Justice Zappala?"

"No, I do not."

"What was Judge Silvestri's effort in these proceedings once the case was assigned back to him?"

Pass said, "Judge Silvestri attempted to, I suppose the best way to describe it, mediate the dispute, attempt to get the parties to come to some resolution of the various issues that were dividing them."

"Did he indicate to you, that is, Judge Silvestri, that he was communicating with the Supreme Court regarding this matter?"

"At one point in the litigation," Pass remembered, "I can't recall exactly when it was, he had indicated that he had had a call from the Supreme Court and they were concerned about what was going on in this matter, because the contract had not been settled, there was no resolution of the dispute, and I suppose that was the genesis of their concern."

Returning to the subject of the meeting hosted by Zappala with all parties to the strike, Costopoulos asked Pass, "what did Justice Zappala direct, suggest, advise, whoever was present to do?"

Pass recalled Zappala telling a representative to the Port Authority "that the court did not have jurisdiction, and there was a question as to whether (city Solicitor Conturo) could file a lawsuit in the Supreme Court directly. I believe Justice Zappala said that she could not, and that she could refile it in the prothonotary's office in the Court of Common Pleas and then the procedure would be to have it brought before the Supreme Court."

"As counsel for the labor unions at that time in this action," Costopoulos asked, "did you feel the position of your clients were substantially compromised as a result of the Supreme Court's action?"

"I think that the Supreme Court's decision was clearly erroneous, in my opinion," Pass responded. He complained that the high court, by ruling the Port Authority Act unconstitutional so that the city could sue, had gutted his union's ability to bargain. "And obviously as a result of that decision, the legislation which was passed here by the General Assembly was ruled to be unconstitutional and really has left the union with very, very little bargaining power. In that sense, yes, I would say we have a very difficult situation in bargaining in the future."

Hadn't Pass previously described the decision as a corrupt decision? Costopoulos asked. This drew an objection from the house managers, who said, "It's both a leading question and it's opinion testimony." God forbid we have any members of the public offering opinions about this corrupt charade. The senate committee allowed the witness to answer.

"I don't want to say and I have never said it was a corrupt decision," Pass responded. "I said, and I have said this many times, I think it is a clearly erroneous decision, it's an incorrect decision. And I think it is bankrupt of any legal logic and principles. I mean, I really believe it was a very poor decision. Of course, someone can say you're ruled against that that's the case. But I firmly believe it was a very improper decision."

Costopoulos produced a document.

"Let me direct your attention to your interview with Trooper John Kelly," Costopoulos said. "I show it to you, Mr. Pass, for the sole purpose of refreshing your memory."

Again the house objected, again was overruled. Costopoulos handed the document to Pass.

"Have you had the opportunity to review the statement of Trooper John Kelly attributed to you dated January 26, 1993?"

Costopoulos asked.

"Yes, I have."

"And the statement that I've shown you refreshes your memory as to how you characterized that ruling of the Supreme Court at that time?"

"It does not change my memory at all," Pass countered. "I never told Trooper Kelly that I thought it was a corrupt decision." (In fact, Pass was one of several witnesses who'd imply at the impeachment hearings that Trooper Kelly had mischaracterized or outright fabricated their earlier statements — either Kelly was a careless and imaginative note taker, or these witnesses now were fearful of a protected Zappala.) "I said I thought the decision was clearly erroneous, it was contrary to all principles of precedent, and I thought it was bankrupt legally. But I never saw that statement, I might say, until about two weeks ago when it was sent to me, and I certainly have never — I was not the author of that."

"I have no further questions," Costopoulos said.

The house managers, as always running protection for Zappala, tried to get Pass to say that he was inexperienced in King's Bench matters and perhaps nothing so unusual had happened after all. Hadn't Zappala merely voted with a majority of justices to rule the Port Authority Act unconstitutional? Pass was asked. What harm had been done? the managers seemed to ask. "And the 2,700-member union that you represented is still active and well in Allegheny County?" one of the inquisitors, Democratic representative Michael Gruitza, of Sharon, asked. "Yes," Pass offered. What the hell then, right? the house managers seemed to say.

In redirect examination Costopoulos asked Pass, "Are you concerned that your truthful testimony before the senate impeachment committee may have some repercussions from the Supreme Court of Pennsylvania and Justice Zappala?"

The managers objected, and were again overruled.

"I would hope not," Pass said. "I would hope that it would not have any such repercussions. I don't know. I don't have any reason to think that it would, but I don't know, obviously."

"Did you have those concerns when you were interviewed by Trooper Kelly?"

"No," Pass replied. "I think I pointed out to you my concern.... I told you I did not feel that we — I represent a lot of labor unions in the state — that we should become involved in the dispute that is ongoing here today, and because of whatever might come out of it, our clients may become caught in the middle of it."

"Let me direct your attention to your interview with Trooper John Kelly," Costopoulos went on, handing Pass the document. "And would you tell the senate impeachment committee what your recollection was then, and is now regarding how your testimony might hurt you?"

"Well," Pass allowed, "as I said previously, my concern, as I told Trooper Kelly, was in this particular political dispute, or whatever it is, and I really have not followed it too closely, but I did not want to become involved because I did not want to have our clients in any way involved in this particular proceeding for, I suppose, fear that we would somehow be looked upon one way or another by any member of the court or any participant here, for that matter. Just we didn't want to get involved, period. I guess that's the best way to put it."

In late March 1992 the Democratically controlled city of Pittsburgh brought its King's Bench petition to Zappala. Only three months later, in early July 1992, the Democratically controlled city of Philadelphia would do the same. Philadelphia attorney Howard Scher, credited with thinking up the King's Bench maneuver for the city of Philadelphia in the PLRB case, was called as a witness by the house prosecution team. Scher described himself for the committee as an attorney specializing in "complex litigation" for his firm, Montgomery, McCracken and Rhoads. "I guess what no one else wants to do, I do," Scher said.

Scher described the political, and economic, problems created for the city when its unions requested the state labor relations board initiate a factfinding procedure in the middle of contract negotiations. The newly installed Rendell administration had wanted the old contract to lapse so it could impose a new contract in keeping with its budget. The PLRB factfinding procedure would, by law, automatically delay such an outcome. Millions of dollars in contract savings were needed, the Rendell people said, to keep the city within budgetary restrictions imposed by a newly created bail-out authority, the Pennsylvania Intergovernmental Cooperation Authority, or PICA. In the impeachment hearings the unspoken question would become whether there had come to be much too much intergovernmental cooperation.

Talks with the troublesome unions stretched on, Scher testified, into June 1992, "and the city's unions had requested a factfinding procedure be instituted. And it was in that context, after that had happened, that a partner of mine, Ken Jarin, asked whether I would be interested in helping advise the city on a pro bono basis, which is how we were representing the city at that time. I think we still do. And to help them develop a litigation strategy to respond to the union's request for factfinding."

Scher explained that a team of volunteer lawyers had been assembled by Rendell to aid in the city's recovery from, well — the Wilson Goode administration. "Mayor Rendell had asked major firms in the city to volunteer to assist in various aspects," Scher said. "Well, shortly after I was consulted by my partner, Ken Jarin, we had a number of conversations, internal, with lawyers with whom I worked regularly, both in the litigation area and Ken Jarin in the labor area ... and I conceived of not a very unusual strategy but I conceived of the strategy. The city wanted to be able to be free to terminate — to have the contract, the labor contract, expire when it was scheduled to expire, June 30, 1992. And they wanted to be free to proceed with implementation of a labor compensation package that would be consistent with their economic plan. And it was my job, as well as the other lawyers with whom we worked, to try to come up with a way that would get the city to be free to do that."

Scher recalled that a member of the legal team suggested

instituting legal action in either Common Pleas or Commonwealth Court. The object, Scher said, would be "to seek an injunction to prevent the PLRB from requiring us to participate in factfinding and thus let us be free to proceed with the implementation of the new labor compensation package. I suggested that we use the King's Bench power, the King's Bench petition. That would go directly to the Supreme Court, and I knew that ultimately were we to make an application to Common Pleas or Commonwealth Court, it would wind up, whoever won, in the Supreme Court anyway. I knew that we had the capability of getting to the Supreme Court directly because it was an extraordinary situation for the city of Philadelphia, and the King's Bench powers are specifically designed to address extraordinary public concern situations.

"It was my judgment and it was clear that the requirements of PICA to have a balanced budget and to operate within a carefully planned economic environment, and the stay mandated by the Pennsylvania Labor Relations Act in the event of factfinding were allowed to go forward, caused an impossible conflict.

"And it was extraordinary because I think the city, I don't remember the numbers precisely, but the city's proposed labor compensation package would have saved the city $2 million a week from that which the current contract, the contract that was to expire on June 30, 1992, required. So that $2 million a week was money once spent which could never be recouped. So as every day passed, every week passed, the city was $2 million further in the hole in their economic plan, deviating from their economic plan."

Scher explained he had been exposed to the King's Bench maneuver several times over his career, not always with the expected results. "I know I was familiar with that process, which is extraordinary by definition — extraordinary. Not peculiar, just extraordinary." Perhaps, Scher said, he'd first been exposed to the powers of the King's Bench as far back as 1971 or '73, while he worked in the city solicitor's office. He recalled he'd participated in a King's Bench petition "early in my career at Goodens, Greenfield, which would have been between '73 and '77.... The party adverse to us was a very prominent political figure, and we didn't believe we could get a fair trial by a Common Pleas Court judge in that particular county. And so we went directly to the Supreme Court and asked the Supreme Court to hear the application, stay the proceedings of the court below, and assign a new judge. I believe the Supreme Court denied the application and assigned a new judge. So we achieved the result that we sought."

Two other times in his career Scher had appealed to the King's Bench. Once, representing the Philadelphia Board of Realtors, he sought to have the court rule a city real estate tax unconstitutional. Another time, Scher said, he "represented the Court of Common Pleas of Philadelphia County, in a labor dispute again, and filed a King's Bench application with the Supreme Court in which the Supreme Court acted by granting the stay and remanding the matter to the Commonwealth Court for original proceedings, for hearings on the application. Those are the only King's Bench applications that I can recall."

So here clearly was a man who knew something about King's Bench. Yet apparently few, if any, of the other pro bono attorneys working for Rendell's city hall were familiar with the obscure and archaic maneuver.

In the 1992 PLRB case, Scher said, "I was the one who recommended it, and there was resistance on the part of the other lawyers who were participating because they just weren't familiar with the procedure." Scher had to read the other lawyers the book and verse of the obscure law. "I cited them the statute, and I showed them where it's written in the rules, published rules, published statutes, and I explained to them my understanding of the King's Bench, which derives from the pre-revolutionary time, the adoption of the powers that that particular court had in England before the revolution."

In his mind, Scher said, the city budget crisis was an extraordinary emergency, justifying the use of King's Bench powers. King's Bench, Scher said, was "tailor made for this situation because it was a matter of great public concern, and it was one in which the Supreme Court would ultimately hear the merits of the case in any event."

Though a lower court had not yet been involved in the PLRB matter, Scher said he was undeterred in filing the King's Bench petition with the high court. Scher explained he had a tactical, as well as economic, reason for filing his petition. "There is an unusual aspect to this procedure," Scher said, "because once the petition is filed, it places jurisdiction, meaning power, originally in the Supreme Court. When the Supreme Court has original jurisdiction of the matter, I believe it operates as an automatic stay of the proceedings in the court ... or tribunal below. And we argued in our petition that the PLRB was a tribunal to which the King's Bench power applied."

"The objective," Scher explained, "was that on June 30 when the contract expired, the city (would) be able to implement its best offer, which would have saved the city $2 million a week. My recommendation was, upon filing the petition, which is why we filed it with such urgency to try to get it in as soon after July 1 as possible, upon that filing, the city had the power to implement its last best offer and begin to realize the savings of $2 million a week or so."

The actual filing was mundane, Scher said. "I asked a lawyer in my office, maybe even a filing clerk, to take the, you know, the petition, that's what we had filed, and bring it to the prothonotary's office. There's a prothonotary's office in Philadelphia in city hall, the Supreme Court prothonotary, and to drop it there on the counter. To file it. It's filed in a miscellaneous docket, and that's what we did. I did nothing else. I did not call any justice, I did not call the prothonotary, nor do I believe and nor do I know of any other contact with any justice or any prothonotary regarding the filing of the petition."

Lightning this time would strike with Scher's quiet petition left on the prothonotary's counter on July 8, 1992. The question would come to be whether Justice Zappala had been tipped off to expect the filing five days before by Senator Fumo, who'd taken the plane ride to see the justice on July 3.

Though Scher insisted he had personally contacted no justice about his filing, he allowed that he had kept Mayor Rendell's chief of staff, David Cohen, appraised of his progress. Scher described Cohen as Philadelphia's vice mayor. Before entering the mayor's office Cohen had been a private attorney, Scher said, and "I was in a case with him probably in the early '80s." At the time of the PLRB King's Bench filing, Scher said, David Cohen was "like the vice mayor. He's a very important person in the city of Philadelphia."

It was Cohen, on July 2, 1992, who had arranged a plane for Fumo to fly up to Lake Erie to see a vacationing Justice Zappala. It was also Cohen who was Scher's contact at city hall. Scher allowed he had kept Cohen abreast of the timing of the King's Bench petition, reporting to him.

"Did you have any contact with Mr. Cohen at any time during your involvement in the city of Philadelphia-PLRB case?" Scher was asked.

"I believe so," Scher replied. "I recall his role essentially was to ask me whether it was done yet. I don't mean to be facetious, but basically he wanted reports on the status of the filing, whether we had filed the application. I reported to him as developments occurred in the case. Sometimes I reported to him. I think most of the time Ken Jarin reported to him or someone else gave him reports."

Scher tried to play down the politics behind his use of the King's Bench maneuver, yet politics always seemed to be part of the equation. Scher had intended the King's Bench filing to serve as a mechanism by which the Rendell administration could unilaterally impose its contract conditions on the unions. Someone at city hall apparently had cold feet. It's one thing to employ politics to attain a favorable court ruling; in today's media-driven society it's another matter to actually *use* such an ill-gained ruling.

"Was the stay that had been granted ever used by the city of Philadelphia to implement the last best offer?" Scher was asked.

"The city, even after the Supreme Court expressly granted the stay and ordered briefing," Scher replied, "did not implement its last best offer, and that was the summer of '92. We then briefed the matter, it was decided by the Supreme Court in mid-September, and the city did not even then implement its last best offer until some period of time thereafter."

It would turn out that the Rendell administration had worried about adverse national publicity should it implement its best offer at the same time as the Philadelphia Eagles were playing a Monday Night Football game.

Scher explained, "My recollection was that the city was not interested in creating what would have resulted — what did, in fact, result in a labor dispute while the Dallas Cowboys and the Philadelphia Eagles were playing on Monday Night Football because there was a fear that pickets would be set up outside Veterans Stadium and that perhaps some of the football players who were sympathetic to unions, or just people generally, wouldn't want to cross picket lines to attend the game, so nothing was done. I don't know whether that was really the reason, but nothing was done until well after the Supreme Court had decided to grant the relief, the substantive relief that the petition sought."

"Is that the complete extent of your interaction with David Cohen, what was talked about?" Scher was asked by the house managers.

He replied that sometime "after the Eagles game, when the mayor was announcing that within 30 days certain medical benefits and so forth would be reduced and certain holidays would be eliminated, and so forth and so on. I remember at that occasion I did meet, you know, face to face with David Cohen. That's about the only time I can recall."

The defense cross-examination of Scher lasted only several minutes. Costopoulos didn't seem to believe Scher. The trial again returned to the lucrative world of bond underwriting.

"Mr. Scher," Costopoulos asked out of the gate, "has your law firm done bonding work for the city of Philadelphia?"

"My honest answer is the only answer I give, but I don't know," Scher replied. "I don't believe so."

"Well, then, if you don't know, you don't know. I'm not

interested in what you believe."

"Okay. I do not know."

Costopoulos asked Scher to detail his conversations with David Cohen. "He had asked you when you were going to file the King's Bench petition, didn't he?" Costopoulos asked.

Scher hedged. "I don't recall him asking me that question, no," he replied. "I can't tell you honestly that I do. I don't recall him asking me, 'Has it been filed yet?'"

It would turn out, however, that Cohen and Rendell had been aware of the exact timing of the filing of the King's Bench petition. "When was he (Cohen), according to your testimony, aware that it was going to be filed?" Costopoulos asked.

"I don't know, but I can give you a very educated guess, if you want it." Scher added, "Because the mayor signed an affidavit to the (King's Bench) petition.... Prior to its being filed.... Attached to the petition is the affidavit of Mayor Rendell, and it may say the date on which he swore to the accuracy of the contents of the petition."

"Is the David Cohen that you're referring to before the senate impeachment committee the same David Cohen that arranged for the Brobyn airplane to take Senator Fumo to Justice Zappala's on July 3?" Costopoulos asked.

Scher espoused knowing nothing about Fumo's plane ride to see Zappala. Accounts of the plane ride by this time had been splashing across the state's newspapers for almost two years. Yet Philadelphia attorney Howard Scher, who claimed he specialized in complex litigation, testified he had no awareness of any stinking plane ride involving Vince Fumo that had occurred the stinking week before Scher filed his stinking King's Bench petition.

"I don't know to what you're referring."

"Are you aware that there was a flight on July 3, 1992, that took Senator Fumo to Justice Zappala's vacation home on that date?"

"I do not know that," Scher said.

"You don't know that?" Costopoulos retorted. "Okay. I have no further questions."

The house managers seemed to hurt their own case when they called as a witness James Crawford, chief counsel of the Pennsylvania Labor Relations Board. He'd been with the agency, in one position or another, since 1972, when he completed law school, he said. Crawford recounted the events that led to his agency's initiation of its factfinding powers in the 1992 dispute between the city of Philadelphia and its unions. The PLRB's jurisdiction in the matter "arose under Act 195 of 1970," Crawford said. The statute applies to public employers, such as Philadelphia.

By statute, Crawford explained, "Factfinding is set forth in Article VIII of Act 195. Factfinding is the third step involved in the collective bargaining process. All the bargaining procedures and processes relate to the employer's budget submission date, which is the date generally where employers adopt budgets, and many collective bargaining agreements negotiated in the public sector begin and end with these budget submission dates.

"Article VIII of Act 195," he continued, "requires that in the first face-to-face negotiations between the employer, the public employer, and the representative of the employees must begin 171 days before the budget submission date. The parties then have an obligation to bargain face-to-face without the intervention of any third party neutral for a period twenty-one days.

"After twenty-one days of negotiations, at the 150th day before the budget submission, the parties are obliged, under Article VIII, to involve the (PLRB's) Bureau of Mediation. In attempting to seek resolution to the dispute, a mediator is then assigned to the case and participates to try to mediate the dispute toward resolution. That procedure statutorily is twenty days, which takes the bargaining process down to 130 days before budget submission."

Crawford said that though the statutory provisions call for an application for factfinding within 130 days of the budget deadline, "It has been our experience, however, that very often the parties start the bargaining process later than directed and do not invoke the bargaining procedures at the time frames where they're obliged to do so."

In the case of Philadelphia's 1992 labor dispute, Crawford said, the city's budget deadline, set by its Home Rule Charter, had been March 30, 1992. This meant, he said, "the parties should have been discharging their collective bargaining responsibilities as early as November, November 1991." As it was, the PLRB wouldn't become at all involved in the dispute until June 1992. Though statutorily incorrect, this tardiness wasn't particularly unusual, Crawford reiterated.

"Does the statute provide that you have to begin PLRB factfinding or at least apply for PLRB factfinding at least 130 days before the budget deadline?" the house managers asked.

"On its face," Crawford answered, "those are the statutory provisions. In practice, until the court's decision" (involving the King's Bench request which ultimately ruled that the factfinding process had begun too late) "factfinding almost universally was invoked beyond the time when the statute provided."

The collective bargaining procedure that should have begun in November 1991 had been delayed mostly for reasons of high politics, and high finance, Crawford explained. A picture emerges of totally broken government, where no one much cares, or can afford to care, about niceties such as written law. "Those were the waning days of the Wilson Goode administration," Crawford said. "The Rendell administration assumed office in January. There were other things happening that affected the bargaining process. There was the PICA legislation, which obliged the city to develop a five-year plan for their finances.

"It was my understanding," Crawford continued, "during this time period, at least, that the Goode administration was not developing a five-year plan because they were leaving office, and the Rendell people had not arrived yet, and that's at least one reason why the bargaining was not taking place, because of the impact, the overwhelming impact of discharging the city's PICA obligations. So there was a period of time after January when the Rendell administration assumed office when they were developing their five-year plan, obtaining approval, and bargaining started in earnest, I would say, in the spring of 1992."

AFSCME, Crawford said, was "the bargaining representative of the employees involved, represented two units of employees who were then negotiating. One unit, which is generally referred to as the blue-collar unit, another unit, which was the white-collar unit. On, I believe it was June 17, the Labor Relations Board received a request for factfinders for both of those units." Factfinders were appointed on June 26, 1992. This date was not only past the factfinding deadline, but also fell after the city's budget submission date.

Could the city implement new contract terms when a case goes to factfinding? Crawford was asked.

"It is the board's position," Crawford said, "that a public employer has no right to implement any provisions that would be an offer or last offer consistent with its bargaining position, at least during the period when the parties were engaged in the Article VIII impasse resolution procedures. And they would include bargaining, mediation, and factfinding. At that time, there was other litigation pending in Commonwealth Court raising the question of once the Article VIII impasse resolution procedures are exhausted, may an employer implement its last offer?

"At the time, or at least in June of 1992, that matter had been argued before a panel of the Commonwealth Court. Later, it was argued en banc before the Commonwealth Court, and the court issued an opinion, I think around the end of December 1992 or January 1993, in which it found that an employer could not implement its last offer, even after exhaustion of the Article VIII impasse procedures."

The managers asked, "It was settled law that if PLRB factfinding was ongoing, the city could not implement its last and best offer?"

"Yes," Crawford said. "You say 'settled law.' I don't think there was any appellate litigation directly on that point, but I think it was pretty well accepted by virtually all quarters that at least while the impasse procedures are ongoing, that no last offer could be implemented."

At the time of the King's Bench application, Crawford said, "the Labor Relations Board was appealing a Commonwealth Pleas Court decision in a case involving the Philadelphia Housing Authority where a judge of the Court of Common Pleas of Philadelphia had reversed a labor board decision and determined that an employer could implement a last offer after exhaustion of impasse."

"So the city would have had some authority for implementing its last and best offer after impasse if this matter had not gone to factfinding as of June 26, 1992?" the managers asked.

"Under that decision."

"To your knowledge, is that why the city filed the lawsuit?"

"I would assume so."

"What was the date that the then-current labor contract was due to expire?" Crawford was asked. "When I say 'then-current,' I'm referring to the labor contract in effect in the spring of 1992."

"My understanding was on June 30, 1992."

"So that on July 1, 1992, the city could have implemented a new contract?"

"I think that was the city's position."

"Was the new contract going to represent a decrease of benefits to the employees?"

"It's my understanding that the city was seeking concessions from the unions with regard to both units," Crawford said. Howard Scher, representing the city, no doubt believed that the stay issued by Supreme Court would allow the city to implement its last best offer, Crawford said. He continued, "Mr. Scher's firm, I might add, was counsel of record in the other case involving the Philadelphia Housing Authority that was pending in Commonwealth Court, and they were intimately familiar with that legal proposition."

Crawford went on to testify that the handling of the PLRB case through the Supreme Court appeared to be both "extraordinary," and "outside the mainstream." "I think it was outside the mainstream the way questions of this sort were raised and decided," he said. "We've been sued before. Usually we end up in court when someone appeals one of our decisions. Sometimes we are in court because we get sued by somebody, and it's pretty much outside the mainstream when we're sued at all. It's very much outside the mainstream when we are sued originally before the Supreme Court of Pennsylvania."

Crawford described the handling of the case by the Supreme Court as extraordinary in that the "King's Bench powers of the court are reserved as a matter of law to matters that are already pending in a lower tribunal of the judiciary. The Labor Relations Board, as an executive branch agency, is not part of the judiciary, so we felt that it was extraordinary for the court to attempt to take up a matter that was pending in another branch of government." This argument had been part of the PLRB's original, preliminary objections to the high court's interjection in the case, Crawford pointed out. "We further argued that this matter we thought was a fairly routine matter for the injunctive powers of the Commonwealth Court," Crawford went on. "Under Pennsylvania Judicial Code, the Commonwealth Court is the designated court for actions to enjoin a state agency, of which the Labor Relations Board is one. We further contended ... that this was not a matter of immediate public importance which the rules regarding the King's Bench powers we thought were limited."

The unspoken implication of Crawford's testimony was that the attempted use of the King's Bench powers was a blatant, yet amateurish (and ultimately self-defeating), overreach of power on the part of the Rendell administration. What was going on here, and why had the Rendell people sought the King's Bench powers? In the final analysis the King's Bench episode seems to have been just a side gambit involving Rendell's efforts to confront organized labor in Philadelphia. He had campaigned as willing to stand up to labor, and to balance the city's books (a sizable portion of which is predicated on labor costs). Only touched on in the impeachment hearings were the other labor cases involving Philadelphia that were pending before the courts in the same time frame as the PLRB case.

In the aforementioned case involving the city's housing authority a ruling by a panel of Commonwealth Court had been expected in late June. A favorable ruling in the housing authority case would have allowed a public employer to implement its last best offer once the bargaining process had run its course, thus negating much of labor's ability to negotiate. This was the housing authority case involving Howard Scher's firm alluded to by Crawford, the same firm that originated the King's Bench ploy in the PLRB case. A favorable ruling in the housing authority case would have laid the groundwork for the Rendell administration to lawfully implement its last best offer once the Supreme Court had issued its stay in the PLRB's King's Bench proceedings.

As July 1, 1992, approached many of the city's labor contracts were lapsing, and the city's lawyers looked with increasing interest to the housing authority case. Many city attorneys turned out at a hearing of the Commonwealth Court panel on June 18, 1992. One interested attorney described for me a courtroom gallery packed with Philadelphia lawyers. It became apparent to those present that the ruling might go against the city — which ultimately happened before Commonwealth Court months later. By that time, late June 1992, the city's strategy for dealing with the unions was already in play and it was too late to stop the train. The King's Bench application was filed several weeks later, in early July. One also shouldn't underestimate the psychological impact of a successful King's Bench application. By displaying it had a wire to the state's high court the Rendell people meant to send a message to the unions and other comers. In that respect the Democratically controlled state Supreme Court was all too happy to comply, and to reach down a helping hand.

In the PLRB case, the King's Bench application, ironically, set the city back a few paces.

"As it turned out," Crawford told the impeachment committee, "the matter was decided slower than it would have been had the city participated in the factfinding. The factfinding would have concluded after the board's appointment of factfinders in late June. The matter would have concluded at least before the factfinders in early August. After the report is prepared by the factfinders, the parties have two ten-day consideration periods in which they can accept or reject the reports. Maximum of ten days. It can be shorter. So conceivably, had the parties completed the factfinding process, the matter could have concluded as early as, say, August the 10th." Crawford pointed out that the city had filed papers with the court stating "their contention that maintaining the status quo under the terms of the old contract was costing the city $2 million a week, compared to their last offer." But the city did not immediately implement.

After the Supreme Court ruled on the merits of this case, Crawford was asked, did the city then immediately implement the new contract terms?

No, he repeated. "The court didn't offer its opinion until mid-September," Crawford said, "and thereafter the city maintained the status quo for some period until the implementation in late September."

Until after the Monday Night Football game.

Crawford, like Joseph Pass, the union attorney from Pittsburgh, was interviewed by a State Police investigator in early 1993. Notes taken by the State Police investigator indicate both Crawford and Pass expressed concerned (to put it mildly) about the handling of the Port Authority and PLRB cases. Crawford and Pass, like the attorneys on *both* sides who handled the turnpike's Wagman case, were not called by Ed Dennis to testify before the grand jury that indicted Rolf Larsen for drug use. These were some of the victims of Zappala's brand of justice, yet *grand jurors never got to hear from one of them.*

In this supreme court matter there was a repeat of the grand jury manipulation and withholding of evidence that we saw in the video poker case. The obvious question is this: If key witnesses and evidence were withheld from the grand jurors, how could they possibly reach dependable conclusions concerning allegations of case-fixings involving Justice Zappala, and the fairness and integrity of Pennsylvania courts?

CHAPTER 22

Put Your Keen Eye to This

At last the day came when the house managers called Justice Stephen Zappala as their witness before the impeachment committee. The senate chamber that morning was packed. The air crackled with anticipation. Here was the heart of the show. Disgraced Larsen, already removed from the bench and smeared on drug charges, would take on his court nemesis Zappala in the well of the state senate.

"The first witness the house managers call today is Justice Stephen A. Zappala of the Supreme Court of the Commonwealth of Pennsylvania," Undercofler cried. Zappala was over in the house chambers, no doubt made to feel much more welcome there than Larsen. "It will be just a moment while he walks over."

"Fine," Greenleaf said.

"May it please the committee," Costopoulos rose to say, "in the event that Senator Fumo is present in the building, we're requesting that he be sequestered during Justice Zappala's testimony." The ridiculousness and impossibility of the request spoke volumes.

"We're not going to grant that motion," Greenleaf responded.

Zappala came in. He was a big man, in his sixties, thinning gray hair, small forehead, slightly drooped shouldered, big in the schnoz. He had an amiable, easy-going gait that betrayed a man sure of himself, a man not many had opposed. The committee and the house prosecutors oozed with deference for him. The house managers proceeded to lob a full inning of softball questions designed to demonstrate that Zappala had done no wrong, that Larsen had inexplicably gone bonkers and leveled absurd charges at his fellow, amiable jurist from Pittsburgh. Zappala gave a memorable performance. He began by outlining his background. City of Pittsburgh grade school. Duquesne, Notre Dame, Georgetown. Passed the bar in '59, practiced with his father and brother, Frank. "In 1968," he said, "I then became involved in county government, took over as director of what they call Bureau of Community Development. Remained with the county government until 1975, went through different divisions of the county, which ultimately resolved itself by me becoming the county solicitor in, I think, 1973, '74.

"In 1975," Zappala continued, "I left the county government, went back into private practice for a period of about two to two and one half years. Then after that I went, attempted to run for the Court of Common Pleas of Allegheny County, ran in the election in 1979, won both nominations in the primary, took office on January 1, 1980. Being a member of the Court of Common Pleas in 1980, sometime in early 1982 took a run at the Supreme Court of Pennsylvania and was elected in the fall of 1982 and have been on the Supreme Court since then. I served to today with one retention election already having occurred in the year 1991."

The house managers proceeded to stroke Zappala. He purred back like an old smoothie, displaying in turns self-effacing humbleness and erudition. When Larsen later got a whack at him in cross exam the fur would be rubbed the other way and we'd see suppressed white-hot anger and eructation.

The managers appointed the Republican counsel, Undercofler, to examine Zappala. Undercofler started off by asking Zappala about allocaturs, the process by which the justices vote to hear a case. They would establish that it takes three justices for the court to hear a case; obviously, their argument went, one justice, acting alone, can cause little or no mischief. Yet Larsen contended that Zappala managed a block of votes (and Joseph Pass's testimony indicates that Zappala wasn't above suggesting that he controlled blocks of votes.)

"Justice Zappala," Undercofler asked, "we've heard testimony throughout this impeachment trial concerning allocatur jurisdiction within the Supreme Court. Would you please describe and explain the court's discretionary jurisdiction?"

"As I understand it, counsel," Zappala replied, his sentences sometimes tangled, "allocaturs are at the discretion of the court and filed with the court itself. An allocatur petition normally requires that of three justices in order to approve a grant for the purpose of having an argument. If three are not on the grant, then, of course, the allocatur would die and there would no longer be any further proceedings before the court itself." He explained that each justice received "anywhere from 1,200 to 1,400" allocatur petitions yearly, each justice taking turns receiving the petitions, "by a wheel or some fashion." Of those, he said, only nine to ten percent were granted yearly.

"Would you please explain for the committee how it is that cases are chosen to be heard from the pool of allocatur petitions that are filed, when clearly there are a number of meritorious claims and they are not all going to be heard?" Undercofler asked.

"Well, normally it's done by the justice himself preparing what we call a proposed grant," Zappala explained. "That proposed grant is then normally circulated to members of the bench. The proposed grant initially, or should initially, have some issue which either is attractive to that particular justice or had some relevance as to the jurisprudence of the commonwealth.

"When that petition is circulated, as I indicated before, we have a rule which you need two additional joinders. There are times whenever you have an interesting point that you do contact the justice and indicate the issue which is being raised and whether or not that justice would take a hard look at it."

Here Zappala came alive with a spark of early legal memory. "I learned my first quick lesson on that from the famous Chief Justice Sam Roberts," he said. "Sam was beautiful because if he had an issue — and he was an outstanding jurist — Sam would indicate, put your keen eye to this, young man, because it may be of interest to you. And normally it would be of interest to me, and normally it would be of interest to the chief justice at that time, Sam Roberts.

"The mere fact that the court will entertain the allocatur and grant it does not mean that those particular justices actually are interested in the issues themselves," he went on. "It still has to be argued and disposed of. However, the mere fact that you get it up on the list is a tremendous advantage to the parties involved."

Still, he said, the justices might in the end vote against you after hearing the arguments. "You may have a change because some of the justices had not looked at it that closely." He agreed with Undercofler that, in this process, a certain amount of discussion must occur between the justices.

"But again," Zappala added, "remembering the discussions and the talk between the justices is predicated upon issues and not personalities. That is important to the court. And again, I reiterate, if there are issues which I think are important — and I'm considered to be a liberal on the bench in the criminal field, I would talk in terms of maybe trying to do something on the wiretapping, on the body tapping, on other areas of criminal law, and I have asked other justices, Would you take a look? If they do, fine; if they don't, fine, too. But I guarantee you, it's never been looked at on the basis of who was bringing the allocatur up."

Now the house managers steered the testimony to the subject of Rolf Larsen. Undercofler asked Zappala to describe his relationship with Larsen when Zappala had joined the bench in 1983.

"I think we had a normal relationship, and over a period of several years he and I became a little more friendly," Zappala replied.

"Did you develop any kind of friendship with him?"

"Oh," Zappala said, almost with a sigh, "I thought it was a friendship. Over the years he had been to my house several times. We had invited him to different functions. I think he had attended either one or two of the children's weddings, and as late as October 1992 he sent my wife a contribution to the Discovery 500." In the summer of '92, when Zappala was undergoing his third back operation, Larsen had sent him get-well greetings. In mid-October 1992, Zappala went on, Larsen "circulated a fax as to his brother, his twin brother's condition relative to his heart. And I had called him and indicated that if he needed anybody in the Ohio — I think it was the university complex hospital — I would be glad to give them a call and see if I could arrange something, and he told me he needed no further help, and that was the extent of it. But that's as far as I can take you as to the relationship until mid-1992, as far as October."

Had there been a change in their relationship? Zappala was asked.

"Somewhat," Zappala replied. He recounted that he "unfortunately" became the senior judge in Larsen's disciplinary matter. The duty had therefore fallen on him to personally inform Larsen that Justice Cappy and he had voted to uphold the reprimand against their fellow jurist. The house managers took the opportunity to list the seventeen petitions or motions for recusal that Larsen had filed over the years to dismiss the other judges or lawyers involved in the disciplinary matter. The list would consume more than three pages of impeachment transcripts.

Zappala recounted how he'd gone to see Larsen in the latter's office kitchenette on October 13, 1992. "He and I sat down, I told him the court had reached a verdict, I said that you may not like it, but we are going to sustain the reprimand. I think we are absolutely correct. I think it will do justice to you and to the court.

"Mr. Larsen indicated he did not like it," Zappala continued, "he thought it was wrong, he indicated that common criminals got more fair treatment than he did, and then he said, 'I'm going to do what I have to do.' And I said, 'You do what you damn well please.' At that point, I got out of that place. That was the extent of any conversation."

Zappala denied having told Larsen during the October 13

kitchenette meeting that he had done anything wrong in the handling of various cases, including the Port Authority and PLRB cases. The house managers then led Zappala through the cases in question. Undercofler asked him to recall the transit workers strike which led to the employment of King's Bench powers.

"Two things happened," Zappala began. "I think, if I recall, the transit strike was on, and also there were no newspapers in the city of Pittsburgh. I think both were on strike or something was going on, but as the strike was progressing, it became public knowledge to the TV media and radio and so forth that the city was somewhat beginning to be paralyzed to the extent specifically that the elderly were not able to get out of their homes, people were not being able to be treated in hospitals, other people were having great difficulty getting to their job sites, and in a simple word, I think you would say that the city was getting close to being in chaos at that time."

Zappala, asked to explain the King's Bench jurisdiction in the Supreme Court, replied, "Well, King's Bench jurisdiction, there's two, essentially. There's King's Bench, and you also have plenary, both by statute. King's Bench is regarded more as the much broader, and it came from the old common law days where you are the king's court and you could do no wrong and whatever the king wants to do, you go and do it. It's almost an absolute power that the court has in order to protect, quote, the fiefdom — or the crown. And it's never been altered or changed, either by constitution or statute.

"Interestingly," he went on, "they then supplemented that with the plenary powers of the court to reach in at any given time because of necessity, and so forth, so that a petitioner could come by either way, King's Bench or by plenary jurisdiction. Both of them are not — are rarely used except in extraordinary times. But both give the court the ability, if they deem it appropriate, to move where necessary to cure something which has been caused by some wrong. That's as simple as I can put it."

"Is there any major difference between a King's Bench case

or a plenary jurisdiction case?" he was asked.

"King's Bench says you can do basically almost anything, and that's pretty wild," Zappala replied. "Whereas plenary, you have to take it on the position that there's a case or controversy at issue, so that there is something pending within your court system, one more or less has to have an overlay of what we call jurisdiction, there has to be something there for you to reach down and take it. Whereas the King's Bench says just go grab what you want, bring it up, do what you have to do, resolve the issue and dispose of it."

Zappala denied having done anything improper in either the Port Authority or PLRB case. Nor, he said, had he misused the King's Bench powers in either case.

"Did you at all depart from the ordinary procedures utilized by the Supreme Court in handling plenary or King's Bench petitions?" Undercofler asked.

Zappala answered, "Absolutely not."

He'd just finished explaining that the King's Bench powers were "pretty wild," and that each justice, for all he knew, had different procedures for handling King's Bench petitions. With all-sweeping, extraordinary powers like this, what are "ordinary procedures?"

Zappala continued, "And to emphasize, as I tried to point out, there never was an individual order signed by this justice. Everything in the Port Authority case was done as court action. And if I be chastised, then other members of the court should likewise be chastised as to what may or may not have occurred. But there was absolutely nothing which occurred relative to this case. They are called extraordinary, they have to be extraordinary and move that way, because if they are not extraordinary and the relief that you want can't be granted, then you're wasting the litigant's time, you're wasting the court's time."

It was true, Zappala allowed, that he had met privately with the separate parties in the Port Authority case, but it was in the context of a larger meeting, with all interested parties in attendance, that he had had private words with each side, "sort of shuttling in and out," as the prosecution characterized it.

Zappala explained that labor disputes in Pittsburgh often were handled in this way, with judges acting almost as arbitrators or referees between the two cloistered parties. Why have separate "conversations" with each party? he was asked. Zappala spoke of the power, elective and otherwise, of the labor unions. Justice Zappala replied that "the reason for the conversation was whether or not there was an issue that could be resolved amicably that you could get the strike settled. You've got to understand, in western Pennsylvania, as a trial judge, there are consistently — or were at that time, this goes back — a great sentiment between labor and management disputes, and the Courts of Common Pleas of Allegheny County were somewhat reticent in trying to impose injunctive relief because of the unions in western Pennsylvania.

"So normally the practice in our county and some of the surrounding counties was try to sit down and negotiate without formally going into court to resolve the issue," Zappala went on. "Because no matter what the issue you resolve, you're going to have a winner and you're going to have a loser. Somebody is going to be happy and somebody is going to be mad. And in western Pennsylvania, don't make the unions mad. It's as simple as that."

Zappala here, between the lines, was making the interesting case that, rather than being a political judge, he was willing to take political heat. He was saying that he, Justice Zappala, was willing to stand up to the unions.

As for head-to-head, one-on-one meetings with the two parties, he said, that "was the practice. But it is always done with the consent of the parties and both parties available for discussions."

"Did you consider those discussion of counsel, where you were shuttling in and out with their consent, to be ex parte communication?" he was asked.

"Absolutely not," he replied.

As for turning away the city of Pittsburgh's first petition for King's Bench jurisdiction, Zappala said he'd been concerned that there was "no case in controversy in any other court in the

commonwealth. Could we," he asked, "under the plenary juris-
dictional powers, bring the case directly to the Supreme Court?
If I recall correctly, my gut reaction was we could not do that.
That would be inappropriate." Zappala recalled, on the other
hand, that at the time of the Port Authority case Larsen had
either said or had written "something to the extent, don't
worry about sending it down or sending it out, you can merely
reach in and take it by the King's Bench powers. I thought
about what he had said, but I said, thank you, no, thank you. I
still thought the appropriate way was to dismiss the existing
petition without prejudice, and then let the city decide whether
they want to come back," after they had refiled with a lower
court. "I did say that I thought it was an issue that I had no
problem referring the same to the Supreme Court of
Pennsylvania."

Even so, Zappala added, he didn't guide the case, or advise
Pittsburgh officials what to do next, as they didn't have to be
"rocket scientists" to figure out what to do.

As for the Philadelphia/PLRB case, Zappala testified he
didn't remember much about the circumstances surrounding
the case, "except," he said, as with the Port Authority case,
"that they were having again, quote, great labor problems." As
with the Port Authority case, Zappala insisted he had done no
wrong.

But name and nature of King's Bench powers mean that
the court can do no wrong. In this case the King's Bench powers had been requested, and granted, even though no lower
court was hearing the matter. Undercofler asked, "Was there, in
your judgment, or was there pending a significant issue as to
whether or not the city could file a King's Bench petition in
connection with a matter before the PLRB?"

"Remembering what I just discussed," Zappala replied,
"and this is in all deference to the committee and to where I'm
seated, the law is not interpreted as to what the law is until the
courts interpret what the law is. In this particular case, as I
understand, there was not a Supreme Court decision as to

whether or not you could reach into the PLRB because that's part of the executive branch of government. Whether we did do it or didn't do it, that's still the prerogative of the Supreme Court. So as far as I was concerned, although it may not have occurred, once the court did it, that became the law of the commonwealth. And they reached in under the King's Bench power and they would resolve the issue."

Zappala said what was "important about the issue" was whether the PLRB could implement factfinding after the 130-day cut-off period. "Is the 130-day discretionary or is it mandatory?"

Inconsistencies begin to show in Zappala's testimony. Only a few months before, in the Port Authority case, he'd wisely rejected summarily employing the "pretty wild" King's Bench powers in the Port Authority case, "thank you, no, thank you." Now suddenly, for some reason, no such worry seems to cross his mind. Zappala's explanation for his sudden change of heart seems high-handed, and borders on the abuse of power. Because they can do it, they did it, was his answer. We judges make the law.

How had the PLRB matter been resolved by the court? Undercofler asked.

The court, Zappala replied, "Just grabbed it and took it up. The court says we're going to do it, and we're going to do it. That was the end of it. Now, from here on in the law of the commonwealth says the PLRB is like any other agency, we can take it, whether you think it's governmental or not, belonging to the executive branch of government, until the Supreme Court gets reversed by some other court, some other Supreme Court at a later day."

Zappala had set the date of July 30, 1992, for briefings to be filed in the case because, he said, he wanted everything out of the way before he underwent back surgery. Was this accelerated briefing schedule at all unusual? he was asked. "Not as far as I'm concerned," he replied. "Because in cases like this you don't assume plenary jurisdiction or King's Bench jurisdiction and wait seven months to get something accomplished. You get it done today and you get it done tomorrow, because the effect of the proceeding and the effect upon the litigants is of no moment if you stretch it out four, five and six months. The whole purpose is extraordinary and to move the matter. And it doesn't bother me at all. It may create a problem for counsel in preparing their briefs, but I have never heard them scream or holler. They comply."

As things turned out, the PLRB's chief counsel, James Crawford, points out, the court's "accelerated" look-see into the matter took more time than would have factfinding. The PLRB then asked for reconsideration of the issue, which was denied on November 6, 1992. Zappala pointed out that Larsen, on October 15, 1992, dissented in the reconsideration ruling. This dissent fell two days after the October 13 meeting in Larsen's kitchenette, Zappala pointed out, "in which I supposedly mea culpaed to these various matters involving this case, and that he would have had to have personal knowledge, and by not bringing to the court's attention was not only a violation of the code, I think it was a violation to every member of the court."

Justice Zappala was asked about Russell, Rea & Zappala, and the involvement of his two sons, Stephen and Gregory, in the investment firm. "Could you identify what Russell, Rea & Zappala is?" Undercofler asked.

Zappala maintained he knew "absolutely nothing" about RR&Z, and nothing about what his sons did with the firm.

"Russell, Rea and Zappala, I'm assuming, is a financial institution," Justice Zappala replied. "I do not know and could not say here under oath exactly what they do. I do not know anything about Russell, Rea. I know nothing about any subsidiaries. I know nothing about any of their workings. Absolutely nothing. Nor do I have an interest, nor have they given me anything, and more importantly, nor have I ever asked for anything."

At first Zappala seems engaged in harmless exaggeration and hyperbole. To say he knows "absolutely nothing" about RRZ is, in a word, untrue. For one, he certainly has an interest where his sons, his brother, *his family* are concerned. Elsewhere in his testimony Justice Zappala expresses keen awareness of the Pittsburgh newspaper strike, so, like all politicians, he must read the papers. In a front-page November 27, 1986, article Pittsburgh Post-Gazette reporter Gary Rotstein quoted anonymous aides to Governor Richard Thornburgh as saying that Justice Zappala had personally lobbied for the appointment of his longtime family friend, protégé and former legal partner James Dodaro as turnpike commissioner; Dodaro in turn had loudly pushed RR&Z as the turnpike's main underwriter. The Chicago Cubs' third baseman Joe Tinker throws the ball to second baseman Johnny Evers, who throws the ball to first baseman Frank Chance — didn't Tinker help get the ball into the hands of Chance? Aren't they after all on the same team? "Stephen Zappala played a key role in leading Thornburgh to place Allegheny County Solicitor James Dodaro, a Democrat on the Turnpike Commission, according to Thornburgh aides," the Post-Gazette reported. "Fellow Democratic Commissioner James Goodman said Dodaro pushed for Russell, Rea & Zappala to be made the Democrats' senior underwriter on the ($807 million) bond issue (of 1986), worth up to $1.5 million in work for the firm." (I, incidentally, spoke with Post-Gazette reporter Gary Rotstein, who said he stands by his reporting, though he would not disclose the Thornburgh administration sources he cites. Rotstein said it would not be hard for a serious investigator to track down the sources.)

Can we believe that Justice Zappala never read that newspaper article? That he never read *any* other coverage of meteorically growing RR&Z?

"Did you tell Justice Larsen at any time that you participated in getting bond underwriting work from the city of Philadelphia for Russell, Rea & Zappala?" the justice was asked.

"I have never told Justice Larsen that," Zappala replies, "I have never told a person that because that is absolutely a lie. And I have never spoken to a public official, and I have never asked anybody to help my sons or help my brother. *That's not the way we operate.* So the answer is not only no, it's a bald-faced lie." (Emphasis mine.) In one breath Justice Zappala suggests his family, as a unit, has a way of operating, of attending to their mutual, common and familiar interests, yet in another he maintains they share no common interests.

On the subject of RR&Z and his sons involvement in the firm, Justice Zappala descends to outright, and demonstrable lies.

"Have you ever heard of a company by the name of S & G, Inc.?" Zappala is asked.

"Yes I have," Zappala replies. "S stands for Stephen, G stands for Greg. They are my two sons. They're both lawyers. They have a consulting business that works in conjunction with their uncle, and that's all I know." Their uncle, of course, is Charles Zappala, of Russell, Rea & Zappala — the justice's brother. A few moments earlier he'd said, "I know nothing about any subsidiaries."

This reply brought a chuckle from the visitors' gallery. A man sitting beside me in the gallery turned, smiling, and whispered what seemed to be on everyone's mind. "Justice Zappala must be the first Italian father in the history of the world who doesn't know what his sons are doing," he snickered.

In one breath Justice Zappala says he knows "absolutely nothing" about RR&Z or his sons' involvement, while in the next he says he's bought stock from his son, who was working for the firm.

"Have you ever had any occasion to do any business whatsoever with Russell, Rea & Zappala?" the justice was asked.

"You're going to get me in trouble with my wife again," Zappala replied. He said he's bought "a little stock" from one of his sons. "I have two securities," he said. "Lackawanna Water and Sewer and I think Allegheny County bond, General Fund." He received no discount from his son, he said. "I found out about that after the investigator," Zappala said. "And my wife asked me why we didn't. And I said, you go talk to your son. He's the one who sold it to you."

The house managers rested their gentle questioning of

Zappala, and the committee adjourned for lunch. Next it would be Larsen's turn. I had a quick bite in the capitol and returned early to the senate chamber, where I ghosted around the hallways. I hoped to speak with Larsen or Costopoulos before the committee reconvened but those two, when you needed them, were scarcer than true justice in a Pennsylvania courthouse. I went so far as to walk into the senate cloakroom, even onto the floor, but no dice.

Not ready to rest my case, I scribbled off a quick note to Larsen. "Ask Zappala about the Wagman case," I wrote on a piece of note paper, signing it. I folded the paper and asked a senate secretary to delivery the message to the defense team. I suspected the house and senate managers would see this open note before Larsen would. I'd done all I could; now I withdrew to the visitors' gallery and watched as the participants drifted back from lunch. Larsen and Costopoulos finally reentered and whispered about like surgeons preparing for an amputation. Zappala came in and retook the witness stand. He half filled his water glass. The house managers, meanwhile, sat in a line at their table, their faces painted with concern, their hands prepared to hit their overworked objection buzzers. It seemed like a nasty episode of the Family Feud. And so it was.

Larsen rose, took his place at the questioner's dais. Zappala began pouring himself half-filled glasses of water from a pitcher at his table. I'd count, over the course of Larsen's examination, four or five refills. "Mr. Justice Zappala," Larsen began, "would you give us an overview of recusal on the Supreme Court of Pennsylvania?"

"The overview of recusal is set forth in the Goodheart case as articulated by the chief justice, and prior to that time, it was set forth in Septa vs. Reilly," Zappala replied. Zappala snapped back at Larsen; he sounded irritated, angered, impatient. "And I don't think I can articulate it any more than as set forth in the opinion, because if I were to paraphrase it, I may be misunderstood. And I think you know as much about recusal as I do. But that is what I consider the polestar case recusal."

"Well, would you tell us what rule you applied to you in recusal?"

"I apply the rule which is enunciated by our court, Supreme Court of Pennsylvania, and is understood to be what the law of the commonwealth is."

"And what is that rule?"

"You read the opinion, Mr. Larsen, you know what the rule is."

"I'm asking you."

"I told you what it is. It's enunciated in the Goodheart case."

"Well, will you please tell us what that rule is?"

"Would you want to get me the opinion?"

"Sure. You don't know it without the opinion?"

"I do not want to be misunderstood."

"When you sit on the bench, do you have this opinion with you?"

"When I sit on the bench," Zappala snarled, "normally a recusal petition is not made. And if it is, it's done prior to when I sit on the bench. And if it is, then I will dispose of it accordingly."

"If you're on the bench," Larsen pressed, "and in the course of your observations, whether at the beginning, in the middle or what have you, you perceive something, can you recuse yourself without somebody filing a petition to have you recuse yourself?"

"If you're asking me are there incidents where, during the course of oral argument, something is divulged which triggers the conscience of the jurist or the justice to react, the answer to your question is yes. One specific case was the Philadelphia Suburban case. Are you acquainted with the case at all, Justice Larsen?"

"Please don't ask me questions," Larsen replied.

"Well, I'm asking you, are you familiar with the case?"

"No, I'm saying, please don't ask me questions."

"Because that was the case—."

"Excuse me," Larsen addressed the committee. "Would the

chair direct the witness not to ask the attorney questions?"

"That's true," Greenleaf peeped. "Let's just leave it as questions and answers. Proceed from there."

Zappala replied that the December 1992 Philadelphia Suburban case, "as I interpreted it ... had to do with some type of underwriting or bonding, I had thought. I had taken a position, without doing any further interrogation or creating a personal problem myself, I did not participate in that case and got up and walked off. Unfortunately, my judgment was wrong, because it had nothing to do with bonding. It was a tax case dealing with a capital stock transfer. Now, to put that question that you asked in proper perspective, if, in fact, there is something which comes to my attention and I cannot render a fair decision, then I am duty bound to do something as far as removing myself or anybody else who may be sitting on that bench as far as recusal."

"Can you sit on cases," Larsen asked, "using the Goodheart standard, where you know and are friends with an attorney who is advocating one of the positions in a case?"

"Are you talking about Billy Bresnahan?" Zappala replied, oddly.

"No, I haven't asked you a thing about Billy Bresnahan." Larsen continued, "If you have a friend who is an attorney and he's advocating a case in front of you, can you sit on that case without violating the Goodheart standard?" Then, "Could you sit on a case where an attorney friend happened to be a litigant?"

Zappala asked Larsen to define friend.

"I'll use the dictionary meaning of friend," said Larsen.

"All right," Zappala said. "What's the definition?"

"'Friend,'" Larsen read, "'one with whom one has a close relationship.' Is there a distinction between a lawyer friend as an advocate and a lawyer friend who is a litigant?"

"There is no distinction," Zappala finally put forth. "A friend is a friend. If it impedes or impairs your sense of fairness, whether he's the litigant or the attorney or anything, then I think the same principle would apply."

"So," Larsen asked, "you can sit on a case and participate in the case if you have a lawyer who is a friend who is also the litigant if you feel that you can judge it fairly, is that what you're saying."

Zappala replied, "whether he's a friend, a litigant, an enemy, if you cannot judge the case fairly, irrespective of the moniker or title you've given the person, then I think you would be duty bound to get off the case."

"And conversely, you're saying, I presume, if you can judge the case fairly, you can stay on the case, is that right?"

"That's where the gray line is," Zappala answered. "That becomes a matter of conscience and a decision to be made by the court."

"Does each individual justice make that determination for themselves?"

"Yes."

Are there no objective standards? Larsen asked.

"No," Zappala replied. "I think there are objective standards, to the extent that you are still subject to what occurs around you. You could very easily take a position that you personally will think that this may not be inappropriate, but to the eye of the outsiders, it may be very inappropriate simply because what is out there looking at you. In other words, the impropriety simply of the relationship may be sufficient. So it's not just strictly your subjective thought; you must go and see what the objective basis is, too. *It just may not seem fair.*" (Emphasis mine.)

"So you're talking about the appearance of impropriety?"

"That's right."

Larsen directed Zappala's attention to the previously mentioned Goodheart case, which dealt with pensions for judges. The case pondered a two-tiered pension plan that gave judges who'd joined the judiciary before March 7, 1974, a pension nearly twice the size of those who'd joined later. Larsen asked Zappala to recall that Zappala and Nicholas Papadakos had been the only justices who'd joined the bench after the cutoff. Yet Zappala and Papadakos had voted on the case.

This line of questioning brought a round of staunch objections from the house managers. Their cover-up radar, always flashing, began to signal incoming. Undercofler complained, "we've not objected to the general questioning with regard to recusal, but now we're into *individual* cases in the court." (Emphasis mine.)

The house managers clearly didn't want one thing above all else — they didn't want Zappala questioned about cases he may have improperly handled for friends, associates or family. If everything, after all, was on the up and up with Zappala, what did Zappala (or anybody) have to hide? Why forbid any questions if there were honest answers? This impeachment supposedly was about unfairness and impropriety in the courts, yet the managers would brook no discussion of sundry mysterious cases run by Zappala. Before the eyes of the public they were protecting Zappala, as Zappala had been protected all along. The stakes — financial and political — must have been steep to keep their judge so onerously afloat.

Chairman Greenleaf allowed Larsen to continue his line of inquiry "as long as the object of the questioning is in regard to the recusal process." But, "it's not relevant," Greenleaf cautioned, "if this is to pursue whether any particular justice should or should not have recused himself in a particular case." (!)

Larsen attempted to proceed, establishing that Justices Zappala and Papadakos had voted on the Goodheart case, which had given those two the same high pensions as the other justices on the court. Undercofler quickly objected, this time squeaking, "Mr. Chairman, I renew my objection. This does not sound to me like recusal theory, it sounds to me like a review of a specific case."

"Well, it is," Larsen countered, "because recusal came in later on this, with a petition."

Chairman Greenleaf now tried to silence Larsen. Greenleaf said he saw no reference to recusals in the articles of impeachment, "or that there should have been a recusal in certain matters. I don't believe that the articles of impeachment deal with that particular area. So we're concerned about the relevancy of it all."

Here Greenleaf, always shaky and uncertain, displayed an appallingly poor grasp of the articles of impeachment, over which he supposedly presided.

"I think the reference in the articles of impeachment," Larsen reasoned, "include the fact that I should not have participated in some cases. And the result of that is, or the conclusion is that I should have recused myself. And that's in the articles of impeachment."

"There's nothing in there that says you should have recused yourself," Greenleaf said.

"Well, if one shouldn't have participated, one should have recused oneself," Larsen said.

The bully boys on the prosecution bench chimed in, "Mr. Chairman, the failure to recuse is evidence of a much more serious pattern of conduct, according to the allegations."

"I have before me Article 1," Greenleaf said, "and the article deals with the allegation concerning tracking certain petitions and the practice surrounding that alleged practice. I don't see anything in the article that specifically—."

"Well, it talks about recusal," Larsen cut him off. "It says (Larsen) didn't recuse himself when the same was heard on the merits because of his association with an attorney involved in the case."

Greenleaf at last saw the light. "Objection overruled. Proceed," he said.

"Now," Larsen began again with Zappala about the court pension case, "you and Mr. Papadakos participated with a full court in that case?"

"That's correct," Zappala said.

"And is there any question in your mind that you and Mr. Justice Papadakos did have an interest in that outcome?"

"Individually or as a class?"

"Individually."

"There was an interest which was both class and individually, yes," Zappala replied.

Larsen pointed out that the judicial salary board then filed motions for re-argument, "And one of the grounds they alleged was that you and Mr. Justice Papadakos had improperly participated in the case, and as a result, the Goodheart case you're referring to for the standard of recusal is in response to the petition for re-argument, is that correct?"

Zappala agreed that this was so. He told Larsen he had trouble recollecting the composition of the three-member panel that had handled this re-argument.

"I'll show you the opinion," Larsen replied, moving toward Zappala. Zappala seemed like a heavy galleon in the water, only half-protected by the fleet, while Larsen was the quicker man-of-war, tacking this way and that for the attack.

"No. that's all right," Zappala said. "That's all right. I don't want to see it."

Undercofler, the house prosecutor, chimed in, "Object again, Mr. Chairman, to the questioner walking around the room and delivering documents, as we've raised before."

"I would like to point out," Larsen responded, nodding at the prosecution table, "that they have eleven people sitting over there today, which is less than they usually have, so they have a lot of manpower to hand things out. There are just three people here on this side, and I'm not trying to—."

This petty exchange typified the sophomoric mentality driving the proceedings. "That's all right," Greenleaf chimed, sounding more and more like Mr. Rogers, "I think Justice Larsen certainly can deliver to the witness any documents that he would like to be examined by the witness."

(Later during Zappala's testimony, when Zappala objected to terminology used by Larsen, Larsen complained, "I would like the witness, he has a lawyer beside him, six feet away from him, and he has a battery of house lawyers here, and he has house members who are lawyers who represent him, and I don't think a witness should be posing objections." This brought a quick objection from house managers. "Mr. Chairman," Undercofler said, "let one member of the battery here speak for a moment, if I may." But a member of the committee, Hardy Williams of Philadelphia, broke in to defend the legislators. "I think we ought to make it clear that we as a body have determined that the witnesses, except for private counsel, have no lawyer represent[ing] them," Hardy railed. "I want that to be clear. I would not want the public to think that's the case in this proceeding." Undercofler, obviously sensitive to the issue, would go on to elaborate, "for the record," that Zappala's lawyer for the proceedings was William Lamb, who was seated next to the justice, while, on Zappala's other side sat the justice's law clerk, Dawn O'Brien, "who is there to assist him if he needs to find documents." Undercofler continued, "I represent that the house lawyers and managers do not represent Justice Zappala, but we have been given permission to talk to him by his counsel." To casual observers in the visitors' gallery, watching the house managers freely interact with Zappala, they all looked thick as thieves.)

Larsen handed the opinion to Zappala. "Now," Larsen asked, "where in that opinion does it set forth the standard for individual recusal?"

"Well, if you read the entire opinion as to the reconsideration, I'm pretty sure the chief justice set it forth in a very articulate fashion," Zappala replied.

"Is it not a fact," Larsen went on, "that there is no standard set forth in that opinion that you cite as the polestar for recusal, and what is set forth is that a litigant cannot complain when they knew that a justice had an impediment to fairly deciding a case because there was an interest involved."

Zappala snipped that this was "a law school discussion," then proceeded to read from the opinion. "'Under our law, a strong tradition has been established which recognizes that each judge has a primary responsibility for determining the validity of a challenge to his or her participation in a given matter.' It goes on to say that, 'Where there is a question of impartiality of one or more of the justices, the individual justice's responsibility is to make a conscientious determination whether he or she can impartially assess the issues in question.'"

Zappala turned testier. "But again," Zappala complained, "if you want to discuss a law school critique on the case, you be my guest. But I don't think this is the proper forum, Mr. Chairman. I think it's highly inappropriate. You have a decision. This decision is written by the Supreme Court. You can interpret the decision. For me to re-interpret it I think is highly irregular. And my answer is very simple. The standard set forth to recusal is set forth in this opinion. If I'm wrong, I'm wrong. But I think we will be here until tomorrow. And if you want me to do that, I'll be here until the day after tomorrow."

The discussion begins to take on the air of the Mad Hatter's tea party. "I object to the witness making objections," Larsen piped. "If he wants to talk about tomorrow and how long it takes to answer a question, I think he ought to discuss that somewhere else and not in response to a question." One begins to see what the atmosphere must have been like in a courtroom with the likes of these two.

"I apologize to the chair if I am out of order," Zappala offered.

At this point prosecutor Undercofler spits out what certainly must stand as the most ridiculous and corrupt utterance of the entire impeachment odyssey, which is saying a lot.

"Mr. Chairman," Undercofler opines, "I think it's a very significant point. These proceedings are on the record. Justice Zappala makes reference to a case. To attempt to have a single justice interpret that case now under these circumstances in the abstract, or even in the specific, is to perhaps to impact the law of Pennsylvania."

One may well ask the point of impeaching a judge in a public forum such as the state senate chamber if the public can't hear a discussion of the handling of individual cases. Undercofler here is saying, So what if a judge is a crooked brigand, if his rulings are patently unfair, they are now state law and must not be rehashed before God and man, who may discover the depths of our system's depravity. What's the good, he's saying, of our public discovering the dishonesty of our laws and of our lawmakers? What benefit do we have in knowing we've been deprived of our basic right to impartial justice? If we're not here to get at the truth, Mr. Undercofler, why are we here?

So you can get paid? Merely to waste everyone's time and lynch Larsen, perhaps? Why talk about injustice, Undercofler is saying — let's get on with the lynching.

There's only one problem with the lynching. The facts are on Larsen's side. He proceeds to walk Zappala through two cases involving Zappala's allies, cases where Zappala did not recuse himself. Larsen does a good job of laying down "evidence of a much more serious pattern of conduct" involving his former fellow justice, to use the words house prosecutors aimed at Larsen.

Larsen asked Zappala about a case involving the aforementioned attorney William "Billy" Bresnahan. Bresnahan had represented Zappala in a 1990 case involving the length of Zappala's term in office. "And did Mr. Bresnahan represent you?" Larsen asked.

"He represented me at that time, yes," Zappala replied. Had he paid Bresnahan? Larsen asked. No, Zappala replied.

Had Zappala sat on any cases, "either during the allocatur stage or the opinion stage, where there's arguments where the case was submitted in which Mr. Bresnahan was the attorney, subsequent to 1990?" Larsen asked.

"If I recall correctly," Zappala replied, "and I think somebody could tell me if I'm wrong, there was a case that was mentioned here involving Erie or somebody, and that I supposedly referred that case or something. In checking our dockets, I did not sit on the case, but what I did was prepare the allocatur which denied his petition to the Supreme Court."

"So you participated in the allocatur stage?" Larsen asked.

Zappala volunteered, seemingly as a prepared speech, "Now, let me also say that Mr. Bresnahan was formerly an assistant county solicitor who worked for me in Allegheny County, that I had known him as a fine lawyer, that he had never, never been involved with any private litigation prior to, during, or after this particular proceedings, that I have no social relationship with Mr. Bresnahan, and I do not consider that case isolated to put me in a position of exercising what is claimed under the Goodheart case, of removal because of recusal because of, quote, a friend."

"It did not create an appearance of impropriety?" Larsen asked.

Zappala splits hairs. "No, it didn't," he said, "because other than the one petition that Mr. Bresnahan had presented, there was no nexus to any relationship between Mr. Bresnahan and myself."

"And the only reason you would recuse in a situation such as that would be because of an appearance of impropriety, is that correct?"

"But the appearance, again," Zappala replied, "is a generic term. It doesn't just come out of the air. It has to be affixed by some factual predicates. Now, the appearance simply could be that he had represented me in some other fashion. He had represented members of my family, he was a social guest at my house, he had been seen in my company for more than one occasion, he is known to be a personal friend of mine. That isn't in this record."

"It may not be in the record," Larsen said. "My question is that based on your perception of him representing you and him having worked for you as a county solicitor, assistant county solicitor, under your direction, that was not sufficient to create an appearance of impropriety, in your mind, is that correct?"

"Absolutely not," Zappala replied. Then, "He would need a better friend than me, then."

Had Zappala, "as a matter of course," recused himself from other cases handled by any of Bresnahan's law firms? Larsen asked. No, Zappala replied.

How would Zappala know this? Larsen asked. "Do you flag cases?" Larsen asked, harking to the impeachment allegation that this was Larsen's practice.

"We all use the term 'flag,'" Zappala said. "They asked me, do I have a special list. Flaggings and listing are two different things, in my mind."

Larsen next explored Zappala's relationship to Senator Fumo. Hadn't Zappala performed a wedding ceremony for

Fumo? Larsen asked.

"Yes."

"When was that?"

"Allison's got to be four or five," Zappala replied, mentioning Fumo's daughter. "Probably in the late 80s. '89, '88, '89. I really don't know."

"A case came up to our court with Senator Fumo?" Larsen asked.

"His father's case?" Zappala said.

"No."

"Oh, okay."

"With Senator Fumo as a litigant in child support brought by his former wife," Larsen said.

"Yes."

"And that case was filed in the Supreme Court in September— or December '89, and disposed of in September 1990, and you participated in that, is that correct?"

"As to the allocatur, is that what you're saying?" Zappala asked.

"Yes."

"Yes, to the extent that I did nothing," Zappala said.

"Well, you didn't recuse yourself?"

"Yes," Zappala said. "I did nothing."

Larsen next visited another curious and enlightening episode of Zappala jurisprudence, known as the PICA case. PICA, we recall, is an acronym for the Pennsylvania Intergovernmental Cooperation Authority, the agency created to bail Philadelphia from its financial turmoil. Philadelphia labor unions took PICA to court in 1992, saying that the agency's budgetary demands for city labor costs violated collective bargaining laws. The unions argued that workers were unfairly locked into PICA's budgetary demands before bargaining could run its course. The PICA case ran in the courts concurrently (some say in strategic tandem) with the city's PLRB case.

Zappala's brother Charles was underwriting bonds for PICA when the justice sauntered in on the case. In the PICA case we see the usual list of suspects, with one enlightening addition to the cast of characters. The Philadelphia Inquirer finally awoke from its editorial coma and got involved, with surprising results.

"All right," Larsen asked. "Now, there was a case that you referred to as PICA?"

"Yes," Zappala said.

"And what was that case about?"

"That," Zappala said, "was an interesting case where the legislature implemented the underpinning of the funding for the city of Philadelphia. It impeded upon existing contracts with employees in the city of Philadelphia, and it required, I think, a special board and a special financing in order to retain the vitality of the city of Philadelphia.

"The case, if I recall," Zappala continued, "was argued in Philadelphia. It was a most interesting argument. I sat on the case. We came back to Pittsburgh. I was assigned the case to write. Our office received a call from the Philadelphia Inquirer, some young reporter. He wanted to know, through my clerk, whether or not I was aware that my brother's firm was one of the twenty or forty or sixty underwriters. I told him I did not know that. I thanked him for his telephone call. I immediately notified the chief justice, and the case was taken out of my chambers. That's all I know. And I think the chief justice retained it, and I don't know who wrote the opinion. That's all."

"And then you recused yourself?" Larsen asked.

"Because that was the first time it was brought to my attention, yes," Zappala said. "I think that the reporter — if it weren't for the reporter, nobody knew of the underlying so-called investment bankers or bond — I don't know what it was. But that's what happened. That was the PICA case."

"When you say there were twenty or forty underwriters, where did you get that figure?" Larsen asked.

"That's my recollection of the conversation from that reporter as to my brother's firm being one of twenty or some number of agreed-to underwriters," Zappala replied. "I think that was the term, for the total bond issue, whatever it was, for the city of Philadelphia. That's all I know. Again, I'm not swearing to the accuracy, I'm just telling you what I recall, but I think was told."

"You didn't become aware that the legislature picked who the underwriters were going to be in that matter?" Larsen asked.

"No, sir. I had no idea."

"Objection, objection!" Undercofler protested. No use letting the public know that the legislature was the paymaster.

"Overruled," Greenleaf said. "He answered the question."

"I have absolutely no idea who picked them, how they picked them, what they did," Zappala volunteered. "I have no idea."

The truly interesting aspect of the PICA case was the dispatch with which Zappala bowed out after having received the phone call from the state's largest daily. One has to wonder how fast Zappala would have recused himself from the turnpike's Wagman case, the Port Authority case, the PLRB case, the Bresnahan case, the Fumo child support case (how many child support cases, by the way, end up before the Supreme Court?) and God knows what else, if only the Philadelphia Inquirer hadn't been asleep at the switch.

After spinning these curious tales and splitting these hairs, Justice Stephen Zappala descends the slippery slope to outright lies and fabrications.

"Now, whenever your brother was involved in underwriting," Larsen asked, "did you make it a rule to get off that case?"

Here Zappala, on the floor of the state senate, having sworn an oath to tell the truth, tells an outright lie. "Anytime my brother was involved in underwriting," Zappala lies, "I would not know it unless it was specifically brought to my attention. Because the term 'underwriting,' I cannot define. The number of transactions they have, I cannot define. And I leave it to the discretion of those who may be the litigants to raise the issue. I do not know and I can't tell you."

Why then had he recused himself from the PICA case if he didn't know what underwriting means? Larsen asked. Zappala said, "in the PICA case it was specifically brought to my attention. But more importantly, to even stay away from the sense of impropriety, I being the majority writer of that opinion, or hopefully, I think would have created some problem for the court and for me personally, and I would then err on the side of caution and I would not have participated."

That being the case, Larsen asked, why "didn't you make it your business to know what bond issues, in what municipalities those bond issues were being underwritten by your brother?"

"Because if we go back to the Goodheart case," Zappala said, "we are only held responsible for that which we may know. I don't think the law requires me to go and be an investigator as to what we don't know. But more importantly, the law also dictates that the litigants themselves have some minimal obligation. If the litigants know and don't raise it, so be it." He added, "I am not going to be the policeman and walk around and try to find out."

"What if the litigant doesn't know who owns bonds?" Larsen asked.

"Unless I know, Mr. Larsen," Zappala replied, "I would tell you that I don't think I could in any way be unfair in the disposition. But if I am told, yes, I think I would then look as to whether or not I would recuse myself, if it had an impact. But simply because it's there and nobody brings it to my attention and I don't know about it, I don't think I'm held accountable for any reason of being unfair or impartial in the disposition of the issues."

In fact, several attorneys complained to me that Justice Zappala in various cases himself advised litigants that his brother Charles was underwriting an entity involved in a dispute before the court, and then went on to ask if this association bothered any of the litigants. I wrote in *When the Levee Breaks:*

"Several times, when matters concerning an entity funded by his brother's bonds have come before the state Supreme Court, (Justice) Zappala has asked opposing counsel whether they mind if he hears the case. This has happened 'six or seven times,' one (turnpike) attorney told me. In one recent case involving a television reporter who was injured on the turnpike, I'm told Zappala from the bench pointed out that his brother sold bonds for the turnpike and asked if either party minded his involvement. Neither party at first objected. After arguments had been heard, the TV reporter's attorney did object to Zappala's involvement. The late objection was disregarded. 'You're supposed to object at the start of a case, *before* arguments,' one attorney snickered. 'Not after you give a lousy argument.'

"Despite Justice Zappala's apparent sensitivity, there remains the inherent potential for the perception of conflict and unfairness whenever he hears a case involving his brother's interests. The turnpike's lawyers aren't going to object to Justice Zappala hearing a case. They secretly feel it's to their interest that he's involved. An opposing counsel is also unlikely to raise objections. 'You're not going to tell a judge he may not be impartial,' one attorney said. 'If a judge is supposed to be anything, it's impartial.' By questioning a judge's impartiality you're questioning his integrity, an action that may return to haunt you next time you find yourself before that judge."

The turnpike case mentioned above involved a television reporter named Susan Jellig who'd injured herself on the toll road, leading to the suit, which wound its way up the state Supreme Court. Turnpike attorneys who spoke with me, as well as Jellig's attorney, Lawrence Ludwig, of Scranton, all dispute Justice Zappala's claim that Zappala was unfamiliar with the entities for which his brother underwrites bonds, leaving it to the litigants to inform him of any conflict. In the Jellig case, the attorneys for both sides agree, Zappala *himself informed the litigants* in open court that his brother was the turnpike's underwriter, and then the justice went on to ask if either side had a problem with this conflict.

Lawrence Ludwig, Jellig's attorney, recounted for me Jellig's opening argument, which was presented to the Supreme Court by a second attorney. Ludwig, agreeing with turnpike attorneys, told me, "Justice Zappala, at the commencement disclosed that his brother was the underwriter for the turnpike. At the time we weren't sure what he meant by 'underwriter.' The other attorney thought he meant some sort of insurance underwriting. Later, once we understood what it was, we filed a motion for Justice Zappala's recusal."

Ludwig recalled that Justice Zappala volunteered the information in open court, before the litigants, the lawyers, court employees, the public, and the other justices. They all know what Zappala's about. Zappala's statement in *Jellig* was hardly a secret, and easily verifiable. Ludwig suggested the case records on file in the court prothonotary's office might even include Zappala's statement. Of course, as in the Wagman case, no one involved in the impeachment of Larsen was interested in taking a five minute walk over to the prothonotary's office to view the stinking records, or to spend a few minutes on the phone with attorneys for Jellig or the turnpike. Not the newspaper reporters, and certainly not Undercofler or Moses, the house special counsel who had been paid hundreds of thousands of public dollars and who held the public trust to do it.

The important point is this: Justice Stephen Zappala outright lied when he testified, "Anytime my brother was involved in underwriting, I would not know it unless it was specifically brought to my attention. Because the term 'underwriting,' I cannot define. The number of transactions they have, I cannot define. And I leave it to the discretion of those who may be the litigants to raise the issue. I do not know and I can't tell you."

Justice Zappala obviously isn't your run-of-the-mill liar. He committed perjury while testifying under oath in the senate chamber of Pennsylvania. Not one of the house or senate prosecutors, paid large sums of money by both political parties, called him on it.

Other avenues of Larsen's cross-exam were less fruitful. Zappala made the expected round of denials. He denied wrong-doing in the Port Authority and PLRB cases. Zappala said he was the court's "budget guy," and that's why Fumo had flown up on the plane provided by the Philadelphia mayor's office. He denied that he and Fumo tried to run over Larsen in front of the Four Season's hotel, denied hearing a doorman shout a warning to Larsen as the car went by. Larsen seemed truly amazed, to everyone else's amazement.

"Did you hear the bellman yell, 'watch out?'" Larsen asked Zappala.

"Can I ask, are you kidding me?" Zappala replied.

"No, I want you to—"

"I never heard a bellman," Zappala said.

"Let me be— excuse me—," Larsen sputtered.

"I never heard a bellman," Zappala repeated.

"Just wait a minute, please, okay?" Greenleaf interjected. "It's a question and answer. You're both talking at the same time and the stenographer can't take it down."

"I withdraw that question," Larsen said.

"No," Zappala countered, "I answered the question, senator. The answer is no, I never heard anything."

What, after all, had Larsen expected Zappala to say?

Larsen concluded by questioning Zappala about the latter's influence over the judicial disciplinary board, which supposedly polices the state courts. "Did one of your daughters ever work for the disciplinary board?" Larsen asked.

The house lawyer, Undercofler, immediately and predictably objected. No use letting the public think the disciplinary board was a sham.

Chairman Greenleaf seemed as concerned about this line of questioning as Undercofler. If the courts were crooked, and the disciplinary board was under Zappala's sway, why were they impeaching Larsen for alleging as much? Why were they all here?

"Is there a relevancy to this, Justice Larsen?" Greenleaf

asked. "Certainly, we've tried to give you an opportunity to ask every question. I don't understand where this is gong and what relevancy it is. If it is, we'll let you ask the question."

Larsen said, "If one's putting one's relatives in employment in the Supreme Court Disciplinary Board, then it develops there is some degree of control there. That bears out one of the allegations I had."

"I renew my objection," Undercofler said. "I'm aware of no such allegation."

"Which allegation are you referring to?" Greenleaf asked. These guys didn't seem to have a firm grasp of this saga.

Larsen recapped, "I've been charged with falsely swearing to a statement that I said, and I'm going to have to get into, that Justice Zappala had control through (John) Doherty in the disciplinary board system."

"Is that part of the recusal motion?" Greenleaf asked.

"Yes," Larsen replied. "It's part of the charges that that was false, and they brought Mr. Doherty in and he testified to that."

Undercofler recalled, "There's an allegation made by Justice Larsen that Justice Zappala and Justice Cappy, acting in concert, engineered the appointment of John Doherty as chief counsel of the disciplinary board."

"Well, that's not—" Larsen started to quarrel.

"Wait a minute," Greenleaf succumbed. "Just a minute. The objection is going to be overruled and we'll let you ask the question."

"All right," Larsen said.

"My understanding," Zappala replied, "is that when my daughter Dana Lynn got out of school, she worked as a receptionist for the disciplinary board for four months and then left there immediately and has since been and is currently employed by Blue Cross/Blue Shield of Western Pennsylvania."

"And how did she get that job with the disciplinary board?" Larsen probed.

Undercofler coughed, "I would object at this time because this is just so trivial, Mr. Chairman, that it strains reason to say that this is relevant."

"The objection is sustained," Greenleaf ruled.

Larsen, with that, rested his examination. "That's all I have," he said. "Note my exception, please."

The lawyers for the people, such as they were, had no further questions, and Greenleaf dismissed Zappala. "Thank you, very much, Justice Zappala, for being here today."

Zappala grudgingly rose. As the justice made his way out of the senate chamber the house attorneys, Republican and Democrat, flocked around the justice to bid him farewell. Here was the entire drama, and the people's dilemma, in miniature. Attorneys Moses and Undercofler, Piccola and Dermody, shamelessly fawned as they pumped Zappala's hand. Zappala's face betrayed obvious anguish, and the house lawyers looked to be consoling him. You could see that Zappala was upset that he had to appear, and these ambitious party lawyers who betrayed the public's trust by unfairly smearing Larsen appeared not to want the justice to hold any of it against them should they one day appear in his crooked courtroom. Onlookers in the visitors' gallery leaned over the railing to gawk down at this shameless display of one-sided Pennsylvania justice. The house lawyers practically were slobbering over Zappala, obviously uninterested in whether Pennsylvania courts were fair and impartial, not caring whether Zappala may have hurt the state, its people and its courts. They unabashedly sided with Zappala, and against Larsen. See you in court, judge, they seemed to be telling him.

From time to time we all fall down. It is a measure of our capital with others whether, in our moment of vulnerability, we are helped back up, or kicked in the teeth and knocked far down. And here the house lawyers of both parties were picking up Stephen Zappala, dusting him off, even as they were attempting to nail the lid down on Rolf Larsen. Sorry we had to call you in, judge, the lawyers seemed to be telling Zappala, but we had to get the bastard. While the lawyers solicitously pumped their man's hand, Larsen sat at his table, stone faced.

Stephen Zappala nevertheless left the senate chamber of

Pennsylvania a permanently damaged public figure. (Though, ironically, this gross abdication of justice would strengthen his family's hand in Pennsylvania. After all, the Zappala clan could say, hadn't they'd been given a clean bill of health by a massive, million dollar investigation and weeks of exhaustive impeachment hearings?) Nevertheless, Larsen had punched Zappala's ticket, trapping his former brethren into telling outrageous lies in the state's most august chamber. Any honest examination of Zappala's record will show him to be a dishonest, untrustworthy jurist. His only hope is continued institutional, deep-rooted corruption which, in Pennsylvania, may be a safe bet. In the bargain Larsen exposed the overwhelming, stupefying, stone-headed corruption of the bi-partisan leadership of our general assembly. Not a bad day's work, even if it cost him his career.

There were things that Larsen didn't cover in his cross-examination. I of course would have liked to hear the turnpike's Wagman case discussed. The Jellig case certainly would have made for fascinating conversation. There were, in short, entire avenues untouched by Larsen.

Larsen's cross-examination of Zappala made clear the political nature of the men who hold seats in our state's high court. Both Larsen and Zappala came across as small-time pols who rose through a political system. Neither man, nor any of the house lawyers, seemed particularly learned of the law, of society, of human nature. All, in the end, came across as beer hall politicians, products of democracy. These were not our finest, our fairest minds. Rolf Larsen had lifted the curtain. Behind the curtain was appallingly little of an elevated nature.

CHAPTER 23

Joke of a Joke

The impeachment trial, at least in substance, ended with Zappala's testimony. Proceedings would drag on in the state senate for six more weeks. Oh, other witnesses gave testimony, but the impeachment quickly de-evolved from a mere nasty, mean-spirited joke to a joke of a joke. Three of the biggest players in the scandal — Senator Vince Fumo, Philadelphia Mayor Ed Rendell, and Rendell's chief of staff, David Cohen — steadfastly refused to take the impeachment trial seriously enough to show up and testify.

House prosecutors had served a subpoena on Fumo, but (predictably) rested their case without calling him. Bill Costopoulos announced he wanted Fumo on the witness stand, that the state senator's testimony would be the "cornerstone" of the defense. At the height of the trial Fumo suddenly dropped from sight. It soon developed that Fumo was vacationing out-of-state in Martha's Vineyard, Massachusetts. Fumo soon demanded $1,000 from Larsen to charter a plane to fly back to testify. Here Fumo stood accused of demanding a chartered plane from the mayor of Philadelphia to fix a case, and now he was demanding $1,000 to charter another plane to deny everything.

Costopoulos angrily refused to shell out the thousand bucks. He raged on the floor of the senate, "We are not going to get ourselves in a position where we have to bargain or pay for anybody's testimony." The stand-off dragged on for days. Costopoulos in time told the increasingly embarrassed committee he'd ask for a mistrial if Fumo wouldn't honor the subpoena. "Should he fail to appear," Costopoulos said, "I intend to file a motion in the nature of a mistrial because we think this is fundamentally unfair. One of your very own ... is flaunting these proceedings."

Fumo's lawyer, Philadelphia attorney Robert Scandone, made an appearance before the committee to say that his client eventually would show up, yet predicted Fumo's testimony wouldn't shed much light. As for the air fare, Scandone intoned, "I'll send a bill to Mr. Costopoulos. If he doesn't pay it, the sad part is the senator will be stuck with it." So sad, so sad.

Fumo at last dropped his demand for cash and finally showed up empty handed before the committee, but not without first stipulating in a letter to Costopoulos that he wouldn't discuss certain matters. This stipulation in the end was backed-up by the senate committee, which sided with house prosecutors in limiting the scope of Fumo's grilling. The committee forbade the defense from questioning Fumo on many matters it characterized as irrelevant to impeachment articles, including whether Fumo regularly had his office checked for electronic bugs, Fumo's knowledge of the circumstances surrounding Larsen's prosecution for drugs, even Fumo's relationship with Justice Zappala.

"I was shut down," Costopoulos afterward complained to reporters. "We were not allowed to develop the political dimension in this political prosecution."

Fumo, for his part, on the witness stand predictably denied everything. He said Rendell's chief-of-staff had purloined him a plane as a favor. The resulting trip, he said, simply was an occasion for himself and Zappala to discuss court budgetary matters. He denied discussing the PLRB case with Zappala.

"Not only did I not discuss the case, I didn't know the case existed," Fumo told Costopoulos. "I'm offended you would suggest I would try to impugn the integrity of a Supreme Court justice by bringing it up." Yeah, right.

Ed Dennis's report, incidentally, apparently contradicts Fumo on this point. Dennis quotes Chief-of-Staff Cohen as telling investigators, "Cohen acknowledged that the airplane trip occurred five days before the city filed the *PLRB* case. He also acknowledged that the city was making plans to file the suit at this time. Further, he acknowledged that the city regularly briefed Senator Fumo and other key legislative figures during the course of the labor dispute which gave rise to the PLRB case, and that these briefings may have included the city's litigation strategy."

Vince Fumo has spent a career cultivating the (mostly overblown) notion that he is a king-maker of our state courts, with a hot-line leading to judicial benches across the state. Power is the perception of power, and Fumo likes people to think he has a wire on every court, a finger in every pie. Fumo's denial that he discusses cases with state judges no doubt provoked snickers in law firms around the state, the same as a smile would be drawn on the faces of clerics should the pope deny having discussed religion with the college of cardinals. Politicians seeking election to Pennsylvania's high benches must court the Philadelphia machine. That's simply the nature of elective politics in Pennsylvania.

It developed during questioning that Fumo, while vacationing in Massachusetts, had bumped into, of all people, Rendell's chief of staff, David Cohen. It's a small, small world. Fumo testified that the topic of the impeachment proceedings had come up in casual conversation between the two vacationing Pennsylvanians. The two, Fumo promised, hadn't spilled words about the mysterious plane ride to Zappala's summer home.

At least Fumo, in his own good time, accepted and submitted to the subpoena from the impeachment committee. The same couldn't be said for Mayor Rendell or his assistant, Mr. Cohen. The impeachment committee sent the senate's sergeant-at-arms to deliver supposedly enforceable subpoenas demanding the appearance of Rendell and Cohen. At the mayor's office at Philadelphia city hall a city police officer stationed at the door kicked out the sergeant-at-arms. At Cohen's office a secretary did the same. The sergeant-at-arms next tried the office of the city solicitor, who, like the others, refused to be served. The senate's security staff had to phone home for instructions, and ended up dropping the subpoenas on somebody's desk. This amazing twist caused chuckles in the state press, which wondered aloud whether the state senate held jurisdiction over Philadelphia.

This odd turn of events further shook the increasingly shaken Chairman Greenleaf, who pronounced the treatment of the senate's security officer as "outrageous." Greenleaf sounded more and more like Elmer Fudd, or Mr. Rogers. It wasn't vewy vewy funny, Greenleaf lectured. "Senate subpoenas are not something to ignore and treat the way they've treated it," Greenleaf tsked. He pointed out that Larsen's side had somehow managed to serve Rendell a subpoena, yet where were hizzonna and his aide? The committee was forced to recess for one week while Larsen tried to gain the appearances of his last four witness — Rendell, Cohen, reluctant Pittsburgh labor attorney Joseph Pass, and Justice Zappala's son, Gregory. Greenleaf, granting the recess, pointed out that those ignoring senate subpoenas risked serious sanctions, including jail terms. He didn't say who the senate's ultimate enforcer would be — Mr. McFeely or Good King Friday.

Rendell and Cohen obviously weren't too worried. At last they did appear. Both men predictably denied everything, saying they merely secured a plane for Fumo to make nice with Zappala as a favor to Fumo. It was best to placate Vince Fumo in these little social whims, Cohen suggested.

Though Rendell and Cohen finally did show up, this sideshow involving the impotent sergeant-at-arms cost the senate's impeachment tribunal what little mantle of credibility remained. It had become abundantly clear that some of the state's most prominent political leaders were treating Larsen's impeachment as a joke. The public by this time came around to the same opinion. If anyone in the real world spoke of the proceedings it was to remark about the colossal waste of money and time.

Who though could blame Rendell and Cohen? AG Preate's

non-investigation of Larsen's allegations and the subsequent drug charges against Larsen had been a travesty. The general assembly's looking the other way at same had been mob humor. The senate's kangaroo court was a blight on the American continent. Nobody was taking this farce seriously.

Me, I went off on a one-week vacation. I sat on the beach hoping, and suspecting, that the devil would take them all.

The cherry on the cake came when Justice Zappala's son, Gregory, subsequently tied up proceedings for a day or so by taking the impeachment committee to Commonwealth Court to protect his financial records. The court held that if young Zappala felt a request for particular records was irrelevant, Commonwealth Court President Judge James G. Colins would serve as an arbitrator. Earlier, you'll recall, when petitioned by Larsen, the courts had refused to delve into the legislature's impeachment prerogative.

Young Gregory Zappala proved that at least one Pennsylvanian felt secure in taking his business to state courts.

One by one the witnesses had trekked to Harrisburg to testify. Some, who didn't want to testify, got dragged in. Others, who wanted to testify, never were called. Some of the testimony stands out in memory. Psychiatrist Kathleen Dougherty, of the Hershey Medical Center, testified that Larsen was justified in having his doctor write prescriptions under the names of Larsen's employees. "If a doctor makes an ethical decision that it was necessary for the patient," Dougherty testified, "then the doctor would be ethically bound to do that, despite the law." She said the dosages of the drugs Prozac, Valium and Ativan taken by Larsen were consistent with treatment for clinical depression.

An attorney friend of Larsen's, James Schwartzman of Philadelphia, took the stand to deny ever having told Larsen about Fumo's plane ride to see Zappala. Though he was with Larsen the night in front of the Four Seasons Hotel, Schwartzman also denied having witnessed anything unusual.

Schwartzman expressed perplexment that Larsen had filed the charges, and said he was puzzled as to why Larsen continued to insist that Schwartzman had knowledge of these things. According to Ed Dennis's grand jury report, "Senator Fumo ... related that he has a very close relationship with Schwartzman."

One of the most interesting witnesses turned out to be one Ronald Persia, who worked as a doorman at the Four Seasons Hotel in Philadelphia. Persia's appearance on August 17 didn't receive much play in the state press, but it bolstered Larsen's account of curious events in front of the Four Seasons on the evening of December 7, 1992. Persia turned out to be a well-educated young man, holding two bachelor degrees in exercise physiology and nursing. He explained he worked off and on at the hotel for nine years, filling in as a part-time doorman or bellman.

The night in question, Persia testified, Larsen got out of the passenger's side of a car in front of the hotel. Persia approached, but Larsen "waved me off because he was still talk-ing to the driver of the car." Persia returned to the door of the hotel. Shortly thereafter, Persia said, a "dark blue or brown" Mercedes pulled slowly into the hotel driveway. The Mercedes "looked like it was going to stop." As the Mercedes approached the front door Larsen was turning away from the car from which he had alighted. Suddenly the Mercedes picked up speed. The Mercedes was suddenly traveling faster than usual for the hotel driveway, Persia said. "I yelled 'watch out,' or 'look out,'" at Larsen, Persia said. "I wasn't sure if he had seen the car that was coming down that lane or if he knew that the car was not going to stop at the front door. I just— I didn't know if he had seen the car at all." Had Larsen continued moving, Persia said, the car might have struck the justice. "He may have been (struck) if he continued to move forward." Larsen, hearing the warning, stepped back out of the way, Persia recounted.

Persia testified, "Justice Larsen asked me— well, first, he said to me, 'Thanks for yelling "look out."'" And then he looked at the end of the driveway at the same time that I did as the car exited onto Cherry Street." He described Larsen as "very thankful. It was like, (his) expression was like, whew, thank you. I don't know how to explain it."

Approximately fifteen to thirty minutes later, Persia testified, a dark Mercedes resembling the fast-moving car in question returned to the hotel. Justice Stephen Zappala alighted from the passengers side of the Mercedes, Persia testified. Later it would be learned that Vince Fumo was behind the wheel.

Toward the end of the testimony, in mid-August, another of Larsen's lawyer friends, Richard Gilardi, of Pittsburgh, took the stand. Gilardi testified he'd known Larsen since the mid-1960s, when Gilardi had begun his law practice. Larsen "went on to the bench," Gilardi said, and "I got to know him very well. I tried lawsuits for a living, and I tried my first case, I believe, in front of him in 1974, and I tried several cases in front of him, and I became very friendly with him as a result of that." Gilardi went on to help Larsen in his political campaigns. "I represent a lot of labor unions," Gilardi said. "I did support him, I got him labor union endorsements and I supported him financially when he ran for the Supreme Court."

In April 1988 Gilardi won an appointment to the court's disciplinary board for a three-year term, then was re-appointed for another three years. During his second term he became vice-chairman, then chairman of the board.

Gilardi's testimony focused on an odd meeting between Gilardi and Justice Larsen in Larsen's chambers in May 1988. At the time Gilardi was handling two cases pending before the high court.

"I told Justice Larsen that I had two matters pending before the Supreme Court which had interesting issues in them, and I asked him to read the papers," Gilardi testified. "He told me to bring him the cover sheets, which are the captions."

"Did you photocopy the cover sheets?" Moses asked.

"Yes sir."

"And did you take them, as he instructed you, to his chambers?"

"Yes, sir."

"Do you recall when you delivered those documents, per his request, to his chambers?"

"I believe it was in, sometime in May of 1988."

What happened in Larsen's chambers? Gilardi was asked.

"When I went to the chambers and brought — and when I had mentioned it, that I had two interesting cases before the court, I didn't discuss the merits of the case. He told me to bring the cover sheets to him," Gilardi continued.

"I brought the cover sheets to him. When I got up there, he asked me to write my position on the cover sheet. In other words, yes in the case of Driscoll, because my position was advocating the allowance of the appeal. And he asked me to write my position on the Buttermore case, which was no, and in that case, we were opposing the petition for the allowance of the appeal."

At the time, Gilardi said, he didn't think he'd done anything unethical. "Well, in retrospect," he testified, "putting the 'yes' or 'no' on that — I did it and I thought nothing of it because he requested it. And upon reflection, putting the 'yes' or 'no' on it could be construed as having a discussion on the merits."

Larsen's request was strange and didn't make much sense, Gilardi reflected. He pointed out the obvious: the notations denoting Gilardi's position on the two cases certainly weren't needed to help inform or sway Larsen, if that had been Larsen's intent. "I don't know what difference that would make to a justice," Gilardi puzzled. "When he asked me to do that, I thought it was strange, because the petition on its face shows who represents who."

After more than a month of hearings, on September 9, 1994, at 9:30 in the evening, the impeachment committee finally gaveled to a close. Rep. Dermody thanked the committee on behalf of the house managers. Costopoulos too thanked the committee, chief Sergeant-at-Arms Charles Hippensteel and staff (who, Costopoulos said, made them comfortable "through this awful ordeal"), and the stenographers. (An interesting side note is that in early 1996 I went to interview senate Sergeant-at-Arms Charles Hippensteel only to learn that he had been fired from his job and was facing criminal prosecution for an alleged long-running scheme involving the theft of postage stamps from the state senate. When writing about government, I've learned, you have to move fast lest you lose potential interviewees to the jailer.)

"I want to state," Costopoulos concluded, "it's nothing personal, it's strictly professional, but I don't have anything to say to the house managers.

"Regarding Justice Larsen, I want Justice Larsen to know from the day I met him in March of 1993, a year and a half ago plus, I cared about him then and I care about him now, and I've been proud to represent him, and my prayers are with him."

Something about Costopoulos's venom for the house prosecutors doesn't quite ring true. I certainly didn't attend this final session, as it would've taken a firing squad to get me out of the house at 9:30 at night to listen to these jokers. I must have been present at another milestone, such as when the prosecution rested its case. Anyway, I recall Costopoulos going up to the house lawyers and warmly shaking their hands in the senate gallery in the jocular way of lawyers who've rested. Good ol' Bill. Once adversaries, now they're Brothers of the Bar, and all's forgiven and forgotten. Ah, lawyers. Anyone else who'd been fighting tooth-and-nail for months could never so easily brush off the slings and arrows. Lawyers, after all, are advocates for hire, for pay, for money. They only pretend to take sides, to take offense. The rest of us, litigants, citizens, writers, carry our grudges like the true wounds that they are.

One of my strongest recollections of the impeachment trial was of Costopoulos and the house lawyers, at the end of the day, warmly schmoozing with each other and congratulating each other on a job well done. As Costopoulos made nice with the likes of Moses and Dermody and Undercofler and Piccola, Rolf Larsen, as always, as ever, sat alone, by himself at the defense table.

In the end, Costopoulos had put up a good fight. He'd done a creditable job of raising questions about the Zappala bonding empire and the political nature of the impeachment. I know he'd pulled punches. Costopoulos didn't go as far as he could have, and should have in the public interest. Why had he not explored Zappala's indefensible intervention in the turnpike's Wagman case? What other cases had Costopoulos ignored, and why? Perhaps, if we're to speculate, tactical reasons existed for pulling punches: Larsen certainly was already in enough trouble. Why stir up more? Then again, how could Costopoulos justify not digging up every known funny case handled by Zappala? Didn't Costopoulos have an ethical obligation to show Larsen had been operating with just cause when he'd voiced concern about Zappala's questionable interventions? Wouldn't those questions have further undermined the legitimacy of the impeachment process?

Costopoulos's job was to defend Rolf Larsen. Prosecuting Justice Stephen Zappala, or bringing down the House of Zappala, was arguably outside the job description. That job and that public trust rested with state Attorney General Ernest Preate, and his selected prosecutor, Ed Dennis. Personally and professionally, you could argue that bringing down Justice Zappala was too much for Costopoulos, acting all but alone. Some have shared the speculation with me that Costopoulos may have his eye on entering state politics, perhaps to run for the office of attorney general. A prudent, conventional pol wouldn't take on the Zappala bonding enterprise and its underwriting of our legislature and the political parties. Look what happened to Larsen. Perhaps Costopoulos chose not to commit professional and political suicide. You don't throw away your bar license on a single case, one observer pointed out to me. To do otherwise would truly have been to take on the legalized mob.

CHAPTER 24

Star-Chamber Justice

The full senate met to hear closing arguments in the impeachment trial on September 27, 1994. Senator Greenleaf, chairman of the impeachment committee, took the floor to offer the final 260-page report of his committee. The report, Greenleaf pointed out, included some four thousand pages of transcripts, as well as daily videotaping of the proceedings. It did not, however, contain recommendations.

Greenleaf was followed by Senator Hardy Williams of Philadelphia, a member of the impeachment committee. Williams pointed out that the sheer volume of transcripts made it impossible for his fellow senators to render a quick, never mind fair, verdict. Williams said his reading of the senate rules required, "that this report have some recommendations, some conclusions or some guides for the resolution of the body." Williams went on, "We're talking about an impeachment proceeding which is probably more important than any other proceeding that we could conceive of when it comes to evaluating it thoroughly, historically, and fairly. Absent some guide here, we would require all the senators who were not there for six weeks daily to hear this testimony, to judge in the dark, to guess, to speculate, to go by hearsay or news reports, and, indeed, to talk to each other as we're doing, rather than in the light of day. An impeachment proceeding, if it should be anything, should not be a star-chamber proceeding." Williams pointed out that the rules read, "After receiving the report, the senate may...receive additional evidence...before making its final judgment." It might not be a bad idea to hear additional evidence, Williams said. Williams seemed to be the only honest, concerned man in the chamber — at least, the only one who spoke up. A silent honest man is of little value.

Other senators immediately pounced on Williams. Senator Craig Lewis, of Bucks County, another member of the committee and himself perpetually mentioned as a candidate for state attorney general, complained of Williams' assertion "that there may be a perception that things have been conducted in the fashion of a star chamber. I believe that all who observed and participated in the conduct of the impeachment trial committee believe, without reservation, that fairness and impartiality and particularly openness were the hallmarks of the work of this committee." (As one who observed much of the proceedings, I certainly disagree with Lewis. I'm sure most of those I met in the visitors' gallery would also disagree with him. The senate impeachment committee may have been a polite firing squad, quick to offer the blind fold, but that's about the best you can say for it.) "Every action taken, every decision made," Lewis blubbered on, "was discussed and handled in a public forum." So what if the committee suppressed evidence and allowed the house managers to blight democracy by bullying Larsen on an obscene scale?

"To me," Lewis droned on, with every word undermining his own point, "the term 'star chamber' represents inquisitional types of conduct that were conducted in the Middle Ages in which truth or justice or fairness or openness were never to be found, but merely the whim and the caprice of those who held power at the time was brought to bear." I don't think I could have said it better myself. If the shoe fits, senator. "I believe that implying in any fashion that the work of this committee reflected a star-chamber proceeding is not only inaccurate but unfair to all of us who participated in that."

These backbiting preliminaries out of the way, the house managers rose to summarize their case. The hypocrisy of their words rang clearly. As bullying tyrants are prone to do, their false words made mockeries of themselves. Rep. Jeffrey Piccola began by observing that, "the legitimacy of our judicial system as a public institution is completely dependent upon the strict adherence of each judge to a duty of impartiality, respect for the law, and respect for the institution of the court. Our citizens have an absolute constitutional right to have the important matters in their lives decided fairly and properly within the law when they got to court." Piccola went on, "This right to due process and the fair and proper administration of justice is meaningless unless we can count on the independence, impartiality, and integrity of every judge in our judicial system."

Why then had Piccola and his cohorts protected Justice Zappala, when Piccola and his fellow inquisitors knew that Zappala had time and again intervened in cases involving his own brother or his law partner? Why had they prohibited all discussion of Zappala's misconduct? Why hadn't Piccola pursued the Wagman case? Why had they shamefully gone after Larsen's use of prescription drugs?

And so the bully blowhards droned on in the senate, explaining all manner of wonders they had accomplished, and waxing that, with wicked Rolf Larsen out of the way, Pennsylvania's courts were now fair and free of blight.

William Costopoulos, in his closing argument on behalf of Larsen before the full senate, pointed out, "And you know, nobody ever, in the history of this country, let alone the history of Pennsylvania, was charged criminally for getting his medications that he was entitled to in the names of his secretaries. And let me tell you, that prosecution got ugly.

"They charged him with twenty-seven felony counts — one conspiracy count for asking his doctor to do it, and twenty-six different felony counts because he was charged with every time his secretary went to the pharmacy, they added a count. We went to a preliminary hearing in Pittsburgh, Pennsylvania. Those charges were leveled by the attorney general's office four days before the primary. We went to the preliminary hearing in Pittsburgh, Pennsylvania, and we had to deal with a swarm of media. First question, walking through that swarm into the courthouse: 'Mr. Costopoulos, how's Justice Larsen's mind.' Do you think that stigma was a figment of his imagination?

"We went before a magistrate, a committing judge. All he had to do was determine whether there was a prima facie case. And he concluded, and I'm quoting from the record, 'My finding is that these charges that have been alleged against Justice Larsen were not in the course or in connection with his office or employment as a Supreme Court Justice.' And he threw thirteen of the twenty-eight counts out because they went beyond the statute of limitations, and the public record is conclusive from a magistrate that there's not even a prima facie showing that he used his office or his employment.

"We're now stuck with fifteen counts. The attorney general's office jumps up and says, 'Well, we're going to add a count for violating the medical standards in the community.' What does Justice Larsen know about violating medical standards in the community? This wasn't even a crime. All right?"

Costopoulos said the AG's office told him, "'You represent Justice Larsen, we'll give you probation without verdict, we'll give you ARD, under one condition — he resign.' No." ARD, or Accelerated Rehabilitative Disposition, is a probation program meant for first-time offenders.

Costopoulos continued, "The attorney general wanted to deliver Larsen's head to the public. The attorney general was running for governor, but the attorney general had his own agenda, and we're not going to give him Justice Larsen's head to be made pubic fodder out of in his campaign that he cleaned up the Supreme Court, because these charges should never have been brought, not on these facts.

"And you know what the jury did? Justice Larsen had always admitted that he did this. Those fourteen counts were that I did what you say I did. I did ask Dr. Humphreys to give me the medications I was entitled to. And I got them. And the conspiracy was that he asked his doctor to do that, and the overt acts were that which he admitted he was doing. The jury didn't find a reasonable doubt as to whether he did it not not. He admitted it. And what the jury found him guilty of was conspiracy to do that which they said wasn't a crime. And that's what the attorney general's office had left when we were done

— a conspiracy to commit a crime that the jury said wasn't a crime, and we have taken that on appeal."

He said the AG's office next told them, "'Well, Mr. Costopoulos, we got a conviction now. We want twenty-three months in jail.'"

"'You're kidding,'" he said he told them.

"'We want him to pay a million dollars back to the commonwealth because that's how much we paid the private law firms in Philadelphia, having deputized them as attorney generals.'

"'You're kidding.'

"'And we go to court now and we've got to fight to stay out of jail because he had asked his secretary to pick up his prescriptions from his doctor that his doctor said he could have. That's getting ugly. They wanted a million dollars. They wanted to take everything he owned. They wanted to take his home, they wanted to take his furniture. They wanted to take his car. They wanted to take his accounts, because he wouldn't resign and give the attorney general his head.

"The day before we go for sentencing, a phone call comes in. 'We want him removed. We're seeking his removal. That's the first time we heard about that. And you want to know something, Mr. and Madame Senators? In my heart, I'm glad you didn't give that removal order out in Pittsburgh any dignity or respect, because it doesn't deserve it. And that removal order is on appeal, this conviction is on appeal, and if everybody was concerned before this impeachment proceedings went forward that he might win this thing on appeal, you're right."

"Well, what about this commandeering of a vehicle and attempting to run Justice Larsen down?" Costopoulos asked the senators. "All I can tell you about that incident is that something happened. There was a young man that came in here and testified, he was a doorman. His name was Ron Persia. He didn't know anything about politics. He's not running for office. He doesn't hold office. He's just a nice young man that opens doors for a living at the Four Seasons Hotel. And what he testified to was that on the night in question, Justice Larsen was getting out of a car and he was going to walk across the breezeway to get onto the sidewalk and a black Mercedes or a dark Mercedes came close to him at a high rate of speed where he, the doorman, had to yell, 'watch out,' and Larsen jumped out of the way. And it was subsequently learned that in that car were Justice Zappala and Vincent Fumo. Vincent was driving. Do I believe they tried to kill Justice Larsen? No, I don't believe that. Is Vince capable of having some fun? Vince is really capable of having some fun."

The senate chamber erupted in laughter.

"And I like Vince," Costopoulos went on. "But it happened, and Justice Larsen perceived it, rightfully or wrongfully, the way he alleged it in his petition. Ron Persia testified that Larsen got out of the car, a car came around the oval from the street that is parallel to the hotel, and that he yelled 'watch out' to Justice Larsen, who stopped immediately and moved backward, and that if he hadn't yelled 'watch out,' Justice Larsen would have been struck by the speeding car. That's the doorman. It happened. We're not looking for criminal citations. He didn't file a civil lawsuit. He made this averment in his petitions for recusal.

"The reason we're here is because he filed these petitions and he pointed the finger at what he believed to be improper conduct by members of the Supreme Court. You guys are considering a whistleblower statute. I don't know what the status of it is, but if this happens to somebody that steps out of line, we're all in trouble."

Costopoulos rose to great eloquence in this closing statement. He summed up Larsen's successes, his rise to the Supreme Court "at the young age of forty-three."

Yet it hadn't been an easy road. "There was another side to Larsen that not too many people knew about — you certainly didn't, the media didn't, the public didn't — that goes back in time to his childhood years," Costopoulos said. For the senators he sketched a life that contrasted markedly from the privileged, insiders' lives of the Zappala clan. "You know, he was in a lot of pain back then. Our psychiatric schools tell us that that might be due to a chemical imbalance, that it might be due to one's history. Everybody agrees it's due to both. And his history is in his growing up years, in his high school years, when our kids would be out playing, he would go home every lunch time and attend to his ailing mother who was suffering from multiple sclerosis. He would take her to the bathroom, he would feed her by hand, and he buried his mother in her early forties who died from multiple sclerosis. His father died in his early sixties from Parkinson's disease. His oldest brother — he came from a family of five — attends Alcoholics Anonymous four times a week. He's got a twin brother that suffered from a heart attack and is one hundred-percent disabled. He had one sister — he buried her when she was twenty-eight from alcohol and drug abuse. And his youngest brother is okay now, but he was once addicted.

"And this family did not lack abuse, and it was in that environment that Justice Larsen was doing well. A brilliant lawyer, a good mind, a good person, he was the only member of his family to graduate from college. He knew he had pain in him that he couldn't quite define. You know, William Styron wrote a book called *Darkness Visible,* where this brilliant author tried to define the depths of depression and the depths of anxiety. And Styron indicated it's not definable. You can't appreciate it if you haven't experienced it. But it's like every day is gray, even when it shouldn't be. And many days are black.

"And it was that kind of day that Justice Larsen was experiencing when he sought help thirty years ago. He sought help to try to address that pain, to try to rise above it, and I'm proud of him for it. And for thirty years, Justice Larsen has been seeing a psychiatrist almost weekly, and for thirty years Justice Larsen has been taking medication. This isn't a red herring that the defense has come up with to justify or mitigate anything. This is the person Justice Larsen.

"You know, and on the witness stand you really had to watch him testify to appreciate what I'm talking about. The members of the senate impeachment committee saw it. You really had to see him sitting over there at the defense table with ten prosecutors across from him to appreciate and understand what that mental illness can do to you.

"But he made up his mind a long time ago that he didn't want to pass on what he defined as the Larsen curse to his only daughter, age thirty-seven, that he loves very much. And his whole world today as I address you is his granddaughter, Leah, who's four and a half months old. And if there's one thing he's holding on to, it's that grandchild and the love of life and the philosophy that he studied and the treatment that he's received as we speak.

"What's Justice Larsen doing? I'm asked by every member of media, by everybody that walks up to me on the street. He's hanging in there. And that's who Justice Larsen is."

While Larsen was hanging in there, and while Pennsylvania's corrupt lawmakers blubbered bombast on the floor of the senate, about two hundred Pennsylvanians gathered close by in the capitol rotunda to protest their court system and the absurdity of the impeachment proceedings. This rally, I should confess, wasn't a surprise to me. Earlier that summer, as the impeachers were just putting on their shoes, I received several phone calls from women who complained that they and other Pennsylvania women had been unfairly tied up in divorce court for years. They'd been networking and wanted to do something to draw attention to the problems of Pennsylvania's court system. I gave them the names of others I knew around the state who'd expressed the same disgust with Pennsylvania courts, and suggested everybody get together for a gathering in the capitol rotunda.

Three bus loads of unhappy Pennsylvanians showed at the rotunda to share their disgust with the court system. It was the very day the state's lawmakers were in the senate chamber advancing their theory that the courts were now right as rain. Me, I was out in the rotunda with the people. I figured the devil could, and would, have the lawmakers.

It was a an interesting gathering. The protesters filled the rotunda. They weren't just divorced women. It was a cross-section of Pennsylvanians who'd been screwed by the courts. Fathers who'd been screwed in custody or support hearings. Businessmen who'd lost everything to unscrupulous lawyers. Mothers who's lost their kids. Most with endless stories of procedural violations or out-and-out unfairness and lawbreaking in the courts. It seemed a lonely hearts club of those whom the system had failed. And none had been contacted by representatives of the impeachment committees, or the attorney general's investigators, to tell their stories.

They took turns at the rotunda podium sharing their horror legal stories. The only lawmaker in attendance, state representative George Saurman, of suburban Philadelphia, said a few words about the travesty we were witnessing. Several around me shook their heads, voicing amazement that only one elected representative was standing with the people. Among those I met was Norma Jean Johnson, whose husband, a pilot, had filed for divorce in 1991. She complained she's unfairly lost every round in court. With her was Charlotte Bogart, of Harrisburg, whose divorce had been dragging on in the courts for, she said, seventeen years. Both women had a motherly air about them. A principal organizer of the rally, Carolee Medico, from Scranton, shared similar divorce horror stories. Medico's husband was a prominent businessman in his community and she'd lost round after round in court. Another organizer, Humphrey Perez, also of Scranton, told me his background was in the logical world of computer programming. The irregularities in Medico's case, he said, were so far removed from the logical, flow-chart order he was used to, he'd come to realize there was a deep problem in Pennsylvania courts. Perez and Medico had started a reform group, Legal Focus, and were attempting to network with other Pennsylvania court victims.

Another victim at the rally was Larry Hohol, of Wilkes-Barre, who'd sold his medical supply business to a group who, he said, later refused to pay him the agreed upon price. He took them to court, but his adversaries hired a lawyer who succeeded in steering the case to a judge who was a former law partner. Hohol lost in court, lost his business, and went broke. Conflicts like this seem to happen every day in Pennsylvania. The judge in question retired before the judicial conduct board could investigate.

Also present was John Gagliardi, of Clairton, outside Pittsburgh, a warehouse owner. In the 1970s Gagliardi had caught one of his tenants, Bell of Pennsylvania, destroying telephone equipment, presumably to pass along the loss to consumers. He blew the whistle on Bell, which yanked his contract, beginning a twenty-year odyssey in the state courts, complete with outrageous conflicts and one surprise court hearing scheduled on a Memorial Day, when the court house was supposed to be closed.

Also at the rally was Robert Surrick, the judicial reformer and supreme court candidate I'd met that spring at the Common Cause meeting. He laughed heartily at the bombast emanating from the senate chamber. "These guys just want to see how many times they can stab Larsen's body!" he'd guffaw.

This rally was not reported by the state's two large monopoly newspapers, the Philadelphia Inquirer/Daily News, or the Pittsburgh Post-Gazette. The Associated Press incorrectly reported that only "about fifty people" attended the rally. "More than two hundred people were there and signed our register," Medico complained to me about the AP. "We had three bus loads and many more who drove down in their own cars." Small regional papers more accurately covered the event, though these publications were easier for the politicians to ignore. For some reason the largest papers and news service either completely ignored the event or drastically played it down.

As victim after victim of Pennsylvania courtrooms paraded to the podium to tell their stories, I watched two Philadelphia Daily News reporters, John Baer and Robert Warner, walk through the rally without even breaking their stride, up the sweeping rotunda staircase, ignoring the victimized people in front of them. The Daily News, like the Inquirer, is owned by

Knight-Ridder. Warner and Baer, on their way to the lynching, wore identical khaki suits. They were on their way, it's a safe bet, to the senate chamber, to report in their paper what the senators were saying. They didn't appear at all interested in what ordinary Pennsylvanians had to say. These men were on their hurried way to see the settling of scores that had been unpaid for ten years. They were a type of walking dead. They were deaf and blind to the current concerns of current people.

The big surprise came with the outcome. On Tuesday, October 4, 1994, the full state senate finally voted on the seven articles of impeachment lodged against Rolf Larsen. In the end, the senate acquitted Larsen on six of the seven counts, convicting him on only one.

On Article I, that Larsen kept a special list of cases pending before the Supreme Court to help his lawyer friends and political supporters receive favorable judicial review, Larsen was acquitted, twenty-four votes to twenty-five.

On Article II, that Larsen met with Pittsburgh attorney Richard Gilardi in early 1988 and agreed to personally review two of Gilardi's cases, Larsen was convicted, forty-four votes to four. This count involved the episode where Gilardi wrote "yes" and "no" on the piece of paper.

Article III, that Larsen lied to the grand jury "investigating" the high court when he denied ever having discussed the two cases with Gilardi; acquitted, thirty-one votes to eighteen.

Article IV, that Larsen improperly contacted Allegheny County Common Pleas Judge Eunice Ross concerning a pending case involving another lawyer friend of Larsen's, acquitted, twenty-eight votes to twenty-one.

Article V, that Larsen deliberately misused the legal process when he made "unfounded" accusations of criminal and judicial misconduct against Justices Zappala and Cappy, acquitted, twenty-seven votes to twenty-one.

On Article VI, that Larsen misused his position as a Supreme Court justice to induce his employees to engage in a criminal scheme to help Larsen obtain prescription drugs, acquitted, twenty-six votes to twenty-three.

On Article VII, that Larsen's conduct undermined public confidence in the judicial process, acquitted, twenty-three votes to twenty-six.

A majority of senators didn't believe Larsen lied when he accused Justice Stephen Zappala of misconduct. This seems to indicate the senators had problems with Justice Zappala's public conduct. They also refused, much to their credit, to buy into the sleazy charges involving the prescription drugs. (Larsen, curiously, also was acquitted on the charges involving Judge Eunice Ross. Zappala's decision to uphold the disciplinary charges lodged against Larsen for the Ross episode had started the ball rolling.)

The count involving Gilardi was the only one to stick in the state senate. Even this charge was weak and puzzling. Gilardi's involvement in the two cases in question, and the outcome preferred by Gilardi, was no secret.

Nevertheless, having been convicted of this charge, Rolf Larsen was formally and permanently removed from office, and barred from ever again holding public office in Pennsylvania. This would prevent a court appeal from reinstating Larsen.

To some this outcome was puzzling, since Larsen had already been removed from office by a judge. Perhaps the majority of state senators merely wanted to drive a stake through Rolf Larsen's public heart. With the single vote for conviction, they had ensured that Rolf Larsen, ever litigious, would never succeed in overturning his ouster by the court.

A few weeks after the vote I asked several state senators for their thousands of pages of impeachment transcripts. I explained that the transcripts were invaluable for a book I'd been planning. The transcripts ran 3,680 pages long. The state senate, the bastion of public non-service, was charging fifty cents per page. A complete set of transcripts, if purchased through the senate, would cost nearly two thousand dollars. Not too many citizens could avail themselves. In fact, not a single citizen had asked for the senate's service, a secretary told me. I pointed out that commercial copying services only charged three to five cents a copy. "We're not a business," the secretary told me with disinterest.

So I asked two state senators for their transcripts. Both senators agreed. I only had to pick up one set, and could leave the other for reserve. I was directed to a senate office, where a secretary pointed to a large cardboard carton under a table in a corner of the office. The carton was filled with book after book of bound transcripts, prepared by court reporters, chronologically ordered, a book for each day of the hearings, each indexed by key words. The transcripts seemed fresh and unthumbed. None appeared to have been opened or read.

I had to strain to pick up the box. I feared I'd bust my gut as I tottered through the capitol, through the Harrisburg streets, to the parking garage and home. Once home I dropped the box with a thud on the bathroom scale. It weighed nearly forty-five pounds. I rested the box in my study, among the piles of paper documenting a particularly cruel season.

Part Four

A mob is a strange phenomenon. It is a gathering of heterogeneous elements, unknown to one another (except on some essential points such as nationality, religion, social class); but as soon as a spark of passion, having flashed out from one of these elements, electrifies this confused mass, there takes places a sort of sudden organization, a spontaneous generation. This incoherence becomes cohesion, this noise become a voice, and these thousands of men crowded together soon form a single animal, a wild beast without a name, which marches to its goal with an irresistible finality. The majority of these men would have assembled out of pure curiosity, but the fever of some of them soon reaches the minds of all, and in all of them there arises a delirium. The very man who came running to oppose the murder of an innocent person is the first to be seized with the homicidal contagion, and moreover, it does not occur to him to be astonished at this.

Gabriel Tarde
The Penal Philosophy (1912)
Quoted in *Among the Thugs*

A mob is man descending to the level of beast.

Ralph Waldo Emerson

CHAPTER 25

What Happened Here?

Late in 1995 Pennsylvania Attorney General Ernest Preate Jr. accepted a plea bargain involving federal mail fraud violations and resigned from office. He admitted that he had mailed false campaign finance reports concealing illegal cash donations from the video poker operators.

Preate's plea agreement was announced by, of all people, Ed Dennis, now Preate's personal attorney, though paid by state funds. Dennis's statement included words to the effect that Preate was praying and was sure of God's mercy. This was more than a year after Dennis had exonerated the U.S. Justice Department for the siege at Waco, yet only several months after the demolition at the federal building in Oklahoma City.

It seemed jarring to hear Ed Dennis mention God's mercy. Hey Ed, who do you think those kids in Waco were praying to when the tanks rolled in? Those kids the FBI refused to give milk? The kids kept awake by the incessant playing of loud music over FBI speakers in the middle of the night? Who showed those kids mercy. Did anybody hear those kids pray. Who was there to defend those kids? What did you do for those kids, Ed? How's the bank account, Ed? How do *you* sleep, Ed?

In early 1996 Preate was sentenced to fourteen months in federal prison. To the end Pennsylvania's former chief law enforcement officer sounded unrepentant. Preate told the judge his moment of sentencing came on the lowest day of his life, yet, on his way from the sentencing hearing, on the steps of the federal courthouse, he told reporters he could serve the four-teen months in the federal pen standing on his head. To the end he trivialized his misdeeds, filing a brief with the sentencing judge describing his breach of public trust as "a rather simple campaign finance violation." He didn't even address his grand jury manipulations which, after all, had been obscured from the public by his plea agreement. His brethren in the justice administration business had successfully closed the door to scrutiny. No use allowing the public too close a look.

Had Preate not made the plea agreement he would have been indicted. Preate's father, Ernest Sr., of Scranton, died in June 1995, on the week the attorney general was to have been indicted. Preates Sr. and Jr. seemed to have been a study in contrasts. The former attorney general's father, Preate Sr., was welled loved. Preate Sr., born in Pescopagano, Italy, in 1909, was a small town attorney who was fiercely proud of his ethnicity, proud of his working-class roots, a man who helped many people. His son was a bad seed, a spoiled upper-middle-class brat blessed with a gift of gab that aided his career as a trial attorney and allowed him to rise in politics. Unlike his father, there are countless stories of Ernie Jr.'s unthankfulness. Attorneys who helped Ernie Jr. in various adventures, such as his vindictive disassembly of the Pennsylvania Crime Commission, privately complain that Preate Jr. never even called to say thanks.

It's said in Scranton that Preate Sr., on his deathbed, told his son to get the federal investigation behind him and do the time. Preate Jr. put word out that he was really not guilty, that he had accepted the plea bargain to get the feds off the backs of his two brothers, who also found themselves under investigation for their roles in his political campaigns. In Ernie Jr.'s mind everyone's to blame but himself. Ground zero is vacant.

Many questions are left unanswered by the plea agreement. The public never got a full accounting of Preate's crimes against his people and his state. Had AG Preate illegally and unfairly aided other campaign donators? We only get a few peeks behind the law man's door. Federal prosecutors, for example, told the sentencing judge that the state Republican committee had funneled some $60,000 to Preate's campaigns in 1988 and 1989, at least $34,000 of which had been transmitted through the committee by Chambers Development Corp., a suburban Pittsburgh waste management firm under scrutiny by the AG's office.

More to the point of our impeachment story, what of the nearly $20,000 in campaign contributions Preate had accepted from those involved with the bonding firm Russell, Rea and Zappala? Before Larsen's impeachment, when I approached the attorney general's investigators with concerns about Justice Zappala's handling of the turnpike's Wagman case, I was rebuffed. Were other leads similarly ignored? At the time I gave Preate the benefit of the doubt and thought he was merely a dull knuckle head. Now we know he was a corrupt criminal who looked the other way at the dishonest activities of his political donors.

Following Preate's imprisonment the newly appointed state attorney general questioned why Ed Dennis's law firm, Morgan Lewis & Bockius, billed the state $440,000 for Preate's defense. This sum was in addition to the $240,000 Dennis bilked the state for his "investigation" of the state Supreme Court. Dennis's charges for the defense of Preate included approximately $2,000 spent conducting a backgound check of U.S. Attorney General Janet Reno. (Ed, she was the one who ordered the tanks to move in Waco.) Dennis charged state taxpayers more than $100,000 for a single legal paper known as a declination document, sent to federal prosecutors to explain why Preate should not have been charged with a crime. Preate's replacement allocated an additional $25,000 for a deputy attorney general to look into Dennis's billing of the Preate defense. Here we have another investigation of an investigation. Justice never seems to get done when Ed Dennis is involved.

As for Larsen's traducement and impeachment, an obvious question begs to be asked: What happened here?

Larsen, learning of Fumo's plane ride to see Justice Zappala on the eve of the PLRB King's Bench petition, obviously calculated that he had Zappala. In an honest government, with the involvement of honest investigators and prosecutors, perhaps he would have had him. Larsen didn't count on Preate being a dishonest crook, and he didn't count on the involvement of Mr. Whitewash, Ed Dennis.

Preate, we should remember, was running for governor, and no doubt felt a high-profile prosecution involving Larsen could only help his chances. The feds closing in on Preate, the attorney general may not have had the political strength to take on the House of Zappala and its legions of benefactees. The mob after all was screaming for Larsen, and Preate and Dennis obliged by setting free Barabbas.

Others suggest Preate had a more personal agenda, that Preate and his brothers once approached Larsen for help in a private court matter. Larsen had declined to help, and now Preate was paying him back. Does it matter?

Once Preate and Dennis abdicated their responsibility and public trust, and instead floated the drug smear of Larsen, the mob climbed on the rotten vehicle.

I've come to view the impeachment of Rolf Larsen as a case study of mob dynamics. In my life I've found myself involved in many crusades, some popular, some unpopular, some successful and some not. It's certainly nice to win, and it's always nice to have the crowd on your side. In my life I've never felt so lonely as when I decided to stick up for Rolf Larsen.

I came away from Larsen's impeachment with insights into human behavior, and insights into the nature of our government and our constitution.

Our constitution of checks and balances was handed down to us by our founders not because we're such fine fellows deserving of it, but because our founders were keen observers of human nature. They understood that human behavior sometimes sinks to the base acts of animals, and that unchecked power breeds tyranny, greed, corruption and injustice.

We have a broad-based government of divided powers designed with the hope that it will not all fail at once. If one branch of government fails, another section hopefully will correct the failure. We have evolved in that government a professional justice system, meant to keep the business of justice removed from the whims of mobs, politics and passing fancy. Our constitution seeks to protect the rights of all, and seeks to ensure government lives up to standards of conduct. In Larsen's impeachment we saw a breakdown of those checks and standards.

Pennsylvania courts have long been held hostage by politics. Justices Larsen and Zappala after all were politicians, and their day-to-day practice of politics in chambers and on the bench brought about a failure of fairness and justice in state courts. When Larsen made his charges, the investigation moved to the executive branch, where it fell victim to the crude politics of Pennsylvania's elected attorney general's office. From there these collected failures snowballed to the corrupt, bought-and-sold state legislature, where we saw the impeachment. Justice by committee, witnessed first-hand by many of our founders with the excesses of the French Revolution, was feared by our founders; anyone who sat in on Larsen's legislative impeachment sessions can appreciate the concerns of the founders.

Should our three branches of government fail us, our founders guaranteed the freedoms of the fourth estate, the press, to serve as a final institutional guardian. It's the failure of the press in Larsen's impeachment that's both so notable yet so predictable. Pennsylvania, like the rest of American in the late twentieth century, has been victimized by a diminished press, concentrated in the hands of a few powerful interests. Pennsylvania's two large city dailies — the Inquirer and the Post-Gazette — both operate with a government-approved waiver of their monopoly status. Both newspapers held long-time grudges against Larsen. Larsen had lawsuits pending against both newspapers. The overseers of both newspapers had great financial and personal interests in seeing Larsen go down in flames. Larsen, in the end, showed us the corruptibility of both newspapers.

It was only after the drunken orgy was over that the

Inquirer seemed to partly awaken, hung over, and ask in a weak voice if the public had been ill-served by the festivities.

In an August 8, 1994, article in the Inquirer, as the impeachment ground to an embarrassing close, Emilie Lounsberry, the sycophant who'd all along cheered on Ed Dennis, interviewed Dennis's assistant, James Tierney, who'd received $196,840 to traduce Larsen. "Tierney," Lounsberry wrote, "the former Maine attorney general, said he remained dismayed at the continued silence of the court in the aftermath of the scathing grand jury report, which found deep and systemic problems in the way the court operates. He said he was disappointed that the court has yet to implement most of the changes recommended by the grand jury. 'Is any good going to come out of this? I don't know. Was the money we were all paid for this investigation worth it? I don't know,'" said Tierney. "'Reform isn't going to happen by magic.... All the things that I had expected have instead focused on the Justice Larsen minutiae and that, to me, is a disappointment.'"

In this amazing article we see Tweedledum and Tweedledee musing confusedly about what went wrong. How'd this happen, guys? May I suggest that your part in the mean-spirited attack on Larsen's drug usage, and your repeated refusal to look at Zappala's unjust interventions, helped to stir up a lynch mob against Larsen and buried any hope that reform would be a topic of discussion.

Tierney, incidentally, went on to offer commentary for Court TV. I caught him early in 1995 confidently predicting the conviction of O.J. Simpson. Tierney scoffed at the early suggestion that the credibility of the L.A. Police Department might be called into question in the case. A seer for our time. Tierney doesn't understand the growing, deep public distrust of law enforcement. In Pennsylvania James Tierney did his share to create a fair amount of distrust and distaste.

The Inquirer, meanwhile, continues to lose long-time editors and writers. Its owner, Knight-Ridder, based in Florida, continues to trim the budget and defang the once-great daily. In late 1995 Inquirer executive editor James Naughton and managing editor Stephen Lovelady both accepted company buy-out offers and resigned. "Philadelphia Newspapers Inc., which publishes the Inquirer and Daily News, has been under pressure to increase profits for its corporate parent, Knight-Ridder Inc., and plans to cut 230 to 250 jobs at the paper," the Associated Press reported. This is a corporation that acts like it doesn't care about its own people, let alone disinterested Pennsylvanians.

As Inquirer employees continue to jump ship like vermin from a sinking vessel, the question begs to be asked: Who are the out-of-state interests that operate Pennsylvania's largest newspaper and what, besides profits, do they want from Pennsylvanians?

And profits, when you're talking about Knight-Ridder and the Inquirer, are the bottom line. The second quarter of 1996 saw developments in two long-standing libel suits filed against the Inquirer. There was a stunning reversal of fortunes involving the suit by the estate of the late state Supreme Court Justice James T. McDermott. The state Supreme Court on April 12, 1996, reversed a lower court and reinstated a $6 million verdict against the Inquirer for a series on the high court titled "Above the Law."

The Inquirer told its readers, "The 1983 articles were written by Daniel R. Biddle. In part, they focused on two Supreme Court cases in which parties were represented by the Dilworth, Paxson, Kalish & Kauffman law firm, which had contributed $6,100 to McDermott's 1981 election campaign for the state Supreme Court. The articles questioned McDermott's participation in the court's rulings in those cases. The articles also reported that McDermott had sought to assist his son, James Jr., in getting a job as a prosecutor in the Philadelphia District Attorney's Office.

"McDermott denied any improper conduct in any of the issues raised by the articles and contended that he had been unfairly portrayed as a corrupt judge.

"...The (1990) jury awarded McDermott $3 million in

compensatory damages and $3 million in punitive damages. It found that a reprint of a 1983 Inquirer series titled 'Above the Law' was false, but that the articles when first published were not. ...McDermott filed two lawsuits, one in connection with the initial series, the other directed at the reprint....

"...The judge who presided at the trial, Carbon County President Judge John P. Lavelle, threw out the verdict in 1993 and ordered a new trial. The state Superior Court agreed with Lavelle's decision in 1994, saying the jury's verdict was inconsistent and could not stand.

"In reversing those decisions, Justice John P. Flaherty Jr. said in a 10-page opinion that 'it was permissible for the jury to reach different results.'

"Flaherty wrote that the split finding was justified because the reprint was 'enhanced by editorials and cartoons' and was sent to various journalism schools and to a 1984 conference of the American Bar Association and the American Judicature Society.

"...In ordering a new trial in 1994, Superior Court Judge Phyllis W. Beck wrote: 'The verdicts returned in this case cannot reasonably be explained. It is eminently clear that the jury went seriously wrong in its decision-making process.'"

Inquirer editor Maxwell E.P. King released the following statement: "There is no question that we will appeal this case all the way to the U.S. Supreme Court if that's what it takes. We are convinced that these stories represent responsible, truthful coverage of public officials that is protected by the First Amendment.... This is the strongest imaginable public official case. If we can't publish these stories, we can't cover City Hall, Harrisburg, Washington or the local dogcatcher."

Also in April 1996 the Inquirer finally settled the twenty-three year-old, $4.5/$34/$24 million libel suit first filed by Richard Sprague in 1973. The Inquirer had suggested in an April 1, 1973, front page article that Sprague had quashed a 1963 homicide investigation as a favor for a friend, former State Police Commissioner Rocco P. Urella. Urella's son and a friend were questioned in connection with the murder. Sprague recommended against prosecuting the friend and agreed with police that Rocco Jr. should not be prosecuted. Sprague accused the Inquirer of acting maliciously when it published its article. In 1972 Sprague had won a misdemeanor wiretap conviction against Greg Walter, one of the two reporters who contributed to the article. Sprague said he warned the newspaper that Walter had been overheard saying he would 'get' Sprague, an accusation that Walter, who died in 1989, denied.

In January 1996 the state Supreme Court had refused to hear the appeal of the $24 million lower court award, and in February the high court refused to reconsider. In late March 1996 a Common Pleas Court judge ordered the Inquirer to pay Sprague the $24 million.

The noose was tightening. A Superior Court judge then ruled the Inquirer could postpone payment to Sprague pending the newspaper's planned appeal to the U.S. Supreme Court. It was at this juncture that Knight-Ridder threw in the towel and settled for an undisclosed sum, presumably because Sprague, who is 70 years old, agreed to a reduction, or perhaps payment in installments. Inquirer publisher Robert J. Hall told readers, "We are confident that the United States Supreme Court would have ruled in our favor if it took the case, but we also are aware that the court takes very few cases. Closing the book now on more proceedings seems like a sensible thing to do. It's been a long time since the 1970s, and it's time to move on." The Inquirer's desire to put the matter behind it seemed oddly reminiscent of Preate's decision, on the death of his father, to face the music. Terms of the Inquirer's settlement with Sprague were not disclosed. The Inquirer's refusal to disclose the terms of the settlement seems at odds with the newspaper's oft-repeated defense of the public's right to know. Big money flows in strange ways.

These libel suits and their outcomes are of importance to Pennsylvanians, who are hostages both of their courts and their diminished corporate press. At the time of the unfavorable April

1996 McDermott ruling the Inquirer complained to readers, "The (state) Supreme Court decision was the second this year to uphold a libel verdict against The Inquirer. Last month, the high court refused to hear the newspaper's appeal of a $24 million jury verdict in favor of Philadelphia lawyer Richard A. Sprague. Inquirer editor King said the newspaper would not settle the McDermott case."

So now the Inquirer feels itself the victim of an unfair state Supreme Court, the very court, with its one-sided treatment of the Larsen impeachment, the Inquirer had protected and fended from reform. There's the great irony. The Philadelphia Inquirer, to settle an old score and to see Larsen go down, had reduced itself to a lapdog of a corrupt court. In return for the favor, after the dust had settled, the corrupt court had taken its lapdog newspaper out to the shed and whacked it. As Groucho Marx would say, Why's that big bully picking on that little bully?

While undoubtedly Sprague's successful suit against the Inquirer represents skillful lawyering, and while many Pennsylvanians feel no love loss for the Inquirer, truth be told, it's an unfair verdict. Libel law attempts to compensate an individual whose reputation or career has been untruthfully and deliberately damaged. Sprague's reputation and earnings have skyrocketed since he filed his suit in the early '70s. Sprague currently is representing millionaire John du Pont, who is accused in the shooting death of Olympic wrestler David Schultz. Sprague's career and reputation clearly has not been damaged $24 million worth. The outcome of Sprague's case against the Inquirer only further demonstrates that Pennsylvania courts are broken, and underscores the essential problem that the state's judiciary is not grounded in reality, fairness or common sense.

The literal bottom line of the Inquirer's announcement of its settlement with Sprague was that corporate earnings weren't affected: "In a statement, Knight-Ridder Inc., the parent company of PNI, said the settlement would have no impact on earnings, and publisher Hall said money had been placed in reserve as a result of the lawsuit, but he would not disclose the amount in reserve."

Of the three libel actions against the Inquirer of interest to our story there is only one outstanding: the defamation suit filed by Rolf Larsen in 1983. Meanwhile, as I write, several patronage-related lawsuits filed against the Pennsylvania Turnpike are moving through federal courts. One of the suits is a wrongful dismissal suit filed by Jacqueline Verney, the former turnpike attorney who handled the Wagman case, into which Justice Zappala intervened on an emergency basis in 1989. Another patronage suit was filed by Dick Sprague's law firm, asserting that their client lost a turnpike job to a woman who dates state senate President Pro Tem Robert Jubelirer. These lawsuits have finally goaded the Inquirer into a much belated examination of patronage problems at the turnpike.

Inquirer reporter Rich Heidorn told me that his newspaper is planning a series on the turnpike for the summer of '96. Heidorn led me to understand that the Inquirer has no plans to look into Zappala's emergency intervention into the Wagman case or whether the account published in my earlier book of Verney's involvement in the case may have contributed to her dismissal. In these patronage suits the Inquirer is once again hobbled by conflicts. The Inquirer can't write about Zappala's role in *Wagman* without casting doubts on Larsen's impeachment, and the Inquirer's role in the impeachment. And Sprague's involvement in a turnpike patronage suit is another minefield for the paper.

Heidorn angrily denied my suggestion that the Inquirer had a financial stake in ignoring the Wagman case and helping to destroy Rolf Larsen's career and credibility.

I asked the Inquirer's attorney in these issues, Samuel Klein, of Philadelphia, the $50 million question: did Rolf Larsen, the first high court judge to be impeached in almost two hundred years, have a reputation that can be defamed?

"I don't want to comment on that," Klein, the media attorney, told me.

Rolf Larsen's attorney in the defamation suit, David

Armstrong of Pittsburgh, had no problem commenting. Did the Inquirer have a financial stake in seeing Larsen impeached? I asked Armstrong. Certainly it did, he told me.

I began to tell Armstrong about the turnpike's Wagman case, and how I had been unable to get the Inquirer or the state legislature to examine the case during Larsen's impeachment. Stop right there, Armstrong told me, as he had a conflict. Armstrong's law partner, he told me, was turnpike commissioner and chairman James Malone. Armstrong told me he'd grown up with the Zappalas, and had from time to time visited their family's lovely stone house, and that he also knew turnpike commissioner James Dodaro. It's a small state, after all.

Emilie Lounsberry and James Tierney's remarkably confused sigh for judicial reform published in August 1994 by the Inquirer wasn't the only amazing and noteworthy after-the-riot editorial product to find its way into print. Philadelphia Magazine in December 1994 published a profile of Ed Dennis titled: "Special Ed: At the center of the nation's most high-profile cases sits one of Philadelphia's most low-key lawyers." Philly Mag quoted Dennis as saying of his colleagues, "They call me 'Whitewash' and ask me, you know, 'What are you covering up today?'"

After the obligatory Philly Mag suck ups (the magazine is enamored of anyone in the public light), the gossipy, light-weight article goes on to mention what it convolutedly describes as questionable investigations handled by Dennis, including Waco, "Irangate," and other mysteries. They mention that columnist and Nixon apologist William Safire wrote a couple of scathing columns about Dennis. "Just after the release of Dennis' Waco report," the magazine relates, "the Times' Safire wrote two columns accusing Dennis of taking part in a cover-up. (U.S. Attorney General Janet) Reno, Safire posited, needed someone who 'could put her (Waco) fumbling in the kindest light.... Enter Ed Dennis.... A Republican-administration prosecutor — but a member of the Justice establishment on whom (she) had a hold.' The 'hold,' according to Safire, came about because Dennis had been involved in the 'botching' of Justice's Irangate prosecution, a complex case involving $5 billion in illegal U.S.-guaranteed loans made to Iraq — and Saddam Hussein's war machine — between 1985 and 1989 by the Atlanta branch of a bank owned by the Italian government. Safire strongly implied that, in exchange for Dennis's conclusions about Reno's handling of Waco, Reno's criminal division told Atlanta prosecutors to settle for a plea bargain, thereby 'avoiding a public trial that would have exposed the machinations of the Bush-Thornburgh-Dennis crowd.'"

It was a typically smarmy and cowardly Philadelphia Magazine article. Why hadn't the magazine's editors found the courage or leadership to criticize Dennis as Mr. Fix-It while the impeachment proceedings were pending, thus alerting Pennsylvanians to what was coming for their courts? Philadelphia Magazine loves to play it safe by issuing after-the-fact, arm-chair warnings. That way they also get to scoff at the gullibility of the poor-sap uninformed victims. If the editors of Philadelphia Magazine had been entrusted with the midnight ride of Paul Revere they would have stayed at home quivering under their beds, only to arise after the shooting had stopped to poke fun at the newly enslaved stupid sops who'd been too dumb to know what was coming.

The deeper lesson of the Larsen impeachment is that we need to look hard at our diminished press and begin to bust up the media trusts. Rupert Murdoch and the Newhouse family aren't going to raise this issue. These media giants are dependent on corrupt-and-for-sale legislative and judicial branches to ensure their concentrated ownerships — the same as the other monopolistic moguls with whom they rub elbows in the club houses. A state like Pennsylvania, with thirteen million citizens, requires and deserves a much richer press than the two corporate-rag goon-squads that cheered on the lynch mob at the Larsen travesty.

What's the practical upshot of these combined governmental/big media failures? On April 19, 1995, the Pennsylvania Supreme Court again exercised its King's Bench powers, this time to allow a Chester County waste disposal firm, Thermal Pure Systems, Inc., to destroy infectious waste without a permit. The plant is on property owned by Chester Solid Waste Associates, a limited partnership belonging to members of Russell, Rea, Zappala and Gomulka. One RRZ&G executive used to be an officer of Thermal Pure. Thermal Pure had hired as its counsel former state Supreme Court Justice Bruce W. Kauffman.

Commonwealth Court had earlier sided with a citizens group that was concerned about the plant. The lower court, in February 1995, ruled the plant's license invalid until the state could formulate regulations that would allow it to operate within a 1988 law limiting amounts of infectious waste processed in a commercial facility. Following the Commonwealth Court ruling the state ordered the plant to cease operations. Thermal Pure petitioned the state Supreme Court, which stepped in with its King's Bench powers and allowed the plant to continue operating without a license.

When he was on the bench Kauffman once wrote that King's Bench powers should be used sparingly. Representing Thermal Pure, Kauffman argued that Commonwealth Court endangered the public by shutting down the plant.

The case came to light only after the Public Interest Law Center in Philadelphia filed papers saying the public was placed at risk by allowing the plant to process infectious waste without a license. The Law Center also argued that all this made for bad case law, as the concerned citizens had been deprived of an appeal since the Supreme Court is the state's highest. The state Supreme Court doesn't transcribe oral arguments, the Law Center also complained, so there would be no record that could be reviewed should the case be appealed to the U.S. Supreme Court.

State Supreme Court spokespeople say Justice Zappala recused himself from the case, and had nothing to do with granting Thermal Pure's King's Bench request.

I will carry with me many indelible memories from Larsen's fall. I'll always remember those attorneys who worriedly whispered to me that Justice Zappala had improperly intervened in cases involving interests funded by his brother. I'll always remember the moment I first heard Rolf Larsen publicly charge that Zappala was fixing cases involving entities associated with RRZ. I'll remember sending my book off to Ed Dennis, and the phone call I took from Ed Dennis's secretary asking me to send another copy to James Tierney. I'll remember the months of quiet that followed, the lolled sense of security that Preate's men were on the job, looking into Zappala. I'll remember Zappala's friend calling me, looking for garbage on Preate. I'll remember my chance encounter with Commonwealth Court Judge Doris Smith, who'd handled the turnpike's Wagman case, and who told me she too had problems with Zappala's handling of the case, that Zappala's associates had threatened her, that there was nothing to be done but suffer in silence. I'll remember the moment I learned Preate's men weren't looking into Zappala's cases, but instead would charge Larsen with prescription drug use.

I'll remember calling and writing both partisan special counsel hired by the general assembly, John Moses and J. Clayton Undercofler, telling them about the Wagman case, hearing the stunned silence on the other end of the phone, and then hearing nothing more from them. I'll always remember going again and again to the offices of the state representatives heading the impeachment — Frank Dermody, Thomas Caltagirone, and Jeffrey Piccola — and learning there was no mechanism for them to collect evidence on Zappala's misdeeds. I'll always remember Dermody's secretary wearily perched at her Xerox machine, grinding out garbage on Larsen, telling me they were too busy to collect evidence.

I'll always remember Justice Stephen Zappala testifying on the floor of the senate, saying he had no idea which cases involved his brother, that he didn't even know what bond underwriting was.

I'll always remember Larsen's attorney, William Costopoulos, telling me they would bring up the Wagman case, then hearing nothing more from him. I'll always remember Larsen, seated alone in the senate chamber, going down alone, going down his way, going down alone.

There are lessons I'll always take with me. I'll never trust Ed Dennis again, Moses or Undercofler, or representatives Dermody, Caltagirone or Piccola, Senator Greenleaf, or, for that matter, Bill Costopoulos. These men should consider this: By tolerating and aiding a corrupt system Rolf Larsen and Ernie Preate in the end brought about their own fall.

I'd recommend all Pennsylvanians avoid Justice Zappala's courtroom, because justice isn't done there. Stephen Zappala, to point out the obvious, is in no position to ever again cast stones by disciplining other judges. He is vulnerable to more investigations. His vulnerability means that Pennsylvania courts, and Pennsylvanians, are vulnerable.

Rolf Larsen needed whacked. Steve Zappala, weakened by his own corrupt practices, was the wrong guy to do it. In Pennsylvania's corrupt political landscape, was anybody clean enough to do it?

And what of Rolf Larsen? He seems an enigma. He certainly knew more than he, in the end, would, or could, tell. The forces of our democracy, in the end, quieted him.

The hallmarks of Larsen's disease — clinical depression — include occasional deep-seated doubts of the afflicted's worth; not insane behavior, as ignorant prosecutors crudely put forth. Did Larsen the depressive feel unworthy and desire to expose himself, his associates, his government — his creators — as frauds?

Larsen's fall is a story of failed democracy. The failure of our system, the failure of us. That failure began with the election of Rolf Larsen to Pennsylvania's high court. His term was marred in turns by judicial politicking and contentiousness. He did not have the temperament to serve well on the bench. Our democracy mixed politics with justice and Larsen is the concoction we got. A merit selection committee, seeking deliberative, fair-minded judges to serve on an appointive court, almost certainly would have passed Larsen by. The failure of our democracy also includes the story of the disgraced elected state attorney general who egregiously prosecuted Larsen, only to find himself behind bars because of a scheme to raise money needed to seek that office. We mixed greed and reckless ambition with public trust and Ernie Preate and Ed Dennis is the contagion we got.

In the old days this sorry episode in Pennsylvania history would have been cited by monarchists as an example of the inability of common men and women, hobbled by petty ambition, avarice, and fear, to rule themselves.

When he was eighty some years old, the journalist I.F. Stone wrote a compelling account of the last days of Socrates. In *The Death of Socrates,* Stone points out that the Greek philosopher disliked democracy, and didn't think much of the ability of men to self-rule. Socrates did not have to stand trial nor did he have to drink his cup of poison, Stone relates. It was common and accepted in ancient Greece to merely go into exile for a few years until storm clouds blew away. By allowing himself to stand trial for the ridiculous charge of poisoning young minds, Stone writes, Socrates intended to give democracy a black eye for all time. Convicted by a jury of hundreds of citizens, Socrates passed up many opportunities to simply flee the city and save his life. Socrates wanted to die, Stone concludes.

And so it was with Rolf Larsen. In the end Larsen passed up opportunities to further tar Stephen Zappala, as if to give our democracy the final present of allowing us to keep a corrupt judge, planting a poison seed for our future. Larsen, made by our democracy, built up by our media, in the end was brought down by the same forces that had created him. In the process of his grand destruction Rolf Larsen showed us how bad we, and our democratic institutions, could be.

Rolf Larsen wanted democracy to fail.

IF·THERE·BE·A·MESSENGER·ONE·AMONG·A·THOUSAND·

Appendix

·THEN·HE·IS·GRACIOUS·UNTO·HIM·

I. Excerpt from When the Levee Breaks

The following is reprinted from Chapter 13 of When the Levee Breaks, published in 1993.

There can be no inside track to justice, and no perception of an inside track. One-sided justice is no justice at all.

I kept thinking about Justice Rolf Larsen's accusations. He alleged that his colleague, Justice Stephen Zappala, "fixed" and "steered" cases to the benefit of Zappala's bond underwriter brother Charles. I kept thinking about the language Larsen used in his accusations.

Larsen charged that Zappala at various times had met ex parte with representatives of various government bodies, and advised them the "'route' and procedures to use in prosecuting" their cases in "this court." When these suits were filed "in the manner in which Justice Zappala had counseled and directed, Justice Zappala then took charge and 'guided' (these suits) through the Pennsylvania Supreme Court in a 'special' manner." These various cases, Larsen wrote, resolved in favor of the governmental bodies, and against the plaintive, "with the result that (the governmental bodies') financial strength was maintained and thus the bonds that had been handled through Justice Zappala's brother... were rescued from risk and maintained their strength."

I became interested and concerned about the case in which observers said Justice Zappala had gone to bat for the turnpike. He'd issued an unusual "quick" court order and accelerated a hearing through the high court.

I asked one observer about the case. We hadn't spoken for several months. In the intervening months Larsen had popped his accusations and a grand jury sat listening to his complaints. The observer expressed the opinion that Larsen's charges "rang true." Justice Zappala, as far as this person was concerned, had been improperly involved in a turnpike case. What was the name of the case that troubles you? I asked.

"I'll tell you only this: the case involved the turnpike's Mid-County Interchange project." I thought I heard tremors of grand juries and investigations shaking the voice. After some prodding, I learned a little more. The case involved a contractor. Turnpike commissioner James Dodaro, I was told, communicated privately with Zappala about this case. Dodaro was Justice Zappala's former law partner, and he'd pushed the justice's brother to underwrite turnpike bonds. Dodaro instructed the turnpike's legal department to appeal the case directly to Justice Zappala, I was told. Those close to the case were told that the justice would be expecting the call.

The turnpike's $85,600,000 Mid-County Expressway Connection project, in suburban Philadelphia, was financed by "Series A" bonds floated by Russell, Rea & Zappala in 1986. The project began in early 1990 and was scheduled for completion in late November or December 1992, the turnpike's 1992 bond prospectus promises. The project in fact was nearly one year behind schedule. The turnpike and its underwriters in April 1989 had promised investors the interchange would open on January 1, 1992. A delay caused by several lawsuits, and the delay's sudden resolution in court, is at the heart of the story.

"This project provides a direct connection between the Mid-County Expressway (Interstate Route 476) and the Pennsylvania turnpike system," reads the '92 prospectus. "An interchange between these two major highways will provide the suburban Philadelphia area with additional regional roadway capacity and relieve some of the traffic growth problems in the Conshohocken-King of Prussia-Valley Forge area."

The scale and importance of the Mid-County project can be appreciated from information published in the turnpike's 1992 annual report. "In the Midst of Mid-County," reads the report, "turnpike engineers face many challenges." I'd learn that the turnpike's legal department also faced challenges with the project's timely completion. "Groundbreaking ceremonies for the new Mid-County Interchange in Plymouth Township, Montgomery County, took place in late 1989," the '92 annual report explains. "Since then, construction on the estimated $70 million project has proceeded on schedule." Nothing here is mentioned about the lengthy legal delays *before* groundbreaking.

"Mid-County Interchange is situated close to the existing Norristown Interchange (#25) in suburban Philadelphia," the report continues. "The new interchange will be part of a 21.5-mile stretch of Interstate 476 linking the Blue Route with the Pennsylvania turnpike's mainline and Northeast Extension. The project extends eight-tenths of a mile or 4,500 feet on the turnpike's mainline and four-tenths of a mile on the Northeast Extension.

"The project includes the largest single contract awarded by the Pennsylvania Turnpike Commission to date. The Mid-County Interchange will be the largest interchange on the entire turnpike system. Scheduled for completion in late 1992, turnpike engineers project the average daily traffic volume during the opening year at 20,000 to 22,000 vehicles daily.

"A $55 million general construction contract for the new Mid-County Interchange was awarded to Hull Corporation of Syracuse, New York in late 1989. It includes: construction of the toll plaza, utility building, roadway, structures, signing and lighting.

"Mid-County is the first additional interchange on the turnpike's mainline to be constructed since completion of the Scranton Interchange on the Northeast Extension in 1957. The interchange will have the largest toll plaza on the turnpike with a total of 17 lanes for entering and exiting traffic and eight access ramps comprising 4.4 miles." The annual report makes no mention of an interesting fact: the contractor, originally, was not the Hull Corporation. The process leading to the contract award to Hull illuminates problems at the turnpike, and in our state courts.

Funding for this project, incidentally, included the "acquisition and construction of a new eastern regional office," which would be purchased for $2 million plus change through associate executive director S. Michael Palermo's former real estate colleague.

In January 1989, the turnpike advertised for bids to construct highway structures for its "single largest contract" on what it called its Blue Ridge project, part of the Mid-County Interchange. The job was a link in a bustling corridor of interconnected turnpike work funded by the massive $807 million RR&Z bond issue of 1986. It was an especially vital link since it promised to bring in more tolls by connecting to busy I-476. Work was scheduled to begin in the fall of '89. Six contractors submitted sealed bids on April 12, 1989. The same day the commission announced the low bidder: G.A. & F.C. Wagman, Inc., with a bid of $57,944,787. The second lowest bid, from the partnership of Dick Enterprises and Tony DePaul & Son, came in $561,254 higher.

Wagman, of York, in south central Pennsylvania, is a family-owned contracting business. It was founded in 1908 by George Aloysius Wagman, who started out as a sole laborer, hauling stone by hand, building several small bridges over creeks and canals. The next year he took in his brother. George was joined in 1935 by his son, Francis C. "Bud" Wagman. The firm worked on the turnpike back in the late 1930s. It recently built such projects as the sprawling I-95/I-395 bridge over the Patapsco River, near Baltimore's Inner Harbor, and the new Columbia-Wrightsville Bridge over the Susquehanna at Route 30. Landing the big Mid-County turnpike job was a coup, but before the contract could be awarded several complications arose. At the time they seemed like minor complications.

The company's bid had to comply with a new women and

minority sub-contractor law, called MBE/WBE, for Minority
Business Enterprise and Women Business Enterprise. The
statute was designed to facilitate the hiring of disadvantaged
firms. The newness of the law made it somewhat subject to
interpretation. Before Wagman could be awarded its contract
the state human relations commission paid a visit to the company to review its hiring procedures. The Office of Minority
Business and Women Business Enterprise finally ruled that
Wagman was in compliance with the new law. Then another
obstacle presented itself. The new interchange would destroy
wetlands. The turnpike found itself forced to build replacement
wetlands, threatening further delay. Planners from Wagman,
eager to win the job and get on with the project, met with
turnpike officials to suggest ways to proceed while wetland concerns were addressed.

Despite these delays, it seemed to Wagman that it was
working with the turnpike to smooth out the wrinkles. One
participant remembers the perception that Wagman "was on
the same team as the turnpike." The firm assumed it would win
the job.

The contract was scheduled to be awarded by a vote of the
commissioners in a public meeting on June 9, 1989. The day
before the scheduled vote, on June 8, the second-lowest bidder,
the joint venture of Dick/DePaul, along with one its minority
subcontractors, filed suit in commonwealth court seeking an
injunction to stop the award. The competitors claimed that
Wagman was in violation of the women and minority hiring
law, an issue which Wagman officials thought had been
resolved.

The turnpike unsuccessfully tried to have the case dismissed. It argued that Dick/DePaul was a disappointed bidder,
and so legally had no standing to sue. On June 21, 1989, the
turnpike filed a pre-hearing brief in opposition to Dick/DePaul
in which the commission maintained Wagman's bid was proper
and that the public interest favored awarding the contract to
Wagman. "Greater injury will result to the public if the
(Dick/DePaul) injunction is issued," the turnpike argued,

"since it will act to delay the construction of the Blue Ridge Project, a project intended to alleviate traffic congestion around Philadelphia."

The judge disagreed with the turnpike. The next day, June 22, after hearing testimony, the presiding judge, Paul Lehman, of Lewistown, granted Dick/DePaul its temporary injunction.

Observers close to Wagman remember this court hearing as almost tragic-comedy. Judge Lehman was born in 1904, retired from the bench in 1972, and served by special appointment of the court. One afternoon at about 3 p.m. Lehman announced that he could only hear arguments for another half an hour or so, as he had to catch a bus home "to Mifflintown, or someplace," as one observer remembers. A delay of weeks, even months, could be expected. Judge Lehman asked the turnpike's lawyers what the commission planned to do. Turnpike solicitors, fearing endless delay, responded that the commission planned to award the job to Wagman. Oh no you're not, Lehman told them. The judge said he wanted to hear the whole case, no matter the delay, and with his injunction enjoined the turnpike from awarding the job to Wagman. More testimony could be heard almost three weeks later, on July 13, Lehman ruled.

Turnpike planners now feared that thrashing out the disputed minority hiring law in court might delay the important Mid-County project indefinitely. The turnpike after all was pressed to complete the vast interconnected expansion projects — of which the Mid-County interchange was a crucial link — as promised to all those buyers of its bonds. Turnpike executive director Louis Martin took what he thought was the simple way out. On June 27 he altogether rejected the first round of bids, arguing that the turnpike was free to pursue its own best interest, which was to get the job moving. In early July the commission called for the project to be rebid. New bids, the turnpike notified potential bidders, would be accepted on September 12, 1989. The project was already set back five months.

For Wagman this was turning into the state contract bid

from hell. Observers close to the contractor say it was badly hurt by the rejection of its bid. The year before the company committed itself to working on a $90 million bridge and road job on the nearby I-476 Blue Route. Now its resources were stretched. When it bid on the Mid-County Interchange the company was forced to pass up other jobs. Its plate was filling up, and though the troublesome bid on the Mid-County Interchange seemed increasingly shaky, the company would be legally obligated to fulfill the contract should it be awarded.

One observer close to Wagman says the company began to consider the politics of the situation. In the earlier court proceeding before Judge Lehman, Wagman had been represented by an attorney with the Harrisburg firm McNees, Wallace & Nurick — considered by both the company and the turnpike as a Republican firm. The turnpike seemed to be tilted to the Democratic side. Executive director Lou Martin was a Democrat, as were Dodaro and the Zappalas. "We were aware of the connections between Dodaro and the Zappalas," one company official told me. Pennsylvanians accept as a fact of life inbred connections in government and the courts. Why not fight fire with fire? Perhaps the situation demanded a law firm with Democratic "connections," Wagman was advised, someone who "knew their way around." The company was referred to the Philadelphia attorney David Fineman, of Fineman & Bach, because, as someone explained it to me, "there had been a prominent Democrat on the legislature named (Herb) Fineman a few years back. Maybe there wasn't even any connection there." It turns out, I'm told by a member of the firm, there is no relation between Herb and Dave Fineman. There seems to be a slight comedy of errors here.

The new attorney counseled Wagman to wait until the job was rebid and then, if necessary, take the turnpike to court. Company officials all the while feared Wagman had diminished chances for winning the rebid. In a situation where a job is rebid, the competition knows the previous low bid, which now becomes the benchmark for the new bidding. The chances of twice grabbing the golden ring are diminished.

Making matters worse, specifications for the second bid were not identical. The turnpike had rewritten the women and minority hiring requirements to make the language more clear and, hopefully, to avoid the snafu experienced the first time around. Also differing from the first bid, the contractor must now construct a noise wall. Most importantly, a $4 million bridge was taken out of the project. The delay in the start of the interconnection was becoming crucial, observers remember. More than six months had elapsed since the start of the first round of bids. The completion date for the project — if everything went right — now was delayed an entire year. The turnpike, already hurt by delays and pressed to complete the complicated, interconnected roadway as promised to investors, took a bridge out of the bid. The commission negotiated with a Pennsylvania Department of Transportation contractor to build the bridge.

"PennDot was working on the adjoining I-476 part of the project," one participant remembers. "The turnpike's contractor was supposed to do the fill work for the bridges. The lawsuits tied all that up. So the bridge had to be turned over to PennDot."

The turnpike's official explanation for granting PennDot responsibility for building this bridge was that the rebidding and subsequent rescheduling problems created harmful delays for PennDot. Interestingly, nowhere in court records does the turnpike indicate how badly the commission and its investors may have been hurt by delay. Or, for that matter, how badly turnpike investors might be hurt by continued delay.

Wagman officials and their attorney attended a gut-wrenching pre-bid hearing at turnpike headquarters on August 22, 1989. Sensing the difficulties of winning the second round of bids, the company decided to immediately take the turnpike to court.

On August 30, 1989, Wagman asked commonwealth court for an injunction to stop the rebidding and prevent the accepting or opening of the second round of bids. The court was also asked to review the legality of the turnpike's having tossed out the first round of sealed bids. Wagman would be irreparably harmed if the injunction wasn't granted, its attorneys petitioned. Commonwealth court Judge Doris Smith set a hearing date in September at the Robert N.C. Nix, Sr., Federal Building in Philadelphia.

The turnpike on September 8 argued that Wagman had no standing to sue since the contractor was not holding enough bonds and so was merely a disappointed bidder. The commission attorneys cited a 1985 statute which claimed that the turnpike couldn't be sued unless the litigant held at least ten percent of outstanding turnpike bonds.

"It was ridiculous," one participant remembers. "They were saying you had to be holding $50 million in bonds out of a total of $500 million in turnpike bonds before you could take them to court!" (Others say the turnpike was misreading this statute, that it was meant to apply only in the event the turnpike went into default.) Even so, before it showed up in court, Wagman bought some turnpike bonds. "No where near $50 million worth," I was told.

This cited requirement (Turnpike Commission Organization, Extension and Toll Road Conversion Act, 36 P.S. §14[b]) states that a potential litigant in "the event of default" hold "not less than ten percentum (10%) in principal amount of the bonds then outstanding" before the turnpike can be taken to court. This requirement becomes particularly interesting when one remembers that the principal bond dealer is Russell, Rea & Zappala. Today there's more than a billion dollars in outstanding bonds. One tenth of that is at least $100 million in bonds. If one assumes that underwriters receive a lowball commission of 1.3 percent in fees for bonds underwritten, the investment companies conceivably stand to earn $1.3 million should one desire enough bonds to take the turnpike to court. This situation is made all the more untenable when one remembers that the Zappalas' childhood friend, James Dodaro, is a turnpike commissioner. It is made completely ludicrous when one considers that the chief bond underwriter's brother and the commissioner's former law partner is a state supreme court justice, where a lawsuit potentially could be decided. And that's precisely where this suit ended up — in the lap of Justice Stephen Zappala. But I'm getting ahead of the story.

One observer made the case to me that RR&Z would not make money whenever a potential litigant is forced to buy bonds. As chief underwriter, RR&Z made its profit selling turnpike bonds to other brokers when the deal was first cut, and would not profit from subsequent public sale of the bonds, I was told. I pointed out that RR&Z also handled the remarketing of bond issues. If potential contractors (or litigants) thought they must purchase $50 million or more in bonds to protect their standing in the event of court action, the supply of remarketed bonds could get tighter, increasing the value and perhaps the size of an issue, to the benefit of RR&Z.

The point is, nobody at the turnpike seemed to be considering the potential for conflict. No one seemed to consider the bounds of propriety. The great multi-billion dollar Pennsylvania turnpike was starting to resemble a back-woods family business set beside a Southern sheriff's sleepy jail: listen to this commissioner; pay his boyhood friend; if you don't like it, submit to justice from the first one's former partner, who also happens to be the second one's brother....

So Wagman bought a few thousand dollars worth of turnpike bonds to bolster its claim for standing. Events took an interesting turn in court as Wagman argued on behalf of turnpike bondholders, of which it now was one. "As a result of (the Pennsylvania Turnpike Commission's) wrongful conduct (rejecting the first round of bids)," the company's attorneys briefed the court, "(the) public, (Wagman), and other bondholders will suffer the following irreparable immediate harm: a) delay in commencement of construction; b) loss of toll revenues; c) financial loss to bondholders, (Pennsylvania Turnpike Commission), and the commonwealth."

Judge Smith on September 11 sided with Wagman. She disregarded the turnpike's assumption that Wagman lacked standing. The statute requiring 10 percent holding of outstanding bonds to bring legal action, she noted, specifically states in "the event of default."

"The core question involving standing is that a person seeking judicial resolution of a controversy be adversely affected," she'd note in a memorandum opinion. "(T)his court believes Wagman has presented evidence to show that it would be severely and adversely affected."

Smith enjoined the turnpike from opening, announcing or awarding the new bids. The turnpike was furthermore enjoined from continuing with the project until a "final disposition of proceedings filed by Wagman." The construction company was ordered to place a bond of $58,000, which it did. Here it was, almost fall, when the project was supposed to have been getting under way. Instead the interconnection was heading for another lengthy delay as commonwealth court proposed to review everything that had happened to date.

Earlier the turnpike had short-circuited a court review by simply rejecting the first round of bids. Suddenly this short-circuiting itself was up for court review. Turnpike officials decided on the ultimate short circuit.

The turnpike responded to Smith's injunction on September 13 by filing for an appeal before the state supreme court. In doing so the turnpike's attorneys claimed their appeal should operate as what's called an automatic supersedeas. State Rules of Appellate Procedure Rule 1736 provides that the "commonwealth, its officers or a political subdivision," by appealing to a higher court, automatically vacates a lower court's unfavorable ruling, as the appeal "shall operate as a supersedeas in favor of such party." In other words, simply by appealing to the supreme court, the turnpike claimed the right to disregard Smith's order and so award the contract. The turnpike notified seven bidders that on Monday, September 18 it would open and announce the bids. "Wagman was notified by the (turnpike) that its appeal to the supreme court constituted an automatic supersedeas and that the rebids would be opened as planned by the commission irrespective of this court's order," Smith later wrote.

A telephone hearing was held between Judge Smith and the two parties on Friday, September 15. Wagman filed a petition of contempt against the turnpike, seeking to eliminate what it called the "alleged" automatic supersedeas. Wagman argued, and Smith would agree, that the turnpike had no right of automatic supersedeas. By statute (42 Pa. C.S. §102), and precedent, Judge Smith found, the turnpike "is defined as an 'independent agency' as contrasted to the commonwealth or one of its political subdivisions." The turnpike was not the governor or a state agency, Smith ruled. It could not invoke the supersedeas. The practical reasoning for the finding was obvious: Wagman had demonstrated it would be hurt if the job was rebid, and any hearings would be made moot if the turnpike went ahead and awarded the job.

On Monday, September 18, the day the turnpike planned to open the bids for the late job, Smith filed an order eliminating the turnpike's claim of automatic supersedeas and reaffirming her September 11 injunction.

So the awarding of the contract, and therefore the project, came to a grinding halt. For most other parties this court obstacle might have proven insurmountable and costly. The turnpike simply played its trump card.

Three days before Smith's order, the day of the phone hearing, Friday, September 15, executive director Louis Martin began conferring with the turnpike commissioners, including Dodaro. In the event Smith ruled against them the following Monday, turnpike officials wanted to be prepared to immediately have her overruled so the bids for the jinxed Mid-County job could be opened.

Observers say that Dodaro and Martin agreed, should Smith make it necessary, to have the turnpike appeal the elimination of the automatic supersedeas directly to supreme court Justice Zappala. They would out-gun Judge Smith. This would cut costly delay. Those familiar with this case say it is their understanding that Zappala received a private communication about the situation by way of commissioner Dodaro over the weekend of September 15 to 17, 1989. An *ex parte,* or one-sided, communication is the very offense for which Zappala had voted to reprimand his colleague Justice Larsen.

The next Monday Smith issued her opinion reaffirming her injunction and eliminating the turnpike's automatic supersedeas. "It is ordered that the appeal filed by the (turnpike)...shall not operate as an automatic supersedeas." Smith intended to stop the turnpike cold.

In case of this eventuality, higher-ups had already instructed the turnpike attorney handling the case to telephone Justice Zappala's office and ask that Judge Smith be overruled. It was the understanding of a key participant in the case that Martin had received these instructions from Dodaro. The turnpike legal staff was informed that Justice Zappala would be expecting their call, a participant told me.

Justice Zappala's clerk took the call from the turnpike's legal department. Zappala's clerk requested "a piece of paper, a motion to work with," which was quickly delivered. Stephen Zappala, as planned and promised, put the case on a fast track. On September 18, the same day as Smith's order eliminating the supersedeas, while confused contractors waited at turnpike headquarters to present their bids, Zappala conducted an expedited hearing over the phone. Lawyers for the turnpike and Wagman offered oral arguments during the conference call. (The entire turnpike legal staff, I'm told, overheard this phone hearing.) That same day the justice issued an order reinstating the turnpike's automatic supersedeas, revoked by Smith. Before the order could be issued Zappala's office demanded a brief from the turnpike, which created a slight problem. The brief and its amendments by this time had grown to about an inch thick and the turnpike staff faced a logistical problem getting it to Pittsburgh. Before the end of the day the brief was delivered, and so was Zappala's order. The turnpike now was allowed to accept, open and announce the second round of bids. "Zappala wasn't stupid," one party remembers. "He allowed the turnpike to open the new bids but ruled it couldn't award the job until the full court heard the case."

"There was a big ruckus back and forth between judges Smith and Zappala," another participant remembers. "It was the most unusual bid day I'd ever seen. Bidders for the contract were told to bring their bids to the turnpike offices, where they sat in a lobby from 10 a.m. to 3 p.m., while Zappala held his phone hearing."

The obstacle of Judge Smith's stay of the automatic super-sedeas removed, the new bids received and opened, the turn-pike's lawyers on October 18 filed for an expedited appeal before the full court. The expedited hearing was granted, and heard on October 23. (The turnpike's attorneys had not earlier asked Zappala for a full, expedited hearing because, for all they knew, Wagman might again turn out to be the low bidder, thus eliminating the need for further litigation.)

Everyone seems to agree that Justice Zappala helped move things along. By the time the full court would rule on the case the turnpike would have a low-bidder in hand, prickly matters such as the contractor's MBE/WBE qualifications would have been investigated, and the commission would be ready to make the award. In contrast, when Judge Lehman, independent of the turnpike, had to catch his bus to Mifflintown, the turnpike had to fear endless delay — as do most litigants before the courts these days.

It had been very quick justice. "By the time the case was heard before the full supreme court it was so messed up no one could understand it," one participant recalls. "Chief Justice Nix couldn't understand why Wagman was there. He said, 'You are low bidder.'" Nevertheless, the full court decided in favor of the turnpike on October 31. The state's highest court, without issuing an opinion, vacated all of Smith's earlier orders on the unexplained grounds that Wagman had no standing to file suit. How unfair is all this? The turnpike originally fought

Dick/DePaul's court intervention on the grounds it had no standing to sue, a contention that Judge Lehman (and later Smith) disregarded. If Wagman and the turnpike had fought Dick/DePaul before Zappala, presumably the court would have ruled Dick/DePaul had no standing, and Wagman would have won the contract.

But that's not how it happened. The contract was awarded, as the turnpike's 1992 annual report notes, to the Hull Corporation of Syracuse, New York. It was not the smooth award the annual report would have us believe. The story of the one-year delay is mostly the story of a big snarl the turnpike suffered at the hands of the state court system, and a smoothing over the turnpike enjoyed when Justice Zappala intervened.

Judge Smith, for her part, on October 25, 1989, filed a six-page memorandum opinion explaining the reasoning, and citing precedent, behind her actions. In defending her judgments she casts suspicion on the way the state supreme court, and so Zappala, handled the appeal. In her memorandum Smith reiterates her opinion that the turnpike is not a governmental body subject to automatic supersedeas. She brushed aside the assumption that one must buy bonds before suing the turnpike. "Substantial legal questions have been raised in this proceeding primarily relative to the (turnpike's) right to reject the first bid," she summed up. "...The legal questions thus raised by the evidence presented at hearing satisfy the criteria for issuance of a preliminary injunction." Unfortunately for Wagman, the turnpike had luckily found a higher judge who disagreed with Smith.

The project, the schedule, all those bonds, were back on track. Several people told me they were troubled by the expedited nature of the turnpike's successful appeal. One described the speed of Zappala's intervention as very unusual. "Sure," this observer said facetiously, "this sort of quick order happens all the time." Most troubling was the understanding of those involved that Justice Zappala had received an *ex parte* communication about the case, and the equally troubling assertion that turnpike attorneys had been told that Zappala would be expecting their call. This case has the potential to lend credence to Larsen's charge that Zappala "steered" cases in a special manner to help his bond underwriter brother's clients — in this case Charles Zappala's biggest client, the Pennsylvania turnpike.

In the Wagman case, turnpike officials (including Dodaro) figured out a way to get past Judge Smith, and Dodaro's patron and former law partner, Justice Zappala, willingly enacted the plan. Judge Smith, in her memorandum opinion, shot back at the high court, writing that someone's rights had been trampled.

Why, I wondered, had the turnpike found it necessary to bring Justice Zappala into the case? Could this have benefited the justice's brother Charles, who sold the bonds for the stalled project? At various times through the years the turnpike's legal staff have called state supreme court justices for emergency rulings, such as the call to Chief Justice Nix to keep embattled Peter Camiel on the commission. The supreme court is supposed to be open at all hours for emergency appeals. Why was Justice Zappala selected to rule in this Wagman case? Why hadn't Dodaro and Zappala recused themselves? Perhaps as important, why wasn't the turnpike sensitive to the appearance of conflict this might present?

One turnpike official with an interest in the proceedings attempted to defend and play down Justice Zappala's involvement. Charles Zappala's firm, the bond underwriter, wasn't threatened monetarily by the snafu with Wagman, this party argued. The Mid-County Interchange project, underwritten for $85,600,000, was only a small piece of the huge, nearly one billion dollar 1986 bond float, I was told. The difference in bids between the two contractors, furthermore, in the event of a court opinion unfavorable to the turnpike, might have been no more than $5 million — again, in the scheme of things, small change, I was told.

What about the element of time? I asked. Supposing,

instead of the month or so it had taken Justice Zappala and the full court to dispose of Wagman, the case had stretched out for years, as usually happens in courts these days? Might the project have been delayed indefinitely? In April 1989, the turnpike's revenue forecasters promised investors that the interchange would be "opened January 1, 1992." The 1992 prospectus for bonds sold by Charles Zappala's firm had to promise that the Mid-County Interchange would be "operational by the end of 1992." Might a fouled-up interconnection have driven away potential buyers of bonds, and so commissions to Russell, Rea & Zappala?

One turnpike official tried to assure me that investors would have understood a drawn-out delay. The women and minority hiring regulations at the heart of the dispute were newly written and so the court delays would probably have been understandable to investors. This person tried to play down Justice Zappala's involvement in the case. Closeness to a particular justice merely means access, I was told. You simply know where to reach a particular justice. Say, over the weekend.

An observer close to Wagman questions this explanation. "We had to wonder why all these lawyers were trooping to Pittsburgh to see Zappala when there were other justices."

A turnpike official offered a cryptic explanation. This person pointed out that lawyers often view the process of court appeals in a strategic sense. "If opposing lawyers are more experienced you might have to do more things." A less-experienced opponent makes the game easier. This person at first said it was proper for commissioner Dodaro to have involved himself with consultations to bring in Justice Zappala. When pressed, this person seemed unusually sensitive and not forthcoming about the roles played by the two long-time friends.

Another turnpike observer provided an insight into this "strategic explanation" of turnpike behavior in the Wagman case. (Judge) "Doris Smith gave us a bum deal," in the Wagman case, this person explained. "It appeared Smith was wired the other way," I was told, meaning that Judge Smith seemed to unfairly favor Wagman over the turnpike. Here's where partisanship begins to show itself at the turnpike, and in our justice system. I was told that turnpike officials initially viewed Wagman as a Republican firm, as the contractor in some matters was represented by the Harrisburg firm McNees, Wallace & Nurick. The partisan view of the case was further reinforced when Wagman hired Fineman, believed to be a Democratic firm. Again, perhaps a comedy of errors. A few of the Democrats at the turnpike, those close to Dodaro and the Zappalas, viewed Smith's unfavorable rulings in the light of party politics.

Judge Smith displayed apparent favoritism in several ways, I was told. For example, Smith received a post-hearing suggestion, meaning a communication after the hearing, from Wagman's attorney. One participant described the communication as an *ex parte* letter written by Wagman's attorney to Judge Smith. This shouldn't, and usually doesn't, happen. Then there was the matter of her staying the automatic supersedeas, which further maddened the turnpike's legal staff. In the early 1980s, in connection with efforts to keep Peter Camiel on the commission, the turnpike had successfully invoked the supersedeas.

All this angered turnpike executive director Martin, I was told. "Lou Martin sometimes has a big ego," one observer explained. "He had ordered the rebidding of the project and he was mad that Wagman had defied him and had gone to court, and he was upset with the way Judge Smith had treated the turnpike."

This view seemed to set the stage for party one-upmanship. As an observer explained, "It's common knowledge that Dodaro is close to Justice Zappala." If the Republicans (or was it the Democrats?) could "wire" Judge Smith, the turnpike could just as easily "wire" the state supreme court. "Didn't they know we had a wire on the supreme court?" a participant put it. "Didn't they know who we were, what our power was?" By using Dodaro to call in Justice Zappala, this person explained, turnpike officials were hauling out their big stick, playing a trump card, sending a message to others, including Judge

Smith, not to play procedural games with the turnpike in the future. Another message was sent to Wagman, which was viewed as trying to play partisan politics in the court system. "Don't use politics against us," was the message to Wagman and others. "Because we can use politics too, and we can beat you at that game."

Judge Smith apparently got the message, this person told me, as she ruled favorably on the next turnpike case before her. "I don't know whether someone spoke to her," I was told, "or if she simply got the message by seeing how the Wagman case was handled."

All this is bad enough, but should we let the turnpike, Dodaro and the Zappalas off the hook so easily? A deeper explanation of the turnpike's behavior might well lie in the question of whether the Mid-County Interchange would have been delayed by endless court litigation. Plain and simple, might a court delay have cost Charles Zappala money?

What about the money nobody wants to talk about, anyway? Let's say it's true that the difference in contractors was small potatoes, "only" $5 million. What was the potential loss of toll revenues? Upwards of $1.1 million for every year the interchange remained unproductive, according to turnpike projections. Other costs are less clear. What about the cost of borrowing all that money while the whole shebang is held up in court? What about the potential loss of investor confidence? In the real world, interminable delays in the American court system often kill projects. A million here, five million there — certainly, sooner or later, you have to be talking real money. In fact, the 1992 bond prospectus tells us, "Total costs for the (1986 bond float) Series A Projects are approximately $25 million above the original estimate in July 1986, due primarily to an increase in the cost estimate for the Mid-County Expressway Connection." There were problems with relocation of wetlands near the interchange, the prospectus notes. Even so, I was told, the one-year delay was mostly caused by the two lawsuits. "That's what held it up," one participant told me, referring to the court action.

One turnpike observer suggested that a prolonged court delay might well have cost the turnpike and its underwriters additional lost revenue, had not Justice Zappala interceded. Federal tax law requires a governmental agency like the turnpike to spend the proceeds of a bond issue within five years, or the money is subject to a tax, which would certainly cost the turnpike money. The turnpike presumably had until 1991 to spend its '86 Series A bond funds, which financed the Mid-County project. So time was of the essence. A looming court battle in late '89 could certainly have stretched out two years into '91. It happens all the time in American courts. (Justice Larsen tied up his neighborhood condo project with court action for *three full years,* from March 1984 to May 1987, until the developer went belly up.)

What if Justice Zappala hadn't interceded? One observer described a cascading series of events that might well have ended with turnpike administrators and underwriters losing money, profitability, and reputations. A prolonged court delay involving its biggest interchange could lead the public to lose confidence in the turnpike. This would cause the turnpike's traditionally high bond rating to be devalued. Money would then have to be borrowed at a higher interest rate, which would cost the turnpike and its underwriters money (and profit) in future bond issues. Or, conceivably, the turnpike might have trouble peddling its bonds. Higher interest means greater risk. As we were reminded by politicians and bond courtesans in 1986, there is *risk* involved in selling turnpike bonds not backed by the state.

It is perhaps true that potential bond investors might have understood a delay of a relatively small turnpike project. This interchange was not small. It was to connect several major highways to much larger combined projects. (Including, you'll remember, the new eastern regional headquarters purchased through the associate executive director's former real estate colleague.) Any chain is only as strong as its weakest link. The uncompleted Mid-County Interchange structures could arguably have loused up the usability, read profitability, of other projects. Aunt Tilly, or a truck driver, can't drive a three-thousand mile road if a bridge is missing. Who knows the whole interconnected picture?

It became interesting to me that turnpike officials seemed to go out of their way to insist that the integrity of Russell, Rea & Zappala bonds never was threatened by court setbacks in the Wagman case (or helped by Justice Zappala's intervention). Normally, when the bondseller and the judge aren't brothers, an administrator would be quick to point out that a project's underwriters require and deserve protection from harmful delay. You're normally free to look out for your investors, free to hope aloud that they make money, free to say gobbledygook like your fiduciary responsibilities to your bondholders demand quick and timely action to complete a scheduled project. (Potentially troublesome litigation, by the way, must be disclosed by a bondseller in its prospectuses.) Even Wagman, in its court briefing, wasn't shy in defending turnpike bondholders.

In this instance, because the underwriter's interests are so shamefully tangled with a turnpike commissioner and a state supreme court justice, everyone at the turnpike has to disingenuously pretend the underwriter's bacon is never on the line. They have to pretend none of their actions impact the underwriter — an amazing contention. Everyone involved seems uncomfortable and not eager to publicize that money's on the line. (Writer Steven Dickson, of the industry paper The Bond Buyer, complained to me that Russell, Rea & Zappala's representative threatened to sue the publication while Dickson was preparing his article on the problems of the justice and the investment house. RR&Z has threatened to sue at least one other newspaper lately, I've learned. These legal saber rattlings carry the unspoken threat that the underwriter's brother is a judge on the state's high court.)

The truth is, people close to the Mid-County Interchange project say time *was* becoming crucial to the turnpike, so much so that turnpike officials felt it necessary to call in Zappala and take a bridge out of the original bid. If there was no hurry, no problem, no *risk,* why do these things? Show me time and money, and I'll show you risk. If there was a risk, Justice Zappala should have recused himself. He certainly shouldn't have taken an *ex parte* communication.

Justice Larsen alleged that RR&Z bonds were "rescued from risk" by Justice Zappala. Consider this thing called risk. On the one hand, these people argue that sweetheart no-bid bond deals should be awarded because turnpike projects, not backed by the state, are fraught with risk and so are deserving of special, non-competitive treatment by trustworthy "friends." On the other hand, when problems crop up that threaten the timely completion of the project, the same people, to protect their sweetheart bondsellers, are forced to argue that the bond holders or dealers were never placed at risk, and didn't benefit by any inside manipulation. It's risky business, or it's not. Which is it?

Time wasn't of the essence, they tell us, so it didn't matter that Justice Zappala sped things along. Today's open-minded and understanding bond buyers, we're told, would have understood the delay and loss of potential revenue. Dan Cupper's 1990 history of the turnpike (the publication of which was officially sanctioned by the turnpike for its fiftieth anniversary), makes a big deal over a few months' delay of the opening of the roadway in 1940. Politics prevented Franklin Roosevelt from officiating at a dedication, Cupper reminds us. "Bondholders began to point out to the commission that every day the superhighway remained closed was another day without revenue to retire its debt," Cupper writes. Now we're expected to believe the bondholders in 1989 have changed their stripes and don't care about delay, and suffer silence. Yet the bond dealer's brother, the state supreme court justice, bashes heads together to get the show rolling. An expedited hearing before the state supreme court implies that time is of the essence. Which is it?

It's easy enough to argue that Dodaro and Justice Zappala should have recused themselves from the entire Wagman snafu. They should have. More to the point, the bonds should never have been awarded on a non-competitive basis. This would have saved everybody embarrassment.

In the case of *Wagman* v. *The Pennsylvania Turnpike Commission* we're presented with the interesting picture of a government agency run a little too much like a business, overseen with a little too much efficiency. Who knows the whole big interconnected picture? The bottom line, in my mind, is whether the billion plus dollars in bonds floated since 1986, enriching to a few, have cost ordinary citizens faith in their turnpike, their legislature and their courts. Greed ultimately destroys the greedy.

In the end, after all, the turnpike is just a road. Concrete, asphalt, rock and stone meeting earth. Not much different, essentially, from the two-lanes it replaced. What is different is the bureaucracy, the political order, behind the road. At what cost do we drive to Pittsburgh? We suffer our souls to get there in four hours.

The handling of the Wagman case appears to potentially violate the judicial code of conduct. Canon 1, dealing with the independence of a judge and appearance of same, reads:

A judge should uphold the integrity and independence of the judiciary

An independent and honorable judiciary is indispensable to justice in our society. A judge should participate in establishing, maintaining, and enforcing, and should himself observe, high standards of conduct so that the integrity and independence of the judiciary may be preserved. The provisions of this Code should be construed and applied to further that objective.

Perhaps, more to the point, since friends, associates and family of Justice Zappala are concerned here, Canon 2, reads:

A judge should avoid impropriety and the appearance of impropriety in all his activities

A. A judge should respect and comply with the law and should conduct himself at all times in a manner that promotes public confidence in the integrity and impartiality of the judiciary.

B. A judge should not allow his family, social, or other rela-
tionships to influence his judicial conduct or judgment. He should
not lend the prestige of his office to advance the private interests of
others; nor should he convey or, knowingly permit others to convey
the impression that they are in a special position to influence him.

The involvement of Justice Zappala in the Wagman case
certainly gave people I spoke with the impression he could be
influenced by "family, social or other relationships," that
Dodaro and the turnpike were "in a special position to
influence him."

Turnpike employees view the justice as having fixed this
case. Wagman representatives certainly are suspicious. The
Wagman episode convinced one observer at the turnpike that
Zappala was a high house judge, that all lawsuits against the
agency must be filed in federal, not state, court. Justice, and the
perception of justice, has been hurt.

II. Judicial Conduct Board Protects Zappala

On January 19, 1994 I wrote the chairman of the
Pennsylvania Judicial Conduct Board, Judge Joseph Del Sole,
asking the board to "voluntarily investigate widely published
reports of allegations of impropriety involving court cases handled by Supreme Court of Pennsylvania Justice Stephen A.
Zappala....

"A case that concerns me and others is G.A. & F.C.
Wagman, Inc. v. Commonwealth of Pennsylvania, The
Pennsylvania Turnpike Commission....

"In brief, Justice Zappala's involvement and handling of
this case raises questions concerning the perception of fairness
and propriety. On the face of it the involved parties are too
closely allied to foster the impression of a fair and impartial handling of the case by Justice Zappala. Troubling aspects include
the following obvious conflicts of interest: 1) Justice Zappala's
brother, Charles, is a principal in the firm that underwrote the

disputed project and contract, and RR&Z had a direct interest in the swift completion of all litigation and the continuation of the project; 2) Justice Zappala's former law partner and protégé, Turnpike Commisioner James Dodaro, played an important role in seeing that RR&Z receive the above-mentioned no-bid bond work....

"In short, the question before us is whether, to prevent the perception of favoritism, and to uphold the court's obligation for impartiality, Justice Zappala should have recused himself from the Wagman case, and all cases involving clients of RR&Z, and the interests of other close associates, patrons and protégés.

"Justice Zappala's intervention in the Wagman case appears to have potentially violated, among others, Canon 1 and Canon 2 of the Judicial Code of Conduct. Canon 1 requires that a judge "should uphold the integrity and independence of the judiciary." Canon 2 requires that a judge should "avoid impropriety and the appearance of impropriety in all his activities." Canon 2 furthermore states that "A. A judge should respect and comply with the law and should conduct himself at all times in a manner that promotes public confidence in the integrity and impartiality of the judiciary . B. A judge should not allow his family, social, or other relationships to influence his judicial conduct or judgment. He should not lend the prestige of his office to advance the private interests of others; nor should he convey or, knowingly permit others to convey *the impression that they are in a special position to influence him.*" (Emphasis is mine.)...

"I ask that you inform me within a reasonable period of time of your decision. While I understand the law allows me or any citizen to pursue an official complaint, I feel it's your obligation to act."

The Conduct Board refused to act on its own, and instead sent me a complaint form. "Enclosed is a complaint form which should be filled out in as much detail as possible if you wish to file a complaint with the Board," Kenneth W. Finnell, the board's Chief Investigator wrote me on February 4, 1994. They would not voluntarily investigate Zappala.

As the impeachment of Rolf Larsen neared, and Larsen's attorney, William Costopoulos, promised to call me as a witness, a finally filed a formal complaint with the conduct board on August 11, 1994. If I was called before the state senate to testify, I wanted to say I had followed the proper, established channels.

My complaint read, "Justice Zappala should not have intervened in the Wagman case. His brother, Charles Zappala, is a principal in the bonding firm, RRZ Public Markets, that underwrote the project disputed in the Wagman case. Justice Zappala's former law partner and childhood friend, James Dodaro, is a Commissioner in the Pennsylvania Turnpike Commission. These facts alone undermine the public trust and right to a fair and impartial judiciary. Attorneys handling the case for the Turnpike voiced their concern and understanding to me that there were improper contacts about the Wagman case between Justice Zappala and Commissioner Dodaro. Canons 1 and 2 of the Judicial Code of Conduct state that a judge should uphold the integrity and independence of the judiciary, and should avoid impropriety and the appearance of impropriety in all his activities. By interjecting himself in the Wagman case Justice Zappala violated these canons and undermined the public's trust in an impartial judiciary. I have enclosed a copy of my book, When the Levee Breaks; Chapter 13 provides a narrative of the Wagman case. Other documents are available."

The next month Larsen was convicted in the state senate, and I never was called to testify.

I heard nothing from the Conduct Board for *six months,* until I received the following letter, dated February 16, 1995, from G.D. Anthony, Deputy Counsel of the Conduct Board, on the official stationery of Vincent J. Quinn, Chief Counsel to the board. Anthony asked me to reveal my sources and turn over my notes — a request no American writer would take seriously.

Referring to the page numbers of my 1993 book, Anthony wrote me,

"In the complaint you filed with the Board, you forwarded a copy of your most recent book, When the Levee Breaks, Yardbird Books, 1993. After reviewing Chapter 13, I would ask that you answer the following questions.

"On Pages 142-3, you have referred to an 'observer' who expressed to you the opinion that Larsen's charges 'rang true.' Could you please supply me with the name, address, and phone number of this 'observer?'

"On Page 152, you state 'Those familiar with this case say it is their understanding that Zappala received a private communication about the situation by way of Commissioner Dodaro over the weekend of September 15 to 17, 1989.' Could you please supply me with the name, address, and telephone number of the person or persons who related this information to you?

"On Page 153, you state that 'The Turnpike's legal staff was informed that Justice Zappala would be expecting their call, a participant told me.' Could you please supply me with the name, address, and telephone number of the 'participant' who related that information to you?

"On Page 154, you state '"By the time this case was heard before the full Supreme Court, it was so messed up no one could understand it," one participant recalls.' Could you please supply me with the name, address, and telephone number of the 'participant' who gave you this information?

"On Page 157, in the first full paragraph, you referred to a Turnpike official who 'offered a cryptic explanation.' Could you please supply me with the name, address, and telephone number of this official?

"On Page 158, you state '"Didn't they know we had a wire on the Supreme Court?" a participant put it. "Didn't they know who we were, what our power was?"' Could you please identify who this 'participant' was and also supply their address and phone number?

"Further, I would like to know if, in any of the above cases, you documented these conversations either with notes or audio/video recordings. If so, I ask that you forward copies of these to the Board.

"'Please be advised that an inquiry of this nature does not constitute a decision by the Board that misconduct has occurred. If you should have any questions, please feel free to contact me. Thank you."

My complaint had forced the Conduct Board to open a preliminary investigation into Zappala's intervention in the Wagman case. As with the impossible request that I betray sources I'd promised to protect, the board's "investigation" displayed suspect motives.

The Conduct Board, I learned, had contacted the turnpike's former assistant counsel and in-house attorney, Jacqueline Verney, who'd handled *Wagman*. Several months before Verney had sued the turnpike in federal court, alleging, among other things, illegal patronage practices. Verney soon was fired from the turnpike, sparking a wrongful dismissal suit.

I was able, through various sources, to piece together what happened next. The Conduct Board, pursuing its so-called preliminary investigation, asked Jacqueline Verney to speak with investigators about *Wagman*. I'm told that Verney, fired from the turnpike, naturally feared further reprisals from the commission if she spoke about *Wagman*. She told the Conduct Board that she could only talk to investigators about *Wagman* if the Turnpike Commission would wave its attorney/client privilege with her. Verney obviously feared the commission would seek to revoke her bar license if she spoke up. The Turnpike Commission, given veto power over the investigation of itself, refused to allow Verney to speak to the Conduct Board.

The result was that the Conduct Board never spoke with Verney about *Wagman*. The turnpike had no legal grounds to hide behind the attorney/client privilege, since it cannot be invoked to conceal law breaking. The point is, the Conduct Board never intended to investigate.

It was obvious what was happening. The Conduct Board was refusing to develop evidence on its own. Instead it was attempting to pass off its investigatory responsibilities to me, a writer, and Verney, an attorney who was fearful of retribution. It would be *our* fault. The Conduct Board was engaged in a bad-faith exercise meant to protect Justice Zappala. On March 6, 1995, I responded to the Conduct Board in the following letter:

"Dear Messers Quinn and Anthony,

"I found your letter to me dated February 16, 1995 to be outrageous, inappropriate, insufficient, and suspect.

"The essence of my compliant to the Judicial Conduct Board dated August 11, 1994 was that Justice Stephen Zappala violated the Judicial Code of Conduct by intervening in the Wagman v. Pennsylvania Turnpike case, as his brother Charles Zappala underwrote the disputed project and Justice Zappala's long-time family friend and former law partner James Dodaro was a commissioner on the Turnpike Commission. These facts alone make it plain to me and others that Justice Zappala violated Canons 1 and 2 of the Judicial Code of Conduct by failing to avoid even the appearance of impropriety in all his activities. I was furthermore told by attorneys handling the case that Justice Zappala took an ex parte communication from Commissioner Dodaro about Wagman.

"You do not need the names of my sources, or my notes, involving my 1993 book *When the Levee Breaks,* to determine whether Justice Zappala should or should not rule on cases involving the interests of his brother, his friend and his former law partner. As for the allegations of the ex parte communication, I suggest you go to the South Office Building, in Harrisburg, less than a mile from your office, and look up the case in the public records, where the attorneys who handled the case are clearly listed. Ask them. If the Conduct Board and its investigators do not engender enough trust with these individuals to have them speak freely, without fear of reprisal, serious problems with the Board and an inability to conduct its constitutionally mandated authority are indicated. It further suggests the time has come to call in independent, federal investigators.

"I should add here that one state judge and several attorneys involved in the Wagman case have voiced the concern to me that the Judicial Conduct Board, because of ties to Justice Zappala, is unable to properly investigate and rule on these charges. I have been asked by the state judge to contact the appropriate federal authorities to seek assistance in reviewing Justice Zappala's handling of Wagman and other cases, as well as your tardy and ineffective handling of this complaint.

"Public complaints against Justice Zappala's intervention in cases involving his brother's bonding company, Russell, Rea, Zappala and Gomulka, and subsidiary RRZ Public Markets, were first aired by former Justice Rolf Larsen in late 1992. At the time, and during Larsen's subsequent impeachment, at issue was not only the fairness and impartiality of Pennsylvania courts, but also the Judicial Conduct Board's ability to guarantee fair justice to all Pennsylvanians. Also under public scrutiny was the extent to which Justice Zappala may control the activities, or lack thereof, of the Conduct Board.

"My complaint to you was filed on August 11, 1994. After more than six months your inability to act in a timely, responsible matter to disavow Justice Zappala having repeatedly ruled in cases involving his brother's interests amounts to a de facto acquiescence that ruling on court cases involving entities underwritten by his brother, and involving friends and associates, is permissible. I and others find this situation intolerable, and adversely affecting all Pennsylvanians' civil right to a fair and impartial hearing in our courts. We fear Justice Zappala's being allowed to intervene in cases involving his brother's bonding business also holds deep and troubling ramifications to the fairness and stability of the securities, finance and bonding business in our country.

"I now feel it appropriate to broaden and modify my complaint to include the following:

"•Attorneys and the aforementioned state judge have complained to me that the Conduct Board's Chairman, Judge Joseph Del Sole, is a friend and/or protégé of Justice Stephen Zappala. Accordingly I hereby request that Judge Del Sole recuse himself from all proceedings involving this complaint. I furthermore request that all other employees or consultants to the Conduct Board with personal or professional ties to Justice Zappala or Judge Del Sole immediately recuse themselves.

"•I hereby request that three other cases brought repeatedly to the public's attention during Larsen's impeachment, and their handling by Justice Zappala, be investigated by the Conduct Board. These are the cases involving the city of Philadelphia, Allegheny County, and the entity known as PICA (Pennsylvania Intergovernmental Cooperation Agency). In each of these cases Justice Zappala intervened when his brother was underwriting bonds for the involved entities.

"•I furthermore request that Justice Zappala's honesty and veracity while under oath in the impeachment proceedings be examined by the board. Specifically, Justice Zappala testified under oath that he had no idea what his own sons were doing for a living, when many other Pennsylvanians seem aware that the justice's two sons are currently or at one time were involved in RR&Z's bonding business. One of Justice Zappala's sons in fact sold Justice Zappala tens of thousands of dollars in RR&Z underwritten bonds; accordingly Justice Zappala appears to have committed perjury by saying he had no idea what his sons were doing for a living.

"Our patience in the Board's good faith and competence in this matter has all but run out. It is now incumbent on the Conduct Board to make an immediate, clear and unambiguous finding that Justice Stephen Zappala should not interject himself in legal cases involving the interests of his family, friends and associates. Every day of delay is another day when Pennsylvanians are deprived of their civil rights to impartial and fair justice. To continue to delay and make excuses in making this finding is to send a signal to other state judges that they too, like Justice Zappala, are free to rule on cases involving the interests of family, friends and associates. It seems appropriate that Pennsylvanians therefore be publicly warned that their interests demand they avoid taking their legal disputes to Justice Zappala's courtroom in particular, and Pennsylvania courtrooms in general."

On March 21, 1995, I again received a letter from G.D. Anthony of the Judicial Conduct Board, informing me the matter was closed. Anthony and the Conduct Board maintain that I, of all people, failed, of all things, to provide adequate information. The letter gives the Conduct Board's tacit approval to a judge's intervention in cases involving friends and family, which certainly must be good news for anyone with a judge in the family, and surprising news for the rest of us.

"The file in this matter will be closed," the Conduct Board wrote me. "The Board will retain all materials submitted with your complaint, including your letter of March 6, 1995, wherein you declined to supply the Board with any corroborating information."